Caring Hands

Discussions by the Laboratory Animal
Refinement & Enrichment Forum
Volume II

Edited by Viktor Reinhardt
Animal Welfare Institute

Animal Welfare Institute
900 Pennsylvania Avenue, SE
Washington, DC 20003
www.awionline.org

Caring Hands
Discussions by the Laboratory Animal
Refinement & Enrichment Forum, Volume 2

Edited by Viktor Reinhardt

ISBN 978-0-938414-88-9
LCCN 2010910475

Cover photo: Jakub Hlavaty
Design: Ava Rinehart and Cameron Creinin
Copy editing: Beth Herman, Cathy Liss, Annie Reinhardt
and Dave Tilford

All papers used in this publication are Acid Free and
Elemental Chlorine Free. They also contain 50% recycled
content including 30% post consumer waste. All raw materials
originate in forests run according to correct principles in full
respect for high environmental, social and economic standards
at all stages of production.

I am dedicating this book to
the innocent animal behind bars who has to
endure loneliness, boredom and unnecessary distress.

Table of Contents

Chapter 3: Refinement and Enrichment for Primates

Chapter 4: Refinement and Enrichment for Other Animals

Chapter 5: Miscellaneous

Introduction and Acknowledgements

This is the second volume of electronic discussions that took place on the Animal Welfare Institute's Laboratory Animal Refinement & Enrichment Forum (LAREF). This forum was founded in 2002 to serve the international animal care and animal research community for the sharing of first-hand experiences on practical ways how to improve the living and handling conditions of animals kept in research laboratories.

Of 2,866 comments posted between June 2007 and March 2010, a total of 1,912 were selected for this volume. I am grateful to the following animal technicians, animal caretakers, veterinarians, researchers and librarians who contributed these comments: Dawn Abney, Genevieve Andrews-Kelly, Paula Austin, Kate Baker, Jas Barley, Carol Barriere, Sharon Bauer, Vera Baumans, Paula Bazille, Lorriane Bell, Emily Bethell, Eileen Boehle, Louise Buckley, Rebecca Brunelli, Monica Carlson, Jodi Carlson Scholz, Holly Carter, Katie Chace, Lynette Chave, Wendy Clarence, Michele Cunneen, Heidi Denman, Marcie Donnelly, Heather Doviak, Natasha Down, Michel Emond, Thomas Ferrell, Renee Gainer, Joseph Garner, Tamara Godbey, Jennifer Green,

Keely Harding, Deborah Hartley, Harriet Hoffman, Steven Iredale, Jo Keeley, Heather Kirby, Amy Krikorian, Cathy Liss, Jennifer Lofgren, Shelley L. Lower, Elva Mathiesen, Kendra McCafferty, Meagan McCallum, Kathleen McDonald, Darren E. Minier, Robin Minkel, Kim Moore, Erik Moreau, David Morton, Casey Coke Murphy, Kelsey Neeb, Stefanie L. Nelsen, Tadatoshi Ogura, Anna Olsson, Emily Patterson-Kane, Laura Poor, Octavio Presgrave, Kimberly Rappaport, Jillann Rawlins-O'Connor, Allison Reiffer, Cynthia M. Roberts, Susan Rubino, Polly Schultz, Jacqueline Schwartz-Cohoon, Chris Sherwin, Evelyn Skoumbourdis, Adrian Smith, Autumn Sorrells, Daniel Stadterman, Kay Stewart, Lydia Troc, Melissa Truelove, Pascalle van Loo, Pascal VanTroys, Augusto Vitale, Richard Weilenmann and Russell Yothers.

I have edited and arranged each comment as appropriate, summarized into single comments equivalent content from multle commenters, and added in brackets editorial clarifications and supportive references from the published literature. Thanks are due to Cathy Liss, Beth Herman, Dave Tilford and my wife, Annie, for thoroughly checking the text for typos and errors.

Attempts to obtain accompanying photos from LAREF members were only moderately successful. Therefore, I have made extensive searches on the Internet and was fortunate in being able to download most of the photos from Flickr, especially under Creative Commons licenses. I am very grateful to the numerous individuals who explicitly or implicitly gave me permission to use their photo material.

My special thanks goes to Ava Rinehart and Cameron Creinin for preparing the layout and creating the design of this book. Their fine sense of harmony gives this book a touch of beauty that I very much appreciate.

This book has been prepared for everybody who is genuinely concerned about the welfare of animals kept in laboratories and for animal rights advocates who don't know that most animal caretakers and technicians, many veterinarians and some researchers do their very best to refine the traditional, often inadequate housing and inhumane handling practices so that the animals experience less distress.

—Viktor Reinhardt
Moderator of LAREF

Mt. Shasta, California
August, 2010

Chapter 1

Basic Issues

annual usage of animals in biomedical research

You are probably not surprised that the number of animals used/killed in laboratories is amazingly high. The estimated worldwide annual figure was over 115 million in 2005, according to a recent census (Taylor et al., 2008).

You start wondering if the gradual implementation of the three Rs really reflects a decline of the number of animals used and killed in laboratories, or if we are merely running in circles, blindly believing that we are reducing the suffering of animals kept in research labs.

• I don't think there is any data anywhere in the world that is sufficiently comprehensive to allow us to do anything more than speculate about the number of animals used for research at the moment.

• You are certainly right. Since most animals used/killed annually in research labs all over the globe are not officially counted/registered, we can only speculate about the total number. Yet, there are some pretty accurate counts in some countries of a few species, and if you add them all up you get well over 1,000,000 animals used and killed every year (Matsuda & Kurosawa, 2002; Richmond, 2002; Gauthier, 2004). Even with the most commonly used animals—mice and rats—excluded, the United States alone uses more than 1,000,000 legally protected, hence registered, animals per year (United States Department of Agriculture, 2007). This number, I think, is high enough to get concerned, and if you care for other creatures, to feel sad.

- I would definitely agree. It's sometimes difficult to change the minds of principal investigators when it comes to decreasing the number of animals per study.

- One of the things one has to bear in mind is that in the U.S.—probably the primary user of animals in research—it is very difficult to get actual figures of rodents used and it is often only an estimate.

- This is not really surprising when you take into account that (a) rats and mice make up the great bulk of all animals used, and that (b) the U.S. is the only country that explicitly excludes rats and mice in its legal definition of the term animal; this implies that rats and mice don't count. They are not covered by the federal animal welfare law (Animal Welfare Act, 2002) and hence are not listed in the official annual reports of animals used in research (United States Department of Agriculture, 2007).

- One also has to take into consideration that the nature of the research has changed significantly from experimental to the breeding-and-killing—for tissues—of transgenic and other genetically modified/mutant animals. I do not know if the United States has even started to count these animals.

- The rising popularity of genetic modification methods has certainly contributed to the overall increase in the number of animals used in research. The number of genetically modified animals used in research has more than doubled in the last ten years (Ormandy et al., 2009).

- I think the issues at hand are not specific distinctions of different animal categories but the huge number of living creatures killed for whatever research-related reason every year. A genetically modified animal is no less a sentient creature who clings to life than a traditional experimental animal.

cage space

How can we find out if a caged animal—be he/she a rodent, rabbit, dog, cat or monkey—would benefit from additional space?

• Quite a number of studies have been published, showing quasi-scientifically that the legally prescribed minimum space is sufficient, and that the well-being of the caged subjects would not be enhanced by increasing the cage dimensions. The biomedical research industry, certainly, welcomes such studies. However, their results and conclusions are questionable, if not intentionally biased, because the studies were conducted with unstructured cages (Hite et al., 1977; Bayne & McCully, 1989; Hughes et al., 1989; White et al., 1989; Line et al., 1989, 1990a, 1991; Galef & Durlach, 1993; Galef, 1999; Crockett et al., 1993, 2000; McGlone et al., 2001). I think it is quite obvious that an animal, and for that matter also a human, does not benefit from space per se but from structures in the space. Minimum-sized cages are often so small that you cannot provide species-appropriate structures unless you increase the vertical and/or horizontal space.

• It is hard to believe that animals don't benefit from additional space. I wish I had additional vertical space for my marmosets. I truly believe they would benefit from it.

- They probably would, but only if you have placed branches or other structures in the additional vertical space. Those structures would be necessary to make the additional vertical space accessible for your marmosets; they cannot possibly perch in empty vertical space, they need some kind of structure to climb and sit on in the additional space.

5

- Beyond minimal requirements for species-typical body postures and adjustments and species-typical movements patterns, empty space has little value for animals and humans alike; in fact unstructured space induces anxiety [Fredericson, 1953; White et al., 1989; Forkman et al., 2007; Kallai et al., 2007; Lamprea et al., 2008]. Individuals therefore have the tendency to shun open space but keep at the periphery close to the only structure available: the wall or the fence and corners. This behavioral and emotional response to open space is termed wall-seeking or thigmotaxis [moving towards an object and keeping contact/touch with that object].

- The classic Open-Field test [Hall & Ballachey, 1932] is based on this natural tendency of rodents to avoid entering and crossing an anxiogenic area that lacks structures that would protect them from potential predators or raptors.

- I know that elephants can hardly be called a laboratory species, but we recently recorded a statistically significant positive correlation between the gait of zoo elephants and enclosure size: elephants with larger enclosures had more elephant-characteristic extended gaits.

- Your observation is not surprising. You will probably find the same phenomenon in human prisoners kept in very small single-cells. My question relates to all captive animals; so your elephants fit perfectly.

- I have heard—but have no personal experience—of laboratory rabbits breaking their backs when they try to hop normally after being released from cages. Presumably this would be prevented if the rabbits were given large enough enclosures to hop normally and develop a stronger musculo-skeletal system. This type of evidence indicates that for best welfare, the amount of space per se can be important, and it is not necessarily always related to what that space includes.

• Birgit Drescher did studies on bone density in rabbits in the early 1990s and found that bone thinning developed in rabbits confined in small cages for about five weeks [Drescher & Loeffler, 1991; Rothfritz et al., 1992]. The bone thinning was reversible once the animals were placed in pens allowing normal movement. Birgit Drescher's comments to me were: "When you take a rabbit out of a cage and let it run in a pen that allows all movements, it will get physiologically normal and strong bones at any age."

• I experienced this several years ago when I tried to take rabbits out of cages and placed them in a pen. The sentinel rabbit stamped his foot and broke his leg due to osteoporosis.

• I would conclude from this that single-caged rabbits, such as bucks who don't get along with each other, really need rabbit runs—like small dog runs—so as to be able to hop properly and thereby maintaining healthy, strong bones.

• It is not uncommon for adult macaques who, after having lived in small unstructured cages for many years, sprain a joint or break a limb when they are released into a large enclosure. There are people who quote such incidents, arguing that monkeys do not benefit from larger cages.

• We never had animals break a limb or seriously injure themselves, but we did see a lot of very interesting locomotor patterns when some of the monks, donated to my last facility, were released to an outdoor pen instead of a cage. They performed a lot of hopping/bucking, like a horse, and had issues with judging distance when jumping between perches. Many of the monks missed perches and/or sides of the pen when jumping toward them. After about a week, everyone usually figured out jumping and walking in monkey fashion.

   I was always wondering, do the monkeys lose depth perception over time when they do not need it, because there are no structures in their environment, or were all these animals near/far-sighted to begin with?

• You raise a potentially serious issue. Most of us tend to think that the retina and visual pathways develop normally under most circumstances. However, this is not necessarily true when the living environment is not normal. In writing a chapter on the welfare of laboratory rodents, I have found two papers indicating that retinal functional development and visual acuity in rodents can be improved by environmental enrichment (Prusky et al., 2002; Landi et al., 2007). So, rearing animals in standard, non-enriched, laboratory-cage conditions could mean that these animals have less effective eyesight. My feeling is that, because primates are generally more visually oriented than rodents, this could have even more serious consequences for your monkeys.

Legal minimum cage space requirements are usually based on body weight. How appropriate, from the caged subject's point of view, are such stipulations?

- Legal minimum space requirements should be tailored in such a way that species-specific and species-adequate furniture can be placed in the enclosure without blocking part of the space that the occupant(s) need for free movement and free postural adjustments. I see no difficulty that would hinder experts from coming up with prescriptions of basic furniture for each species, for example shelters for rodents and amphibians and elevated resting surfaces for birds, cats, dogs, rabbits, and nonhuman primates.

- One factor that is important but is consistently overlooked is age. Very young animals need far more space than heavy or obese ones!

- Yes, juveniles need to have more space than adults, let alone adults who are overweight. Young animals are much more active and typically want to play; to do that, they need extra space. Most countries, including the U.S. [United States Department of Agriculture, 2002a], do not take this into account in their legal minimum space stipulations for caged animals.

- In the revised Appendix A of the Council of Europe, minimum floor area is now not only based on body weight, but it also takes into account the need for young animals to play [Council of Europe, 2006]. For example, for mice, the minimum floor area is 330 cm² per mouse, independent of the animal's body weight; this means that young and small, but relatively active mice grow more or less into their cage. Furthermore, the cage must be structured and provided with enrichment; examples are given for each species.

- It may not be enough to stipulate that enrichment must be provided and then list some options. We have this situation here in the U.S. with the Animal Welfare Regulations. To take an example: you do comply with these regulations if you give a single-caged monkey a mirror, but otherwise do not structure the space, for example, with a high perch. Both the perch and the mirror are listed as possibilities of environmental enrichment [United States Department of Agriculture, 2002a], leaving it up to you to pick and choose.

  It does not seem appropriate to lump everything together under the term environmental enrichment. There are things that are biological necessities, such as elevated areas for primates, so they should be legally mandated, while other things such as mirrors may be enriching, hence can be optional.

- That is true; when only the *necessities*, such as nesting material for mice, shelter for rats, social contact for social animals, high perches for nonhuman primates, etc. are listed as examples of environmental enrichment, there is no option to get away with enrichment for which the animal has no real need, for example toys or mirrors. I saw little play balls for mice, as if mice would need those to express mouse-typical behavior patterns.

inanimate enrichment

Most animals quickly lose interest in inanimate objects that have no survival value. At what interval do you rotate enrichment devices to create a novelty effect so that the animals show renewed interest in them?

- In facilities with large numbers of rodents, rotation of enrichment gadgets becomes part of the cage changing routine, that means about every ten days. To exchange the gadgets more frequently would not be practical; it would also not be good for bio-security to open 1,000 or more ventilated cages two or three times a week.

- At my primate center, the enrichment devices are rotated on a two-week on, two-week off schedule.

- At our facility, we rotate enrichment objects and foraging devices for caged primates on a weekly basis. A device is given for two days per week and then removed. Currently there are five different feeding devices and six different non-feeding devices used regularly in our rotation. Our animals usually do not see the same device more than once every 2-3 months.

- We have an enrichment tech who develops a calendar for the animal care staff to replace different toys on a two-week rotation when the cages are changed. All monkeys of the same room have the same toy. In addition to the toy, every two weeks each monkey gets access to a different in-house made foraging device, each for the duration of the two-week interval.

- In my experience, there is one toy that rhesus macaques never seem to lose interest in. I hang paint rollers on the outside of the cages and smear peanut butter or honey on them once every day; it takes the monkeys a long time to pick every morsel of the sticky food stuff off the rollers. Since the animals show no signs of habituation, we do not need to rotate these gadgets.

- Gnawing sticks are also enrichment objects in which macaques do not lose interest over time. The sticks are changing their form and texture due to wear and dehydration, thereby retaining a kind of novelty effect. You don't need to rotate these branch segments, but simply exchange them with new ones when they have become so small that they fall through the mesh

floor of the cage. The nice thing with these natural toys is that they are inexpensive; you can actually cut them yourself from dead deciduous trees. I have done that while working at a primate research center and provided attractive environmental enrichment for more than 700 caged rhesus and stump-tailed macaques at no cost.

- That's the way to go! Doesn't it make much more sense to come up with some kind of enrichment in which the animals do not lose interest over time, rather than investing money and time to buy an assortment of enrichment objects with short-lived novelty effect and rotate them on a regular basis? I think what is true for nonhuman primates is also true for rodents, rabbits, dogs, cats and birds: effective enrichment is much more reasonable than rotational enrichment.

- In my opinion, enrichment should at least focus on species-specific behavioral needs. Toys generally don't do that, which might be the reason why the animals lose interest in them quickly. Experience has shown that the provisions shown here remain attractive for a very long time, probably because they address species-specific needs.

Shelter, gnawing and climbing possibilities for rats

Shelter and nesting material for hamsters

Nesting material for mice

Shelters and hay for guinea pigs

Straw and hay for pigs

Social companions for mice, rats, guinea pigs, hamsters, pigs, monkeys, dogs and cats

- It seems also to me that biologically relevant environmental enrichment intrinsically bears a quality of lasting novelty that most dead enrichment objects are lacking. For example, depending on the species, animals don't get bored from:
  (a) working for food (e.g. food puzzles),
  (b) searching for food (e.g. food mixed with woodchips),
  (c) processing vegetables/fruits,
  (d) gnawing wood,
  (e) interacting with a companion,
  (f) maintaining a species-adequate nest/shelter,
  (g) bathing in sand,
  (h) looking out from a platform/shelf/perch, and
  (i) looking through a window.

  These activities in themselves are biologically important, plus the enrichment object is dynamic or provides entertainment. In a way, such enrichment is not really enrichment. It is a necessity, and as such should be a basic standard provision in the captive setting.

- I could not agree with you more! The word enrichment is often misleading, making us think we are doing something as a luxury for an animal, when in fact it is often essential for the animal's welfare.

Are running wheels for rodents a necessity or enrichment?

- I see a running wheel as a necessity for caged hamsters and caged mice, because it allows them to release the biologically inherent drive for moving around; I am not an expert, but I would assume that in their natural habitat many rodents travel quite a distance within the area of their home territory in the course of a day. The running wheel is not a natural structure, but it promotes the expression of a behavioral drive that could otherwise find little release other than stereotypical movements. I am not sure what the situation would be for rats.

- I think running wheels should be in the necessity category.

  I have had researchers who do exercise studies, and both mice and rats would run over 10 km a night. I was quite surprised at the distances covered by these little guys.

- When I wrote a review on wheel running, I found that the distance run in 24 h by animals in a running wheel can be as great as:

  43 km for rats (Richter, 1927),

  31 km for wild mice (Kavanau, 1967),

  16 km for laboratory mice (Festing & Greenwood, 1976),

  9 km for golden hamsters (Richards, 1966), and

  8 km for Mongolian gerbils (Roper, 1976).

- I would infer from this that rodents have a strong biological need to move their legs over considerable distances. In the artificial cage environment, a running wheel becomes a necessity because it helps them satisfy this need.

Do you use laser pointers as an enrichment tool for animals in your charge?

• One of our ideas is to use a laser pointer to train rhesus macaques targeting to an area that we cannot reach with a traditional target (e.g. a lixit in the back of the cage). We have exposed the monkeys to the laser, just to gauge their reactions. Some of them are interested, some of them don't care, and some of them are fearful at first.

   I have used a laser pointer with our house cat; she absolutely loves to chase it, and never gets tired of it. It's amazing how high on the wall she'll jump trying to catch the light dot!

• I have used a laser pointer with cats, both at home and in the lab. They love it! Having tried a few different varieties, I've found that they don't seem to care what shape or what color the light reflection is, just as long as it keeps moving.

• Laser pointers work very well for cats living in relatively large quarters. To have them chase after the light dot provides species-adequate environmental enrichment for the cats and for the personnel. It's real fun!

   Unfortunately, the laser pointer gets useless when you are dealing with single-caged cats. There is just not enough space for chasing after a target.

• Laser pointers also provide great enrichment for hens.

enrichment versus enhancement

When we refine the living quarters of animals do we enhance or do we enrich their environment?

- U.S. Animal Welfare Regulations use the terms environmental *enhancement* and environmental *enrichment* in their specifications for nonhuman primates. These regulations do not define either of the two terms; environmental enhancement is not used as a synonym for environmental enrichment, but environmental enhancement includes environmental enrichment along with social grouping and restraint devices (United States Department of Agriculture, 1995).

- Environmental enrichment seems to still be the standard term; I always use it as a key word. In text, however, I use something more specific and accurate such as the name of the actual physical change being assessed.

- The term environmental enrichment will still have to be used as a keyword as long as it is the preferred term in the lab animal world.

- When checking the literature it becomes clear that environmental enrichment is the most commonly used term. Why? Probably not because of a preference; I guess people have simply become used to it, without actually questioning its practical value, and the word enrichment has a positive connotation in the public domain.

- We have discussed these terms already. There was a general consensus that *enrichment* may be somewhat misleading when we provision the barren living quarters of captive animals with conditions—furniture, social partners—for the expression of basic behavioral needs, such as foraging, social interaction, seeking shelter, building a nest, or retreating to an elevated refuge area. When we do this, we are not really enriching the environment of the animals but we are addressing basic necessities for their behavioral and emotional health.

  We may enrich a rat cage that is already furnished in species-appropriate ways by adding a toy or some other entertaining gadget. But we do not enrich a barren rat cage by adding a suitable shelter.

- To add some resources to a barren cage is over-egging it when calling it enrichment; hence *enhancement*, to make it slightly better.

behavioral problems

Are caged animals in research facilities showing abnormal behaviors, or are their living quarters in which they live abnormal, hence determining the animals' behavioral expressions?

• Animals in captivity often exhibit behaviors that they do not show in their biologically natural environment. We label such behaviors as abnormal and invest a lot of resources to eliminate them, even though evidence has shown that this is a rather futile endeavor, and stubbornly—and perhaps even intentionally—overlook the fact that it is not the animals' behavior that is abnormal but the human-created, species-inadequate living quarters to which the animals try to adapt but often fail. If we would design more normal, that means species-adequate living quarters, there would be no cause for abnormal behaviors.

• At our facility, we avoid the term abnormal behavior because what is normal behavior in captivity does not necessarily correspond with the behavior in the wild. Behaviors

- are bound to change in an artificial, captive environment. We use the term aberrant for behaviors—such as SIB [self-injurious biting]—that we regard as behavioral problems and hence need to be addressed for animal welfare and/or scientific reasons.

- It seems to me that an animal's attempt to somehow adapt to species-inadequate living quarters are intrinsically normal even if the corresponding behavior appears to be abnormal.

- If a behavior does not normally appear in the ethogram of an animal, then when it is expressed it must be abnormal. If we start describing or accepting abnormal behaviors, such as self-biting or hair-pulling as normal, we give people an excuse to continue housing animals in the conditions that are causing these behaviors.

- Even if the behavioral adaptation is unsuccessful—for example self-mutilation—and looks abnormal from the human point of view, it is certainly not the animal's fault. The animal's response to the given situation—being forced to permanently live in a small and boring cage—is, in my opinion, biologically normal. This doesn't imply that we can accept the inadequate, human-created living conditions that are responsible for the animals' unsuccessful adaptation attempts.

- I would not call self-biting and hair-pulling normal behaviors either; they are most definitively harmful. But sometimes I wonder about stereotypical circling and pacing. The animal is confined in a much too small space, what else can he or she do to burn energy and get exercise, but move in a rather restricted manner. I would call this an *adaptive* behavior; adaptive to the small cage.

  I would most certainly pace back and forth or run in a circle over and over again if I were forced to live in my little bathroom for most of my life; I would do this, just to do something, trying not to go crazy.

- I very much agree with your observation and would also label stereotypical locomotions and movement patterns, such as pacing, somersaulting, circling, rocking, swinging and bouncing as adaptive behaviors. As you point out, what would we do if we were locked permanently in a small unstructured room? The biological drive to move cannot be disregarded; it somehow has to be expressed in action. However, we would have to make a clear distinction between adaptive [non-injurious/harming] behaviors and maladaptive [injurious/harmful] behaviors:
  (a) self-biting leading to no visible tissue damage would be an *adaptive* behavior, while
  (b) self-biting leading to open injuries would be a *maladaptive* behavior.

- I worry that the term adaptive behavior may be misused as a caveat for decreased concern over animal well-being, since it could then be argued that animals do adapt to any living quarters even if these disregard their behavioral needs.

- There are quite a number of quasi-abnormal behaviors that are not an animal well-being concern for me. Repetitive locomotion and movement patterns are probably unavoidable whenever we place an animal—including a human—into a cage. I see those activities as biological healthy attempts to adapt/adjust to artificial, enforced living quarters; the subject *must* somehow express the drive to make use of the legs, even if this implies running in circles, bouncing up and down, or back-flipping. Even in zoos, where animals have much more living space compared to animals in laboratories, repetitive locomotions and movement patterns are not uncommon. I want to argue that we cannot avoid that animals in laboratories develop such stereotypical locomotions; and I would also argue that such activities are not detrimental to the subject.

- It is not unusual that animals and humans develop bizarre, repetitive behavior patterns when they are bored for a long time. Being confined in a more or less barren cage/room is probably such a situation in which parts of one's own body serve to provide some minimum stimulation for the mind. I would categorize such boredom-triggered behaviors not as abnormal but rather as normal attempts to cope with a biologically abnormal environment.

- If an animal develops an abnormal behavior that is causing injury or any other physical or psychological harm, then I would say that the animal cannot properly adapt/adjust to the human-created living quarters. I would classify such a self-destructive activity as *maladaptive* behavior and argue that we have not only an ethical but also a scientific obligation to change the animal's artificial living environment in such a way that (a) the behavior stops completely, or (b) does not show up in any other animal raised and kept in the refined living environment.

   I think we could help laboratory animals more effectively by focusing our effort to *prevent* maladaptive behaviors such as self-mutilation rather than engaging in the futile attempt to stop/eradicate normal adaptive behaviors, such as stereotypical pacing or running in circles.

- I prefer the terms captive or adaptive behavior rather than abnormal behavior, but it will probably not make a difference to the animal what term we humans use.

- Terminology does matter, at least indirectly, to the animals because words reflect human feelings/attitudes. When we say, *an animal shows abnormal behaviors,* we make the animal quasi-responsible for behaving in an undesired manner; something is wrong with the animal, so we try to correct this behavior or make the animal stop showing it. When we do this, we are shifting the responsibility for the problem onto the animal, tacitly disregarding the fact that we—not the animal—created enforced, species-inadequate living quarters that make the animal behave in a strange manner. We—not the animal—created the problem, so it is up to us to fix it!

- The word *vice* used by farmers for stereotypies such as bar-sucking, tail-biting and crib-biting is probably the equivalent to the term abnormal behavior used by laboratory animal scientists.

- In order to have a vice you have to be responsible for your actions, i.e. be a moral agent, hence Aristotle's *vice and virtues*. When we say, *animals show a vice* or *engage in an abnormal behavior*, we implicitly suggest that they are carrying out these behaviors deliberately to frustrate their owners; crib-biting in horses means destroying the beautiful feeding trough that has been given to them. Unfortunately, these terms are often used as if it were the animals' fault to engage in these behaviors that are seen as "undesirable" [e.g. Poffe et al., 1995; Sodaro & Mellen, 1997; Boinski et al., 1999; Lukas et al., 1999; Iglesias & Gil-Burman, 2002].

- It seems to me that both terms—vice and abnormal behavior—imply that something is wrong with animals who show certain activities that are not accepted by their owners.

We use this kind of fault-finding language not only with animals but also with humans. For example, when a child gets engrossed in stereotypical hair-pulling or nail-biting while doing homework, the parents are tempted to let the child know that it should stop pulling the hair or biting the nails; they may—and often do—even punish the child for behaving abnormally, that means not like a *normal* child; so the child gets the message, *something is wrong with me, I am a bad kid.*

Personally, I think, it would be fair of the parents to ask themselves first, "why does our child show this bizarre behavior? Do we, perhaps, overwhelm the child with our selfish expectations of him or her in school?" Most parents don't ask such

sobering yet honest questions. In the end, the child's "abnormality" may have its origin in the parents and not in the child; that would be a completely different story!

Before we claim that a mouse or a monkey shows an abnormal behavior in the laboratory cage, should we perhaps not first ask ourselves, "when we designed the animals' living quarters, did we fail to consider something that is now making the animals behave in a way that they would never do in the wild?" We may find that what is abnormal is perhaps not the animals' behavior—attempts to adapt/adjust—but the inadequate living quarters that we have created and now force the animals to live in.

mood swings

We sometimes feel great, relaxed, outgoing and happy, at other times sad, frustrated, depressed, tense, or impatient. I wonder, do the animals we are working with on a daily basis pick up these mood swings and respond to them physiologically and behaviorally?

• Studying the effects of stress on how rhesus macaques interpret signals in their environment, I think it is possible that monkeys who have a trust-based relationship with people are sensitive to the factors you suggest. However, I suspect most monkeys housed in laboratories do not have the opportunity to develop such relationships with the attending staff so that they could pick up on these subtle emotional signals.

My own research suggests that the way in which monkeys interpret and respond to ambiguous signals varies with the monkeys' own stress levels. For example, following a routine but stressful veterinary examination, monkeys demonstrate a reduced expectation of positive events associated with ambiguous stimuli. In less stressful situations, monkeys demonstrate an increased expectation of positive events associated with the same ambiguous stimuli.

If we were to extrapolate from these experimental findings and take caretaker mood signals as our ambiguous stimuli, then it is reasonable to assume that interpretation of our mood signals

depends on whether or not a monkey feels at ease or stressed. In other words, depressed or stressed monkeys may be more likely to interpret our behavior and expressions as more threatening, regardless of our actual mood. Being stressed creates more stressors! This produces a negative cycle that inevitably leads to depression, despair and illness. This may well be very similar to our own experiences of bad moods or depression, where we interpret otherwise ambiguous events as worrisome or threatening— paranoia being an extreme example.

- Dogs certainly are sensitive to our moods. They very quickly pick up changes, especially visual ones, like a sad or angry face or a depressed body posture. They definitely know the difference between an angry voice and a happy voice. The instant a smile crosses a person's face, a familiar dog will gleefully wag his or her tail.

- You don't need to raise your voice when scolding a dog; your mere look is sufficient to make the dog feel uncomfortable and ready to be forgiven.

- When I am entering a monkey room in a bad mood, rhesus macaques respond to me in such a way that I believe they do sense my emotional energy and respond correspondingly in a rather reserved, apprehensive manner.

- I find it fascinating to experience over and over again how spontaneously and correctly animals—like monkeys, cats, dogs, deer, cattle, buffalo and birds—not only understand what's going on in the human psyche, but also in the human mind. It's a communication beyond words, so there is very little risk of misunderstanding. If you pretend to feel a certain way, the animal will know that you are cheating and will respond accordingly, but you can always be assured that the animal behaves and expresses feelings authentically. The same principles hold true when you interact with human infants who have not yet learned how to play social roles to their own advantage.

radio music/talk

Animals in laboratories are often exposed to radio music/talk while attending personnel are in their rooms or, all day long, while the radio is on in the hallways. No doubt, radio music/talk may help to keep personnel in a good mood, which may reflect in a relatively better performance of their routine work. What about the animals? People do show aversive reactions when they are exposed to radio music/talk that they don't like or that is too loud. They can protest or simply leave; caged animals do not have this option even though the radio music/talk may also be a nuisance (stressor) for them at times.

When your animals are exposed to radio music/ talk, what tells you that they are not bothered by it or, even better, that they actually like the radio music/talk?

- The dogs and cats we are working with do not seem to be bothered by music. Coming from animal shelters, they were originally probably in homes and, therefore, used to the sounds of radio and TV. Hearing these familiar sounds may have a calming effect on them. Whether they actually enjoy the sound of music is hard to say.

- I would argue that radio/TV music and talk should be allowed in rooms of research-assigned animals only if it has been documented that the music/ talk does not disturb the animals, i.e. constitute a variable that has the potential of influencing research data. Choice tests along with behavioral observations should readily clarify this question.

- I play classical music (CDs) in our dog rooms. It is difficult to say if the music makes a difference for the dogs, but I enjoy it and feel calmer!

- Some time ago we exposed mice to pop music, a Mozart symphony, New Age music or no music and scored telemetrically the animals' heart rate, body temperature and activity and recorded manually their behavior. We found no significant difference between all types of music and no music and concluded that music did not make a difference for mice. However, as the attending animal care staff liked listening to music during their working hours, their feeling good might indirectly have affected the well-being of the animals in their custody in a positive way.

- AAALAC once toured a facility where heavy metal played at full volume all day and night. When the site visitors came in, they frowned visibly and suggested this was too stressful a type of music for a transgenic core facility. I indicated the music was IACUC [Institutional Animal Care and Use Committee] approved and they would have to discuss the music choice with the PI [Principal Investigator], as it was his preferred music. When they asked him, he went on for 20 minutes elaborating about the virtues of the loud music to cover the elevator machine room that was right next door.

- It is my experience that rabbits in rooms with low-volume music are much less startled when humans enter the room. Many breeding colonies of mice need music to mellow out the background noises in order to achieve more consistent birth rates.

- I believe the single most important, influential variable in the housing room of any mammal or bird is the human caretaker. We influence the animal by the way we smell, body language and other vibes we humans can't even figure out. Anything that makes us happier makes us give off better vibes and the animals are less stressed and consequently will give better research results. When I am in a good mood, the animals in the room will reflect this in their behavior; they will be relaxed, calm and curious about their surroundings. When I am in a bad mood, they will be restless, alert and reserved when I approach them.

  If I like hip hop music, but the facility says only classical can be played, I may be in the room hating what I am listening to; my feeling of frustration may affect the animals negatively thereby overriding any positive noise-masking effect of the classical music. Conversely, if I enjoy listening to the music, I will probably radiate positive energy that will affect the animals in a positive, perhaps anxiety-buffering manner.

  So, I think you should be allowed to play your favorite music when you are in your animal rooms, but you need to keep the volume at a level that allows you to talk over it if you need to communicate with someone in the room.

- As long as the animals are not exposed to repeated noise—for example their room is located right beside the elevator machine room—the reason for the music is to keep us caretakers or animal technicians in a good mood; after all we humans are potential predators, hence serious stressors for the animals. When the animals are alone, there is no need to keep a radio on. I am not sure if music per se is of any benefit to the animals.

- We used to have radios turned on in our marmoset rooms. After finding out that marmosets, when given the choice, prefer silence over any kind of music (McDermott & Hauser, 2007) we decided to turn all the radios off. There was some concern that the marmosets would be more nervous during any kind of disturbance, but this was not the case. When there was silence, the animals showed no conspicuous alarm reactions when people were talking in the hallways or someone entered their room.

  We now turn the radio on for short time periods only (a) when we expect a sudden noise which might upset the animals, or (b) when a technician is working in the room (to keep the technician happy).

- That marmosets prefer silence to radio is not at all surprising when considering the fact that 30-minute exposure to playing radio is enough to double their salivary cortisol concentration (Pines et al., 2004); it's obviously stressful for them when they have to listen to the radio.

- Audio plays for our cynomolgus macaques all day long. We have a mix of music that is played, from soft jazz to waterfall sounds and instrumental. The volume is set at a specific level, but in each room there are dials to turn the music down or off when a function is accruing or the television is playing. I do see calmer primates—both attending human primates and nonhuman primates—when the softer music or instrumental music is playing.

  We'd had some harder type classic rock songs that were taken off the list, because they made some monkeys very agitated, especially when the volume of the sound was turned up too much.

- We use radios in the study room for as long as the study lasts. In the housing rooms, we have the radio play music one hour in the morning and again one hour in the afternoon. The rhesus monks and the marmosets seem to enjoy listening to music from the 60s, 70s, Disney music, and also nature sounds. I have the impression that the music has a calming effect on the animals.

- It is my personal experience that music in animal quarters does not necessarily make all humans who are exposed to it happy.

Some people like loud rock music, others like soft background music, while others prefer silence. I would assume that animals also do not always share the musical taste of the attending care staff and, perhaps would chose silence if they could.

- I have found in most primate research facilities I have worked and visited (a) that radios or TVs are the main aspect of their enrichment plan and (b) that the animals are generally stressed by people. Often the only contact they have is under stressful situations such as health checks, dosing and sample collection. Unless a great deal of effort has been made to acclimate the animals to research procedures and human interaction, they are typically fearful and defensive-aggressive in our presence.

  The animals can neither control the volume nor the content of the sound that is emitted by the radio. Typically, the attending person listens to programs with people singing or talking. If the animals already find humans stressful, how *enriching* can it actually be for them when they are exposed for hours on end, against their will, to human voices from the radio?

- It is questionable that nonhuman primates, and for that matter any animal species, like radio talk and music as their caretakers do. Being confined in a cage,

not able to escape the source of loud and possibly disturbing music and human talk can probably be quite distressing for them. After all, what is *music* for the human ear is most likely *noise* for the animal ear, and if that's the case it is most likely a source of stress [Barrett & Stockham, 1996; Jain & Baldwin, 2003; Pines et al., 2004; Campo et al., 2005; Burwell & Baldwin, 2006; Baldwin et al., 2007; Naff et al., 2007; Turner et al., 2007].

- I know of one unpublished study in which chimps were given a control box that allowed them to turn the music on and off. Perhaps not surprisingly, the chimps usually chose to turn the music off just like the marmosets of the already mentioned study by McDermott and Hauser (2007).

- It is worth remembering that animals have very different hearing ranges than humans, for whom we have designed radios and speakers. This subject really is one for asking the animals themselves in terms of types of noise/music and the volumes, because they also have very different frequency sensitivities; so, what humans might find comfortable and pleasing, other species might experience as noisy and unpleasant.

construction noise and vibration

Do you think that the animals in your charge get stressed when construction takes place in or near the animal holding facility?

- I can share some anecdotal evidence of effects of construction noise on the animals from my previous employer. While analyzing a rat adjuvance arthritis study, we found a significant and unexplained dip in body weight on one day, followed by immediate recovery over the next two days in all of our rats. When we asked the animal unit whether anything extraordinary had happened with our animals that day, they told us that the previous day, a large PET [Positron Emission Tomography] scan needed to be installed in the building, and one side wall of the building had been opened. All researchers performing behavioral studies were warned in advance, but they did not think it would affect any of the other studies!

  So, yes, I strongly believe that construction noise can stress animals. They might get used to it when it goes on for a while, though I am not sure about that.

- Yes, I do believe that animals become stressed by construction noise.

  We recently had our cage wash outfitted with new tunnel washers. During that time, our nonhuman primates became extremely stressed and agitated. The monkeys alarm-called a lot during the day while construction was going on and many of them developed stereotypies that were not observed previously, like swaying back and forth and charging their own reflections. Others who had already displayed stereotypies—like hair-pulling—before the construction started, increased these behavioral disorders, and some even began self-biting after the construction got underway. We did our best to alleviate their stress and entertained them during the day by providing extra enrichment items like foraging boards and puzzle feeders.

The construction went on for several months during the summer, and I have to say that our primates did not adjust over time. Even after the construction was completed and the noise finally stopped, some monkeys continued with their new stereotypies.

Also, our canine colony seemed very distracted during the construction months. The dogs were much more vocal and less focused during their training sessions; however, they appeared to gradually get used to the noise. Towards the end of the construction, they were again more focused and less vocal.

I should note that the cage-wash area is located on an adjacent wall to both our dog rooms/runs and also our primate suites. These two groups of animals received the brunt of the noise from the construction compared to the other species located farther away.

- The cynomolgus macaques I have worked with did not adapt to construction noise;

they always became and remained conspicuously more reactive and vigilant during periods of loud construction activities.

- I have made the same observations in rhesus macaques. While the construction noise was dragging on for weeks, the animals were much more reactive and restless. I had to stop training them on workdays because they were always on the alert and very distracted; their responses to me were no longer reliable, so the interaction became unsafe.

- We had a lot of noise going on over the last couple of months during construction of a new outdoor monkey area with a swimming pool, as well as a new indoor building for the monkeys. The new digs were built about 30 feet behind the existing facility, so the animals could see and hear everything that was going on.

The rhesus monkeys were stressed out during the first couple of weeks, but their stress levels decreased gradually as they became accustomed to the project. I knew they were stressed out at the first stage of construction, when I observed a lot of pacing, out of character screaming, fear grimacing, even leg-biting and arm-biting—behaviors that these monkeys had never shown while they were in my care. So, during the first couple of weeks, I stayed with them in the indoor area for reassurance; I played some of their favorite movies with the volume up quite high to drown out the sound of construction. The only thing that remained an unwavering stressor was when the concrete trucks arrived. The trucks made a loud beeping noise as they were backing up; the monkeys never became used to that. So during concrete delivery we locked the animals indoors until the trucks were gone. I handed out treats and gave a lot of reassurance during that time. They could still hear the trucks and the beeping, but at least this extreme noise was somewhat muffled.

In summary, I would certainly say that yes, construction activity can be a serious stressor for captive macaques.

• Pines et al. (2004) found that marmosets do not necessarily show any stress-indicative behaviors when they are exposed to loud construction noise even though they experience a physiological stress response as measured in a significant increase of saliva cortisol levels.

• We have been in the middle of construction pretty much constantly for the past ten years. Most of the noise had little noticeable consequence, however, when a classroom building was built across the street from us, the ground was first tamped for three weeks and then pilings were driven for another three weeks. For six weeks the ground vibrated constantly for eight hours a day! We lost at least six months' worth of breeding of the transgenic mice; even the zebra fish stopped laying eggs. Unfortunately we did not have anywhere to move the animals within the facility to shield them from the commotion.

• As an institution we have experienced quite a bit of growth in the past few years. Some animals, particularly mice, rabbits and bushbabies become obviously stressed. The disturbance associated with the construction range from loud noise to strong vibrations felt through the walls and floor. This appears to affect our animals' reproductive cycles and performance. Fewer litters are born and there is more evidence of cannibalism during times of loud construction activities.

• Rasmussen et al. (2009) noted in mice that construction noise decreases reproductive efficiency by decreasing live birth rates.

• Typically, new construction and renovation of facilities are long-term projects that can create an extraneous variable. This is often overlooked because it seems unavoidable. I would assume that construction activities are not only stressors to the animals and the personnel, but the animals' physiological response to them will make any scientific data obtained from them questionable if not altogether useless. Yes, you can install/place noise-buffers, but they are not 100 percent effective and they have no impact on vibrations caused by construction; in addition, most institutions are unlikely to invest extra money to shield animals from stress caused by construction because they are already spending so much money on renovation and new construction. Seems to be a pretty hopeless, extremely counterproductive situation in many facilities.

{Chapter 2}

Refinement and Enrichment for Rodents and Rabbits

environmental enrichment

institutional standards

Does your facility have standards implemented for rodent environmental enrichment?

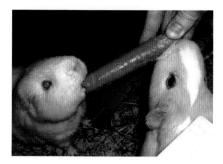

• All our mice get tissue paper and cardboard—usually toilet paper rolls or cut up glove boxes and egg cartons—for nest building and shelter. We also provide chalk sticks for gnawing.

• The cages of our mice are each furnished with a commercial plastic house, a running wheel, and bedding material such as a cotton fiber pad, paper towel or shredded paper.

• The standard furniture of our rat cages consists of one plastic tube serving as refuge and a piece of wood for gnawing.

• We have made it a standard rule that every single-housed rodent (a) has access to a toy that is rotated once a week, and (b) receives daily produce and grain.

When submitting an IACUC protocol, there is a question if the individual animal can receive enrichment or not. If the answer is no, there has to be scientific justification. So far, no investigator has ever insisted that the toy be removed, but some have placed restrictions on food enrichment.

• At our facility:
  (a) the mice get nesting material and a commercial plastic house,
  (b) the rats get a plastic tube and a hardwood block, and
  (c) the guinea pigs get a plastic house, a hardwood block and autoclaved hay.

These enrichment provisions are standard for every animal. If researchers want to opt out, they must provide a written explanation in their protocol; it has to be a very good reason.

We encourage everybody working with our rodents to offer food treats as positive reinforcement after procedures.

foraging enrichment

What are practical options to promote foraging activities in rodents?

- Giving rats large seeds by hand certainly promts much hoarding. I also like to supply them with whole walnuts that they gradually learn how to open. They enthusiastically pull scrunched-up paper out of toilet paper rolls, chew through little cardboard boxes and dig through a pile of shredded paper to retrieve hidden treats. Frozen peas floating in a shallow pan of water is another popular attraction for them.

- For rats and mice, I place high-fiber rabbit food in the bottom of the cage at cage changing; this provides for low calorie, inexpensive foraging enrichment. Hay is also great, both as food enrichment and nesting material.

- Our hamsters receive irradiated sunflower seeds, dried fruit, and peanuts.

- At my institution, the breeding groups of guinea pigs get fresh green grass, vitamin C dissolved in water, and autoclaved hay.

- Based on my two-year experience with a large breeding group of guinea pigs, I can say that guinea pigs relish dandelions and other thoroughly washed green stuff from the garden; they love high-quality hay—the more the better—without experiencing adverse side effects.

- Our guinea pigs relish lettuce, carrots and apples. We've tried cabbage, but some animals don't tolerate it too well, so we stopped feeding it.

- Fresh green stuff is a disease risk, as it can be contaminated; bird droppings are a particular problem. Washing the material in clean running water will remove much of the contamination but it's not foolproof. Many years ago, we fed cabbage and kale to guinea pigs and lost a major colony due to salmonella-contaminated kale that had been washed but obviously not thoroughly enough. We do feed raisins and other dried fruits of human consumption quality to all our rodents.

investigators' permission

At your institutions, do you have to ask permission from the principal investigators (PIs) to enrich the cages of rodents?

- We have a form that all PIs sign, giving permission for enrichment. As more and more investigators become educated about the value of enrichment [for example: Cooper & Zubek, 1958; Diamond, et al., 1964; Bennett et al., 1969; Ferchmin et al., 1970; Carughi et al., 1989; Fernandez-Teruel et al., 2002; Arendash et al., 2004; Cancedda et al., 2004; Green et al., 2004; Neugebauer et al., 2004; Van de Weerd et al., 2004; Sharp et al., 2005; Fox et al., 2006], some actually ask us to provide more enrichment for their animals; this is so nice to see! However, our IACUC will give researchers permission to remove enrichment if they have a convincing reason for it.

- At our facility, it is explained to the researcher that each animal cage has to contain certain enrichment objects or structures. An investigator has to have compelling reasons to keep his/her animals without such enrichment. When we get to know the techs working with the animals, we encourage them to distribute food treats, like cereals and also autoclaved hay, if this does not interfere with the research.

I find that the techs are very willing to give these items to the animals in their charge. It makes all involved feel much better!

- Before adding any kind of enrichment in the cages, we first seek the permission from the investigator to make sure that the enrichment does not affect the experiment. Our investigators have to inform us proactively if there are certain enrichments that must be withheld for study reasons.

- In our facilities, we have begun the process of outlining in our IACUC protocol application forms what we consider to be standard practice, such as provision of nesting materials and shelters for mice, rats and hamsters. Researchers are asked to specify what enrichment provisions they want to be withheld and explain exactly how these enrichments would confound their experiments.

I do see an increased interest and willingness in many of our researchers to provide their rodents an optimal environment, which I attest to a better understanding of the effects of improper environments on research data. There's still much room for improvement, but I think we are moving in the right direction.

- It is my impression that provision of basic environmental features is still not routine in the United States. The implementation of environmental enrichment in a facility seems to depend heavily on the motivation of key people.

- I agree, environmental enrichment is often left up to the individual caretaker; there is no policy that has to be followed. The problem with this is that some animal care staff believe greatly in enrichment while others think it is unnecessary. This inconsistency is probably natural but it is very frustrating; without institutional standards, some animals will have the benefit of having their living quarters enriched by motivated personnel while others have to be content with barren cages because the attending personnel are not interested in providing environmental enrichment.

- At our institution in the United Kingdom, environmental enrichment is the norm. If researchers want to opt out, they must include scientific justification in their project license application so that it can be taken into account by both our internal ethical review process and the Home Office when they consider the license for approval.

- Environmental enrichment is something that Brazilian researchers are not aware of at all. People usually do not give any environmental enrichment for rodents or rabbits, especially if it is a short-term experiment. Therefore, the question of obtaining permission to provide the animals with enrichment does not arise.

rats

amazing social creatures

Is it true that rats are reliably tolerant of each other?

• That rats get along with one another so well is one of the reasons I like working with them. I have never noticed any signs of aggression among rats.

  I have worked with rats in neuropathic research. The animals were always very friendly to each other, even when they were experiencing pain. I witnessed rather affectionate interactions—such as grooming and bringing food pellets nearby—in rats who had undergone surgical procedures.

• We always keep individual rats during the post-operative phase with a buddy to speed up the recovery.

• I have worked with rats for several years but never witnessed that they were aggressive with each other. Yes, they can be aggressive with humans; I have been bitten on several occasions.

- The only time I've ever seen aggression among rats was when someone inadvertently put ex-breeder males together; predictably, this resulted in a major scrap. Unfortunately, this means that once a stud male has been used for breeding, he has to be housed singly from thereon unless he lives in a permanent pair or harem.

  We occasionally get a female who becomes aggressive during the time she has a litter, but that's toward humans, not other rats.

  Diabetic rats can be aggressive toward each other if their insulin is out of control, but that is only temporary and, once insulin is back under control, they become their

usual sunny selves. I believe that obese Zucker rats can be bad-tempered but suspect this is also due to erratic blood sugar levels.

- During my undergrad training, I worked in a pet store for several years. We would routinely put together rats of various ages and genders. I don't recall that we encountered any aggression-related problems when the animals met each other for the first time. To make it even more interesting, we would often use nursing rat moms to foster pups from other rodents, such as hamsters and gerbils; we simply put the new pups in the pile, and the rat mom would take care of them.

- Apart from the jumpy strains, rats are remarkably docile. They can make great children's pets.

- I have always found rats to be the most accommodating of the lab critters: well-mannered, well-groomed, social, affectionate, and intelligent. When it comes to their relations toward each other, I've only ever seen one squabble in 13 years. This occurred when an older female's roommate died and I had a singly-housed girl, who I thought would make a nice friend for her. When I placed them together, the older female did a little song and dance number with a bit of a hiss; but I think that was just to explain that she was Queen Bee. The next day I found them sleeping in their little snuggle patch, as rats do, and they continued to have a happy relationship.

- We humans could learn something from rats in regard to living together rather than fighting against each other.

are rats animals?

Considering the fact that rats are such amazing animals, isn't it outrageous that they—along with mice and birds—are explicitly not covered by U.S. animal welfare regulations (United States Department of Agriculture, 1989)?

• Here is the most recent update of these regulations, including the definition of the term animal:

"*Animal* means any live or dead dog, cat, nonhuman primate, guinea pig, hamster, rabbit, or any other warm-blooded animal, which is being used, or is intended for use for research, teaching, testing, experimentation, or exhibition purposes, or as a pet. This term excludes: Birds, rats of the genus *Rattus* and mice of the genus *Mus* bred for use in research (United States Department of Agriculture, 2002a)."

This language creates a rather bleak situation for the majority of animals used in research, testing and education in the United States.

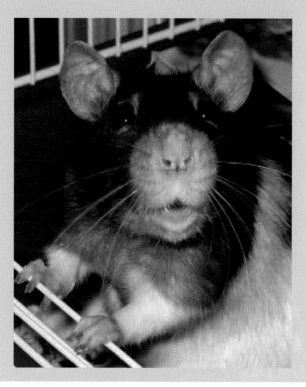

- Many countries have animal welfare laws and regulations. To my knowledge, the situation in the U.S. is an exception: no other country excludes any species in its legal definition of the term animal.

- Why are rats, mice and birds excluded from regulations and oversight? It's a purely economic decision. American research runs on rats and mice. And if birds were regulated, where would the research on chickens, chicken embryos, and pigeons be? In America, our laws are made by the most powerful lobbyists, not by the Congressmen themselves. In terms of animal suffering, we Americans are a lot less civilized than many of our coworkers in Europe.

- I think it is important to add that although the USDA [United States Department of Agriculture] animal welfare regulations do not include mice, rats or birds, the Public Health Service Policy on Humane Care and Use of Laboratory Animals [Public Health Service (PHS), 1996] covers all animals used in research; this includes mice, rats and birds, as well as cold-blooded animals. This policy must be followed by any institution receiving federal funds.

Additionally, many institutions—including private industry groups—are also AAALAC [Association for Assessment and Accreditation of Laboratory Animal Care International] accredited, which uses the the *Guide* (Guide for the Care and Use of Laboratory Animals) as the current standard of care. So, while there are some facilities that do not fall into either of these categories (and there are a few, I will concede), the majority of animal research does follow a standard of care similar to that described in the animal welfare regulations that are promulgated by USDA.

- As a side note, it needs to be remembered that:
  (a) "Animal facilities should [not "must"] be operated in accord with" the Guide and the PHS Policy (National Research Council, 1996, page 2), and
  (b) the NIH [National Institutes of Health], which administers the federal funds, is not an enforcement agency; therefore, the public has no guarantee that the Public Health Service Policy is actually followed by institutions receiving NIH grants.

petting

Rats seem to like it when you pet/groom them. Is there a body area where they prefer to be groomed?

- I used to be a teaching assistant for a rat lab in college, and ended up *pardoning* a couple of rats who became my pets. They always seemed to be soothed by me petting them, very gently and calmly, right at the base of their neck, especially while they were falling asleep. Prior to working with them, I didn't appreciate how very affectionate they could be!

- Rats seem to enjoy having their heads gently scratched behind the ears, and some will lie down for their abdomens to be scratched. If in free mode having an out-of-cage wander on the bench, rats will come up to where someone is working and get in the way until you give in and groom the critter. I find that all of our rats—not just pets—appear to welcome a gentle scratch whenever there is an opportunity. I always encourage investigators to spend some acclimatization time with their rats before they start experimenting with them. This should make them appreciate how amazing their research subjects are and, hopefully, re-evaluate the implications of their planned experiments on them.

- Yes, having the investigators gently handle and groom their rats before starting an experiment is a great idea. An investigator, who has experienced the natural affection of rats and their spontaneous trust in humans, will be very careful not to cause them any avoidable discomfort or harm when conducting an experiment with them.

- If rats have been properly socialized, they will often solicit attention. They seem to love it when you gently scratch them behind the ears, on the head between the ears, and when you give them a mini-massage on the neck. I've had some rats who liked the tops of their front legs massaged too. Males are more likely to sit still for petting/grooming than females.

    I love those little guys! They are really underrated creatures—extremely affectionate and playful, and great learners.

- The rats I have had as pets, and those I have worked with for a long time at work, particularly love to be petted on the top of the head and between the ears. They also give the impression that they really like it when their tails are being stroked from base to tip.

- My pet rats solicit both grooming and play, and they also groom my hands. There are studies showing that rats emit ultrasounds, a kind of *rat laughter*, when they are groomed by hand at the nape of the neck. Rats groom in this manner when they want to play with another rat [Burgdorf & Panksepp, 2001; Panksepp, 2007].

- My rats have always loved grooming me, but they've all been different. I had one girl who would grab my nose with both of her front paws and just lick away. Others liked grooming my eyelashes. Many of them preferred to lick my front teeth—I know, this is a bit gross, but for some reason it didn't bother me, probably because they were my pets. Some licked like crazy, some also nibbled a little bit with their teeth as they would when grooming their own fur. These were very special experiences for me.

- Rats are highly developed social creatures. That they typically establish such affectionate relationships with their human caregivers makes it even less acceptable that U.S. animal welfare regulations do not recognize them as animals.

- I completely agree. I once worked at a zoo facility that bred rats but kept the animals under very poor husbandry conditions. I fought to get better litter for them—they were kept on pine shavings, which are toxic to rats—and suggested that they need bigger cages. When USDA officers would come and do site inspections, they completely ignored the rat room! How can these wonderful, intelligent little creatures be so disregarded and treated as if they were disposable?

- It's so wonderful to witness such enthusiasm for rats! Rats were my first love, but sadly I became severely allergic in graduate school. This is how I ended up with monkeys. I was so accustomed to working with highly intelligent/social creatures that my heart broke when I was told that I would have to find another way to spend my career if I wanted to continue to work with animals. I, of course, love working with monkeys. Luckily, over the years, I have toughened up my immunity so that I can, once again, play with rats. Yeah, I still get hives along my neck when they ride on my shoulder, but it's totally worth it for both parties involved!

- All rat strains I have encountered (Sprague-Dawley, Fischer, Long Evans, Wistar) have enjoyed the scratch behind the ear, but I've only had Long Evans seek/allow their bellies to be rubbed.

- My rats have always loved being scratched/rubbed behind their ears and along the top of the head. Also, a few of them enjoy having their chins and/or upper backs rubbed as well. Then, of course, some will roll over for a good belly rub.

- I need to add another strain of rats to the belly rub list. We had two nude rats arrive at our facility this week, and I was assisting the research group getting used to the proper handling of these new animals. Both of the little guys were more than glad to curl up in my hands for a scratch behind the ear and then wiggled themselves into a position for a belly rub.

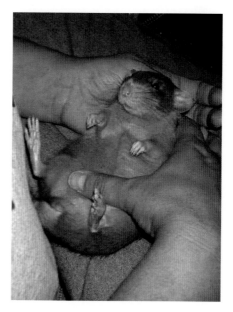

signs of well-being

What are the signs warning you that a mouse, who is neither under the influence of a test drug nor of an experimental procedure, does not feel well? Are these signs the same for rats?

• When I worked with lots and lots of mice, I looked for hunched back, ruffled—or poorly groomed—hair coat as warning signals.

• Aside from the obvious lack of food consumption or lack of urine/feces in a cage, I pay attention to the postures and movements of the mice. Typically their movements are a dead giveaway when they don't feel well. They might be sluggish, or hunched, or their gait might be a bit off.

I also check if they are grooming or interacting with their cagemates. It can take a bit of practice and patience but, once you know the normal behaviors of the animals in your care, you can usually pick up even subtle changes in those behaviors very quickly. Since mice—and rats—tend to be good about hiding their symptoms, this can mean the difference between an easy recovery or a rapid race to the euthanasia chamber.

Unfortunately, none of those signs that I use are well-defined. It's more of the old *I know it when I see it* than look for X, Y, and Z. Obviously, we still look for appetite, weight loss, hair coat, shivering, etc., but in my experience, those symptoms tend to manifest *after* behavioral or movement changes.

- Every veterinarian will endorse your statement: the real knowing does not come from the mind. Yes, this is not a scientific approach to the question at hand, but it has proven over and over again that you often *know without thinking* that something is not right with an animal, that the animal needs help.

- Changes in posture in particular, but also piloerection, are reliable indicators that a mouse does not feel well.

- Isolation from the group, hunched posture and starry coat—hair clumping or standing on end—are, in my experience, reliable signs that a mouse is going downhill. Such an animal *feels* light, compared to a healthy animal, long before you can actually see that the animal is losing weight. Yes, you need to know your charges very well in order to recognize such warning signals before it is too late.

  Introducing a favorite food, such as a few sunflower seeds or some forage mix, is also a good well-being test: if a mouse doesn't try and grab her share, then you may well have a problem at hand.

  Sometimes, you can pick up a peculiar smell in a rat room that tells you that an animal is not well. This peculiar smell is more difficult to detect in mice as they have such a strong odor of their own.

  When I was a young tech, listening to my animals was a good aid to detecting ill-health, as I could hear wheezing/sneezing; this was often the earliest indication of an outbreak of Chronic Respiratory Disease [CRD] and appeared long before any visible signs of the problem.

- We recently put Huntington's mice into enriched cages that contained a climbing rope and a beam. By monitoring the use of these enrichment structures, we noticed a decrease in usage by individual mice several days before any clinical symptoms of disease could be observed, and many days before they actually got sick.

- This is obviously a good way of testing for neurological diseases, without the need to disturb the mice [Carter et al., 2001; Cummings et al., 2007; Quinn et al., 2007].

- We use the ability to run/walk on a beam or cling to a rotating rod as an indication of Prion disease development in mice. The inability to perform these tests and/or the time it takes a mouse to clear food out of a tube reliably shows that she has Prion disease well before any other signs are seen; this has enabled our researchers to refine the end point of the disease dramatically.

petting

It seems to me that mice —unlike rats—do not like to be touched, let alone petted by a human; is that correct?

- Mice definitely are less interested in being petted than rats, but I have found a few who tolerated, perhaps even enjoyed being petted. I have never worked with a mouse who actively tried to get my attention though. I've always loved mice because they're so darn cute and funny to watch.

- While I haven't had a mouse enjoy petting, I had one who seemed to like eye cleaning as a treatment for sore eyes. In the beginning, I had to scruff her to clean the eyes with saline and a Q-tip. After several days of treatment, the little guy would just sit on my hand and lean into the Q-tip for the cleaning. It probably felt good, so why fight it?

- A long time ago, I had a mother mouse die, leaving behind three 15-days-old pups. I did my best to save them and succeeded. Unfortunately, after all they had been through, they were not suitable to be used for research. Well, I didn't want to euthanize them, so I kept them as mascots. There were two females and one male. I felt bad that the male had no buddy to

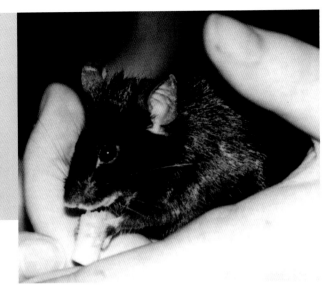

live with, so I took it upon myself to be his surrogate. I assume that he came to like my petting, as he would not run away when I put my hand in the cage to rub his head. He would sit in my hand, while I gave him his daily rub, and close his eyes slightly.

- I used to believe that mice do not like to be held, touched or handled. However, during the past year, I have found that it may all depend on who is working with the mice and how they are being handled. Granted, I would say that 90 percent of the mice at my institution would rather be left in their cages 24/7 without disturbance by human hands, but we have a lab here that has truly happy mice who literally buzz when you hold them.

  I wouldn't have believed that mice could be that way until I witnessed it with my own eyes. I was so amazed the first time I saw this that the person in charge of the mice placed one of them in my hands so I could feel the buzzing. The little mouse then closed her eyes as I gently rubbed behind her head. She even leaned into the direction of the rubbing so I could get behind her ears. I have since referred to this individual as the *mouse whisperer;* he has taught me that there is much more to the mouse than meets the eye.

- Doesn't your own experience strongly suggest that the way animals respond to us depends primarily on us? After all, mice *are* social animals, so there is no good reason why they should shun human contact if they can trust the handler.

  Some years ago we studied the behavior of a large buffalo herd. Initially, many people warned us not to approach the animals without a fence in between because buffalos are supposedly extremely dangerous and have even killed people. After several days of thorough observations from behind the fence, we climbed over and did our studies while moving along with the animals. Yes, we did follow certain social rules that we had learned during our pilot observations, but were able to take our ethological records directly in the herd. It never happened throughout our two-year study that we were charged or put into any kind of dangerous situation by the animals. No, we didn't try to physically contact them, for the simple reason that buffalo, unlike cattle, do not groom each other, hence probably don't like to be touched.

shelter and nesting material

There are various plastic shelters—houses, tubes, and igloos—for mice on the market. Based on your own experience, which is the most species-appropriate and practicable shelter?

- Mice are highly motivated to chew up paper or cardboard to build nests. If this material is provided, I think the pre-fabricated houses are largely redundant. It is the performance of the behavior —building a nest—that is important to the mice, not just its functional consequence of having access to a shelter.

- I would recommend a shelter structure on which the mice can also climb and that has several entrances/exits; the plastic material should be transparent but red-colored so as to avoid disturbing the occupants during the daily checks. Mice appear to prefer shelters without floors. Our mice get shredded paper that they move into the shelter and chew up to form a nest.

We have found that, if you are using plastic shelters, some strains need to quasi-grow up with them in order to use them when they are adults. When we first investigated plastic shelters, we noticed that adult mice rarely used them, but if introduced at the age of weaning, the young mice will accept them more readily and you will end up with almost all adult mice making use of the plastic shelters.

From the mouse's point of view, compressed-paper shelters would be more attractive, but these make the checking of the animals so difficult that we have phased them out in preference for transparent plastic shelters.

- We have never had a problem with plastic tubes for either rats or mice. Yes, the animals can and do chew at the edges of the tube and, after just a week or so, it may need replacing; we have not encountered any teeth or gastrointestinal issues related to that chewing.

- You make a good point about the chewing of plastic; we do see it but, like you, have never encountered any problems as a result of ingestion of plastic particles.

  We also use compressed-paper tubes and shelters; this material is always autoclaved first, so it's very unlikely to be the source of any pathogens for the animals.

- We recently began moving away from plastic igloos to commercial paper huts with several openings. Our staff report that the mice seem to prefer the huts. Different strains appear to customize their hut, adding a *sunroof* or a *canopy*, shredding it completely or using the hut simply as a shelter without damaging it in any manner.

- Taking the standpoint of the mouse, I would certainly prefer reasonably suitable nesting material that I can use to construct a cozy nest at just the right spot of the cage over a prefabricated, heavy, fancy but empty, cold house/igloo that cannot possibly take my personal microclimatic needs into account.

- Van Loo et al. (2005) gave mice a choice of a commercial paper-based shelter (Shepherd Shack™) and a plastic shelter (Techniplast Mouse House™) and noticed that all three strains of mice tested showed a significant preference for the paper shelter. The paper shelter was much lighter (20 g) than the plastic shelter (95 g). This allowed the mice to move it around, manipulate it and change the position of the entrance within the cage. The plastic shelter was probably too heavy for such maneuvering and, hence, never changed its place. The mice also gnawed the paper shelter, occasionally nibbled an extra hole in the side, or shredded part of the walls, using the shreds to strengthen their nest. They could not do this with the plastic shelter. All mice slept inside the paper shelter but never in the plastic shelter. When they slept in the cage that contained the plastic shelter, they did so in the sawdust *outside* the shelter. When tissue paper was provided, the mice dragged the material into the paper shelter and built a

nest, but they never combined this nesting material with the plastic shelter.

- I am not sure there actually is a best plastic shelter; we use several different types that the mice use unpredictably either as a nesting place, a hiding place, or a toilet. What is most important for them, and what they use in a consistent manner is nesting material. Mice love to build nests. When we give our mice Nestlets™ and hay, they typically build a nice igloo-type shelter out of it even if they are also provided with a plastic shelter; I usually find them sleeping in *their* nest but not in the prefabricated plastic shelter.

- I believe that nesting material is more important for mice than a prefabricated plastic shelter. If they have access to nesting material, healthy mice always build a nest and sleep in it. I believe a plastic shelter is useful when several mice are housed together, especially males. If an argument breaks out, the subordinate mouse has a place to hide from the aggressive individual—hopefully out of sight, out of mind. Nesting material doesn't give this kind of cover or protection. We offer both, a cotton fiber pad and a shelter. We use mostly the plastic square houses with several openings. Some mice nest inside the shelter, but many use it to hide from us and from each other, and to climb on. I think both, the cotton fiber pad and the plastic shelter, serve important functions for the mice, so both should be offered to them.

Is it really important for a mouse to build a nest that serves her as a shelter? Is it not enough to give her a substrate, such as half a cotton fiber pad, that allows her to engage in nest-building behavior?

- Suppose we place a mouse in an open field, with access to plenty of soft nesting material and an empty plastic shelter, and expose her to a life-threatening stimulus, for example a cat. I would predict that the mouse will ignore the nice nesting material, because the drive to build a nest is temporarily superseded by the survival instinct, but will swiftly escape into the shelter. I would not conclude from the mouse's response that using the shelter is driven by any higher motivation than building a nest, but that the motivation itself is dependent on the context in which a behavior is *needed*.

  Mice are pretty much always on the alert for good biological reasons, therefore, I do feel that a mouse should be provided with the necessary substrate that allows her to build a proper—that means closed—nest that can serve her as a safe refuge in the event of danger.

- I think your scenario depends a great deal on the type of nesting material available. If you provide a large amount of shredded paper and a plastic shelter, I predict that, in response to the cat, the mouse will run under the paper—which unlike the shelter offers many escape points—and take refuge there, without necessarily building a nest at that time.

  If, however, you provide a cotton fiber pad and a plastic shelter, I agree with you that the mouse will almost certainly escape into the shelter.

  There are many different types of material mice can and will use for nests, from cardboard to electrical cable. Of course, the motivational state for immediate survival (escape from the cat) is different to that of a mouse placed in a cage with little else to do other than perform basic behaviors, such as constructing a nest and improving it whenever new material becomes accessible and can be incorporated.

- In a dangerous situation, mice will go for the shelter, but if the coast is clear they will look for the soft bedding. Case in point is the mice who invaded my garage! I can see where they live: in the small hole near my septic tank entrance. The mice gained access to my garage and were stealing soft materials and bringing them back to the hole in the ground where they live. I can see pieces of the bedding they bring back; they leave trails of the bedding between my garage and their hole. When they are in the garage, my cat is obsessively staring at the walls. I can watch the mice from my window when they scurry about bringing stuff down the hole. But if I am working around the hole, I never see any of the mice come out; their refuge shelter is then much more important for them than the soft bedding.

Mice are biologically programmed to build quite elaborate nests that take various behavioral and microclimatic conditions into account. What kind of nesting material is most suitable for mice to build nests in lab cages?

- Based on my experience with mice, soft paper—not shredded paper—is the most appropriate nesting material for them when kept in cages.

- Van de Weerd et al. (1997) conclude from systematic choice test studies that mice prefer paper-derived materials, such as paper tissues and paper towels, to wood-derived materials such as wood-wool and wood shavings, probably because paper products have a structure that can be converted more easily and appropriately into nests.

- I like shavings along with a cotton fiber pad. It's my experience that mice prefer to build a nest that totally covers them and, when given both materials, most will build this type of nest.

- Nestlets™ are good, but the animals can build much better nests with shredded paper.

- Nestlets™ are 4.8 x 4.8 x 0.5 cm large compressed cotton fiber pads; they are commonly used to offer caged mice the opportunity to build a nest. The nests constructed from one or, even worse, a half of these Nestlets™ have never impressed me, so I am questioning if they can really satisfy the biologically inherent need of a mouse to build a nest.

- In order to cut costs and make mice more visible in research facilities, mice are not given enough material to create a proper nest. A single cotton square is not enough material for a mouse to build a *good* nest, but that is what most mice have to work with.

- Nothing seems to make a mouse happier than building a good nest! But, yes, I agree, the amount of nesting material offered to caged mice is usually pretty scarce.

However, the cage design makes if often problematic to give more. Some mice will construct big nests right next to or around the water sipper tube, a situation that can easily cause flooding of the cage, putting the occupants at high risk if the problem is not noticed and fixed in time. It would be nice to have a cage design for a standard ventilated rack cage that would make it impossible for mice to construct their nests around the water sipper.

- We do use half Nestlets™. We have tried a whole one but the mice love to build their nests under the sipper tube and, by doing so, flood their cage. They never seem happy when wet, so I am thinking they would prefer half Nestlets™ and a dry cage to the wet! Unfortunately, half Nestlets™ are most likely not enough to build a nest in which to hide.

- It seems to me that mice have an extremely strong drive to build a proper, which means closed nest. Whenever a homeless mouse finds suitable or not so suitable material, such as electric wires and some strings under a car's hood, she will not hesitate to build her nest.

  It is very strange that nobody has so far come up with a mouse-cage design with a sipper tube that allows mice to build mice-appropriate nests without risk of flooding. Nest building is such an important behavior for mice that, in my opinion, efforts are warranted to more seriously address this behavior in the research lab setting. As a single-caged monkey is not truly a monkey, a mouse without her nest is not truly a mouse.

- I have the opportunity to give mice just about every kind of nesting material out there. A combination of soft nesting materials and bedding substrates work best for my mice. They seem to prefer paper towels, but they also will use pre-shredded paper, crinkle paper (a commercial product), straw and/or cotton together with the paper towel to form a closed nest.

- Many debilitated mice—transgenic, post-surgical, etc.—cannot use some of the commercial nesting products—such as compressed cotton squares—because they do not have the energy to shred this material and build a nest. I have actually seen such mice sitting on top of unshredded Nestlets™! This doesn't provide for thermoregulation, protection from light or other stressors. I think loose cotton or pre-shredded paper should be made available to such animals so that little effort is required of them to build their nests.

- I have also seen some mice who don't know how to pull the cotton fibers apart and end up just sitting on top of the full sized squares. Sometimes, I'll rip the cotton fiber pad and fluff the edges slightly to see if *starting* it for them helps, but then I find them just sitting amongst the pieces I tore. I haven't noted that this lack of proper response is strain-dependent, but have seen mice of different strains sitting on their Nestlets™ rather than using them as nesting material.

Could it not be that mice need appropriate nesting material, not only to satisfy their strong nest-building drive, but also to construct nests that allow them to conserve heat as needed?

- Gaskill et al. (2009) report "in laboratories, mice are housed at 20 to 24°C, which is below their thermoneutral zone (26 to 34°C)" and thus, "mice are chronically cold stressed." If a mouse is permanently kept in a cage that provides a temperature below the animal's biological thermo-comfort zone, a commmerial, small cotton fiber pad—let alone a half one—will not be enough to enable the mouse to build a cozy nest. She will feel always a little bit cold; this, certainly, would not be conducive to the general well-being of the mouse.

Is wood-wool an enrichment substrate that you would recommend for mice?

- Mice prefer material that is softer than wood-wool. I have witnessed that mice get their paws entangled in this substrate. It can have sharp parts, causing damage to eyes and paws. The fact that wood-wool is not absorbing is a hygienic disadvantage.

- I agree, wood-wool is not suitable for mice; it not only can cause micro injuries but it is often also very dusty, which may create a health hazard for these small animals.

blood collection

From the standpoint of the mouse, what is the least distressing blood collection technique?

- I have found that mice are less stressed when I take blood samples from the submandibular vein versus the saphenous vein. The mouse is subjected to less restraint, for a shorter time. The vein requires hardly any pressure afterwards to stop the bleeding; this again means relatively shorter restraint time. The vessel bleeds far better, especially in small mice, and a bigger sample can be collected if needed. I prefer to use a relatively large 21-gauge needle, because I think it is less stressful for the mouse to be punctured once with a larger needle than poked several times with a smaller needle to obtain a sufficient amount of blood.

- I agree, the advantages of the mandibular method include:
    (a) no need for a restraint device,
    (b) no need to warm the mouse to induce vasodilatation, and
    (c) the technique is relatively simple and easy to learn, and practical especially when you have to collect numerous blood samples.

- We use the saphenous vein approach with large mice who have a good sized vessel, but I also prefer the mandibular approach with small mice who have tiny saphenous veins.

- With the saphenous collection technique you have to use a lot of caution not to hold the mouse too tightly; over-restraint can cause undue stress or even death. I have seen mice being held so tightly that it injured them while saphenous blood was drawn.

- While there are risks and probably pain involved with any of these techniques, I feel that I have more control and get better results with the submandibular blood collection technique.
    I have recently found out how much less stressful it makes the process for the mouse and you if you use the proper lancet. A too large lancet causes too much damage, and with a too small lancet you don't get enough blood. With the correct lancet you can make a good stick one time and get the blood you need quickly, reducing the amount of stress on the mouse *and* you.

- I also prefer the submandibular technique. It is fast, reliable and doesn't require holding off the vessel as does the saphenous technique. Restraint is one of the most stressful things for mice in my opinion. I assume this because they are usually vocal and almost always try to bite!

  The saphenous approach is okay, but sometimes the vessel must be held off for a relatively long time and the mice don't seem to like it all that much.

- I would recommend the tail-incision method for blood sampling of conscious mice. The mouse is placed on the cage lid, head and body covered with a tissue. The tail is bent upwards and with a sharp razor blade a perpendicular, small incision is made at the ventral side of the tail about 1.5 cm away from the tail base. Blood drops are then collected in a capillary tube. It is my experience that the mouse is very calm and hardly responds. When finished, a gauze pad is gently pressed on the incision for a moment before the mouse is returned to the home cage.

- Having applied the tail-incision blood collection many times, I can testify that there is no indication that this technique leads to bone or cartilage damage. However, the incision is so small and superficial that it yields only very small amounts of blood. If larger volumes are needed, I puncture the saphenous vein; for this procedure, the mouse's leg is carefully shaved one day prior to puncture to minimize the stress on the day of the actual blood draw.

- I am going out on a limb and state that I prefer the retro-orbital blood collection technique of conscious mice for the following reasons:
  (a) done by a trained individual, this technique takes less than five seconds to complete;
  (b) you can use a microhemocrit tube;
  (c) if you need to take several samples at different times, the movement of the microhemocrit tube into the canthus is enough to break the clot and allow blood to flow;
  (d) done correctly this technique does not damage the eye.

Performed by well-trained hands the submandibular, saphenous and retro-orbital blood collection techniques are equal in my opinion. Therefore, if you are the best at retro-orbital, you should use this technique; I certainly do.

- As you say, you are going out on a limb!

  How do you measure lack of pain in the mouse when you have to scruff her, holding her so tight that she cannot move? I think the retro-orbital technique should only be done with an anesthetic to alleviate the animal's distress and pain associated with this procedure. This is not a technique for the average vet tech and investigator; it requires extremely skilled and sensitive hands to protect the mouse from serious injury, pain and distress.

- The eye is a particularly vulnerable organ, so just imagining being subjected to a retro-orbital blood collection gives us goose bumps. This is probably the reason why we kind of instinctively infer that a mouse subjected to retro-orbital blood collection must suffer a great deal. It is my experience that this can be the case when the technician or investigator is poorly trained or, even worse, untrained, uses the wrong–size tube, tries to perforate the conjunctiva and is neither careful nor skillful.

  I have taken many retro-orbital blood samples from awake mice and never encountered a serious problem. When you know what you do, and how to do it correctly, you can swiftly collect a sample from a conscious mouse without causing damage to the animal's eye and without inflicting undue restraint stress.

- Personally, I see the risk and trauma to the animal during retro-orbital bleeds without anesthesia as unacceptable. I perform several retro-orbitals monthly yet, I still prefer the submandibular. Done correctly on an adult mouse, it is faster and less traumatic than a saphenous, and less risky than a retro-orbital.

- Even when correctly and carefully performed, the retro-orbital approach certainly causes considerable discomfort to the mouse. Although some people use topical anesthesia, I am not so sure this desensitizes all parts involved in this rather invasive procedure.

- Topical anesthesia for retro-orbital blood withdrawal is not enough. That would be only sufficient for anesthetizing the cornea. The pain comes from penetration of the conjunctiva and the deeper tissue layers. To anesthetize these you need to set a retrobulbar anesthesia, which is a rather painful procedure for humans, and probably also for mice. The best option, in my opinion, is a short isoflurane anesthesia for retro-orbital bleeding.

- At the department where I am now working, retro-orbital puncture is routinely performed under light anesthesia. The technicians are very skilled and, therefore, the procedure causes no problems such as hematoma formation after blood collection.

- I've seen seasoned techs who are so fast and precise with the retro-orbital bleed (the mouse is under anesthesia) that for those mice it seemed to be a fairly benign procedure.

  I'm not as well-practiced and feel that I cause much more morbidity. I personally prefer the saphenous bleed, especially if only a small volume of blood is needed. The mandibular works well—if you can prick once successfully—but I've seen several mice develop large hematomas afterwards, so I think one needs to hold off for some time after the collection, which might be difficult in an awake mouse.

- Some techniques have an inherently higher risk of doing serious damage, because they involve puncturing vessels in the vicinity of sensitive structures. I am of course thinking of the retro-orbital and submandibular techniques. The great advantages of the saphenous technique are that:

(a) you see what you are doing and the vessel for which you are aiming;

(b) you see what happens after the bleed, for example, if there is any hemorrhage, and

(c) the structures around the vein (skin and muscle) are not so critical.

- Based on my own experience as a veterinarian and based on what I have seen in research laboratories, I would argue that the degree of discomfort (physical restraint) and the intensity of pain (tissue poking, hematoma) and stress (duration of handling) experienced by an animal during blood collection is determined not so much by the technique applied but by the sensitivity and expertise of the person who performs the procedure. If you know how to do a procedure correctly, you probably inflict less discomfort, pain and stress on a mouse during retro-orbital blood collection than when you restrain a mouse incorrectly and have to poke the saphenous vein several times before you can collect a blood sample.

  Could it be perhaps that there are not so many people around who do the retro-orbital bleeding correctly as there are people who do the saphenous or submandibular technique correctly?

aggression

Male mice can cause aggression-related problems when you transfer them into a new/cleaned cage. What works best, in your own experience, to minimize or avoid altogether inter-male aggression when you clean/change cages?

- A complete change of the cage bottom reduces aggression; if you then transfer the animals' shelter—or what's left of it—and/or some of their nesting material, fighting will be reduced still further. It seems that some scent markers of the old cage have an aggression buffering effect in the new cage. We transfer our mice directly from dirty to clean cage and see very little fighting; apparently something is working.

  If you put the mice from different cages in succession into the same holding container while you are cleaning their cages and then transfer them into clean cages, every mouse will pick up the scent from other cages and you end up with one humdinger of a scrap. I am not surprised that people who do it this way report terrible fighting problems.

  I should perhaps add the obvious: we make sure to handle the males before the females or at least change gloves after having handled females.

- We have conducted several experiments and found that the following provisions are effectively reducing aggression among male mice [Van Loo et al., 2000; Van Loo et al., 2001; Van Loo et al., 2003]:
  (a) keep the number of mice at three per cage;
  (b) provide two shelters per cage (out of sight means, in general, end of fight);
  (c) transfer some nesting material (tissues) from the soiled cage to the clean cage;
  (d) do not transfer bedding material soiled with urine to the clean cage; this would increase aggression.

- It is my practice to transfer the mice along with their old shelter—if it is still in reasonable condition—directly into a clean cage with fresh bedding. The old shelter seems to mitigate overt aggression in the new living quarters.

  Our mice always get new Nestlets™ in the new cage. A nest building committee is quickly formed and aggression seems decreased because of the chore at hand.

  If the animals get into continuous fighting in the new cage, we don't wait long but check for the primary instigator and remove this individual from the group.

Could you please share more about your experience of removing the aggressor in dysfunctional groups of mice.

- It is not always easy to determine the aggressor right away; I must sit and wait, sometimes for quite a while. If I notice squabbling in a cage, I mark it and will then monitor the mice repeatedly on normal days when their cage is not changed. I mark the cage with a sticker, so the researcher or their techs will also be able to monitor the situation and let me know if they catch the problem mouse. The aggressor typically is the guy who is chasing and initiating an argument with the others. Patience may be required to identify him, but it will pay off. If the fighting has gone on for some time, then the guy with the least or no wounds is usually the culprit. Once we have identified the troublemaker, we take him out of the group.

  When the rascal is removed, I like to keep the sticker on the back of the cage card so I can easily keep track of that group. Typically, another male will take the dominant position of the removed aggressor; I have never noticed that the new alpha male acted as aggressively as the old one, so I never had to remove one of them. It seems that the new dominant mouse is just less aggressive, so fights happen less often and they are usually no longer severe and a cause of concern.

- The following quote from a published article (Emond et al., 2003) supports your observation that removing a particularly aggressive mouse can be very helpful to control aggression:

  "At our Center, two observation periods were set aside daily in order to identify, according to previously described behaviors, dominant mice and separate these when indicated. By reducing or eliminating the number of aggressive acts between group members in the same cage, our social conflict reduction program has led to a 57 percent reduction of mice being reported for clinical signs, death, and euthanasia."

- When I wrote an article on this subject some time ago, we were using conventional cages—no filter tops. This made it quite easy to visually and audibly identify dominance behavior whenever it occurred at its early phase.

  Since then we have been using filter top cages on ventilated racks. Under this new caging condition, we can barely hear the mice fighting because of the filter top barrier and the noise produced by the ventilators. Additionally, when we do spot an aggressive mouse, it takes a few more steps to first remove the cage from the rack and then take off the filter top and the wire-bar lid from the cage in order to access the dominant mouse. By then, most of the time, we have lost visual contact with the perpetrator and it will take many more minutes of patiently waiting to see if the dominant mouse will act up again—or not—or until it is too late and we find injured animals the next working day.

  So, identifying aggressive mice within a ventilated rack system isn't as easy as it is in the old open-cage system described in my article. We are now dealing with more casualties than before.

- Permanent separation of troublemakers is a husbandry intervention that can be useful also in nonhuman primates.

  We had serious aggression-related problems with one of our cynomulgus breeding groups. Close observation revealed quickly that there was one particular animal who instigated almost all fights. Removing this individual resulted in a drastic reduction of overt aggression and the group became oce again relatively harmonious.

- I had to deal with a similar situation in a rhesus-breeding troop.

  There were two female allies—Beta and Witch—who tyrannized most of the lower ranking females of the group. It was quite a terrible situation where we were forced to do something.

  After much consideration, I decided to carefully remove the two troublemakers, one at a time, while taking systematic ethological records over a long follow-up period. I spent many hours observing in order to always be prepared for an emergency situation. I was lucky: initially there was a rise in non-injurious aggressive interactions related to a reshuffling of the troop's hierarchical structure. The alpha female and the alpha male kept their positions without any challenges. This probably held the group together; aggressive conflicts quickly subsided and there was no longer any injurious aggression going on. The troop remained stable and compatible for many years [Reinhardt et al., 1987].

Has anyone had issues with high levels of aggression with FVB mice? If yes, what has worked or not worked to decrease aggression?

• I had serious aggression problems with some FVB males some time ago. I gave them two plastic shelters that have an opening on every side and in the roof, autoclaved hay, a half cotton fiber pad and a bit of shavings. This modification of the males' living quarters reduced overt aggression quite a bit.

• We have very little fighting in our FVB colony; over the years no mouse had to be separated due to fighting or bite injuries.

Our mice are housed in pairs—not trios—in an IVC [individually ventilated caging] system. Each cage has a floor area of 530 cm² and is furnished with a cardboard shelter that is open in the front; this allows good visibility of the occupants by the attending technicians and avoids problems with one mouse dominating the entrance. Generous amounts of shredded paper for nesting are also provided. If pups are present, we offer the mice a small amount of pellets on the floor. We use an expanded diet that is very hard; it keeps the mice quite busy. All cages are checked daily and changed once a week.

Originally we worked with FVBs obtained from a commercial source in the United Kingdom. These mice were far more aggressive than our current FVBs obtained from a source in Germany, so there may be a sub-strain problem somewhere along the line.

• Would you please elaborate a bit on the expanded diet.

• This is a diet that has steam pumped through the mix while it is being pelleted. The nutrition is the same as standard extruded pellets but the resulting expanded pellets are very hard and crunchy and a little chunkier. They are more palatable to the mice, and they are microbiologically cleaner due to the high processing temperature. The only word of caution I would add is that, if you have a strain that produces very small and weak pups, some supplementation may be necessary for the first week or so post-weaning. We give ours a few cubes that have been smashed up so that they are easier to chew and ingest.

Most of our feed manufacturers in the U.K. offer both extruded and expanded diets.

Does access to a running wheel
—without an attached shelter/igloo—affect intermale aggression?

- I found that certain hiding items, such as PVC tubes, reduce aggression, but I have witnessed that access to a running wheel actually increases aggression among male mice.

- Our mice have running wheels, but we still see them fighting and have to separate aggressors. Interestingly, the males continue running stereotypically in circles despite having a running wheel.

Animals tend to compete over a biologically relevant, yet limited resource. Do rodents compete over access to a running wheel?

- I have never noticed any competition, but many times I have seen up to four mice all running on the same wheel together! Sometimes one of them falls off but jumps back on the wheel immediately without being hindered by the others.

   It's the funniest thing to watch. All four mice run on the wheel with their little legs just zooming. If one stops running and the others keep going, the stopped one just spins around on the wheel....weeeee! I also never saw competition, but they are so busy running; I'm not sure they'd be able to fight.

- I have made similar observations in hamsters. Often, two ore more of these critters are running in the wheel; no aggressive competition over a space on the wheel, just a lot of hopping on and off.

barbering

Partner-directed hair-pulling (barbering) is a common behavior shown by mice kept in laboratories; in fact, it can be so common that it is often accepted as normal for this species. If you see signs of barbering (loss of hair/alopecia) in your mice colony, are you concerned about it?

• I have mainly noticed barbering in C57BL/6 mice. Most of the time there is one mouse who has all of his/her hair while all other group members are partially bald. Often, if you remove the barber, the others will grow back their hair, but it also happens that one mouse will take on the role of the group's new barber.

I have noticed that each barber has his or her own style, grooming away hair just between the ears or just on the right flank. It seems that individual styles are copied by others. For example, if a flank-barber is placed in a group of mice with an ear-barber, you'll probably end up with mice who will now be missing hair both between their ears and on their flanks.

To be barbered by another mouse doesn't seem to bother the mice overtly. However, if one considers the mouse's sensory musunculus [analogous to the human homunculus which reflects the relative space that parts of the body occupy in the somatosensory cortex; Vanderhaeghen et al., 2000] a large portion of their sensory input comes from the vibrissae. We could infer from this that, if a barbered mouse lost all of her vibrissae, it might be akin to blinding that important sensory organ.

• Barbered mice are certainly poor choices for any behavioral research, as they will no longer be able to use their whiskers as a biologically crucial source of sensory input for orientation, exploration of the environment, distinguishing objects, locating objects and discriminating the texture of objects. I don't know if the behavioral researchers/investigators are aware of these confounding variables, as many of them were probably taught that barbering was a normal behavior so they could, in essence, ignore it as a confounding variable.

• It is no secret that whisker-barbering will confound an open field test and any behavioral test that requires species-typical sensory capability.

- Barbering/hair-pulling is, in my opinion, a very sensitive indicator that something is seriously wrong with the housing condition of mice or any other species who engages in this compulsive stereotypy. We have become so used to it that we often overlook it as a behavioral problem that needs to be acknowledged and addressed.

- If one is not aware of the fact that a certain behavior, such as barbering, is not normal, then one cannot control for it. In the JAX™ [Jackson Laboratory] mouse info, it says that barbering is a normal display of dominance in mice. Well, if I were an investigator who knows little about mice, I would probably say "hey if JAX says it is a normal behavior then, okay, nothing to worry about; it won't affect my research because it is a normal mouse behavior."

  I have to fight battles daily with investigators who don't believe their animals need enrichment because (a) "they are just mice," (b) "barbering is normal according to JAX" and (c) "barbering does not affect my XYZ research." I would guess most of the enrichment/behavior folks out there in LAREF land have heard these excuses from not so progressive investigators before.

- It surprises me that no earnest published efforts have yet been made to better understand this behavioral problem, develop refinement strategies to prevent it from developing—at least in those strains of mice in which barbering has no genetic component—and perhaps even eliminate it once it has manifested. Do investigators simply not care, because barbering has no explicit economic implications? In sheep, wool-pulling has economic implications, so strategies have been successfully explored and implemented to control this costly behavioral pathology [Reinhardt, 2005].

- There has been research on barbering in mice, but the problem is that it seems to be a multifactorial phenomenon, with both genetic and environmental factors possibly playing a role. The most important difficulty is that you cannot predict which animal is going to show this behavior; it is also not possible to induce it artificially. This means you cannot set up an experimental design with barbering groups and control groups, with and without environmental modifications, as you can never predict which group—perhaps both or neither—will actually display barbering. So it is not that people are not interested, but more a matter of defining your groups in an experiment.

- Although it is often said that barbering is performed by the dominant animal, I dare dispute this. I often observed that not only subordinate but also dominant mice actively offer themselves to get barbered. They would lie down and relax while their cagemate is grooming and barbering them. When the barber stops too soon, he is nudged to resume the barbering.

  Of course these are only anecdotal observations, but it would not surprise me if being barbered would activate some endogenous opioid system and, hence, can become addictive. If this is true, the behavior itself may actually be stress-reducing and less of a welfare problem than we think.

- I am also not convinced that the mice on the receiving end are in pain or that the act of barbering is motivated by aggression. I have often seen the animals sit quietly while the barber completes his task. Some of them seem to actively invite the barber to pull their hair. Over time, barbered mice develop bald patches, but this does not seem to affect their physiological and behavioral well-being.

  We do identify barbering as an unwanted behavior but we don't regard it as an animal welfare issue.

- Regardless of whether having hairs pulled out is painful or not, having naked patches must hamper thermoregulation for a normally furry animal. Mice who live with a heavy barber may have most of their neck and back plucked.

- The mouse who is being barbered is, in my opinion, not suffering all that much directly from this behavior—apart from possibly feeling a little cold. However, I believe the mouse receiving the barbering is probably suffering because she is experiencing the same inadequate housing conditions that make the active mouse engage in the barbering.

- Rather than focusing on the barbered mouse, we should probably be more concerned about the mouse who does the barbering. After all, barbering is not a normal behavior as it is performed in a stereotypical, almost compulsive manner.

- Barbering mice show histological changes in the prefrontal cortex (Sarna et al., 2000) that are seen also in humans suffering from compulsive hair-pulling, a behavior classified as a mental disorder that can cause clinically significant distress (American Psychiatric Association, 1987). The hair-pulling mouse is perhaps also in a state of distress; if that's the case, barbering would certainly be a welfare concern with possible implications for scientific data obtained from affected animals.

hamsters

aggression

Hamsters can create aggression-related problems when they are caged alone (defensive aggression against personnel) and when they are caged in pairs or groups (injurious aggression against each other). What are practical options to minimize aggression in captive hamsters?

- Hamsters are nocturnal animals who want to sleep during the day, when we are active. This implies that we are always waking them up during their sleep cycles so, very naturally, they are grouchy. I always give them a minute or two to wake up and only then will I try to handle them. This usually helps to avoid an aggressive overture.

- We typically put two hamsters in a cage and encounter no real aggression-related problems. I let the two wake up before I reach in the cage and handle them. Some folks like the saying *let sleeping dogs lie*, mine is let sleeping hamsters lie. It occasionally occurs that just-waking-up hamsters are—understandably—grouchy. When this happens, I take a PVC tube section and simply herd them into the tube and pick them up.

- We house six to eight males in large cages where they receive sunflower seeds and have access to gnawing blocks. Generally, there is no fighting, but minor scuffles at cage change occur regularly. They result in a few squeaks and nips, but everyone calms down quickly and goes back to sleep most of the time; after all, they want to sleep during daytime when we do our work with them. The hamsters often sleep on top of one another, suggesting that they do seek close contact with each other.

Occasionally, wounding does occur, and you can typically see the troublemaker. While you change the cage, remove him, and the others quickly resume harmonious communal life. My policy on hamsters is to try housing them in groups but to always be on the lookout, as some animals may get aggressive and need to be single-housed.

As for attitude, hamsters must be handled a lot or they will become feisty. This can range from screeching and teeth barring to actual bites and bloodshed. It appears to me that when left alone, a hamster remembers that he or she is by nature a curmudgeonly, solitary animal, content to be alone.

- These days, most commercially supplied hamsters—in the U.K. at least—have been selected for temperament and seem to tolerate each other if they have been reared together. Previously, we have overcome any aggression towards personnel by regular handling although, in fairness, most of the aggression is just bravado and, if you handle hamsters correctly, they rarely bite.

- In my experience, hamsters are usually aggressive to personnel, but not to each other. In order to minimize aggression against personnel, we gently handle the hamsters regularly before we conduct experiments with them.

pair housing

Is it easier to keep female hamsters than male hamsters in social settings?

- We keep five females, older than 30 days, per cage. They seem to get along with each other quite well, and there is hardly any overt aggression. They always sleep very close together, often one on top of the other. Even when they are eating, we do not see any antagonistic behavior.

- Our male hamsters live in pairs; they are not siblings. They may have a few arguments when the cage is changed, but they work it out; in almost all instances no serious stuff that requires separation.

guinea pigs

group housing of males

By transferring our pair-housed male guinea pigs to groups in pens with more opportunity for social interaction and exercise, we hope to keep their body weight at around 500 g. Our animals get fed chow ad lib, together with hay and a daily ration of carrots and apples; they have access to chew sticks and tunnels. What would you consider to be the optimal housing environment for these animals to help them satisfy their species-specific behavioral needs while also managing their body weights?

- It seems to me that you are already providing your animals relatively species-adequate living conditions. If you offer them the same feeding and structural enrichment when kept in groups, you are already doing your best pretty much.

However, keeping male guinea pigs in groups may cause you some headache. In the wild, guinea pigs live in large harem groups; they do not form bachelor groups, as many other species do, so keeping a group of males permanently together in the same enclosure can be problematic because victims of aggression have no way to leave the territory. Even numerous shelters will probably not be a guarantee that a group of confined guinea pigs will not become incompatible because more dominant males will bully, often quite mercilessly, subordinate males.

- I agree, you already do an excellent job with enrichment, but I would also have concerns with housing males together in groups; this may not go so well.

- Rather than trying to give male guinea pigs more exercise in a group setting so that they don't gain too much weight, it should be possible to achieve the same effect by changing their diet.

- I would not be too concerned about aggression but make sure that environmental factors don't trigger unnecessary aggression among the males.

  I find that the presence of females in the same room is the main trigger for aggression among male guinea pigs. Refuges will not change the males'

behavior; once fighting starts, the integrity of a group can usually no longer be maintained, which is not an ideal situation.

We try to keep our females in a separate room, but if this is not possible, the two sexes are always in separate racks and the males are cleaned out before the females. Even though all our cages have solid floors, it is not uncommon that aggression among males is set off when females are kept in a tier above them.

proper diet to prevent obesity

Guinea pigs love hay and vegetables, especially the green stuff. We usually feed guinea pigs in laboratories hay and greens as a supplement to their commercial pellet diet. Why not reverse it, and make the hay, greens and vegetables the staple diet and supplement it with pellets and vitamin C as needed?

- I think that would be a reasonable approach to prevent guinea pigs from getting too heavy. Unfortunately, it would be hard, if not impossible, to get administrators and investigators to realize that feeding caged guinea pigs veggies/greens/hay in the morning and pellets in the afternoon would be an optimal regimen to control the animals' body weight and provide them with a diet that is much more species-adequate than dry pellets only.

- Yes, it is frustrating at times to deal with PIs and administrators who stubbornly cling to the traditional way animals in labs have been kept, fed, treated and handled. It can be quite a task to break this inertia of tradition; it is worth the effort because it is possible!

- Our guinea pigs only get a pelleted diet and autoclaved hay if the study allows. I would love to see them eat fresh foods, but I guess the time allowance for that may be a problem in some facilities. The washing and preparing of the green stuff for the first feeding, then a second feeding at night, all takes time. Unfortunately some facilities just won't go for it, when it is so much easier and less costly to simply supply pellet food.

- Although it's true that guinea pigs adore their greens, I have been taught that animals housed indoors should be fed a staple manufactured diet in addition to greens so that they get the proper amount of vitamin C. If one were able to provide the animals with veggies rich in vitamin C, there might be a chance that one could lower the amount of manufactured food in the diet. However, I am not sure if the guinea pigs would be willing to eat enough of the veggies to obtain the needed nutrients; this would be a condition for such a diet regimen.

- Wild guinea pigs don't get a balanced commercial diet but they thrive well on natural plants and seeds supplemented occasionally with rain water.

- In order to feed greens, hay and vegetables as a staple food for captive guinea pigs, it is essential to make sure that the foodstuff provides the animals the necessary vitamin C. If this is not possible, supplemental vitamin C is needed.

- In my experience, guinea pigs like a simple vitamin C solution a lot. We dissolve one vitamin C tablet (for human adults) in water. The animals literally suckle it from the syringe voluntarily.

straw bedding

Is it a practicable and safe option to keep breeding groups of guinea pigs on straw?

- I would prefer hay for guinea pigs, as straw may cause eye damage. Hay is softer.

- You can use straw—we give it when we don't want the animals to obtain too much nutrition from foodstuff. However, the straw needs to be wheat or oat straw not barley; the awns in barley straw do, indeed, cause eye problems.

shelter

Rodents have a need for a refuge area, be it a shelter or a self-constructed nest. Do rabbits have a similar need; if so, how can we address this need for animals who are caged alone and for animals who live in groups?

- Our group-housed rabbits regularly use an old metal rabbit cage—with the door removed—as shelter. This cage is placed in the bedded area of the floor pen; the rabbits often sit inside or on top of it. They use a separate area for a latrine, so the shelter is rarely soiled, but if necessary, it goes through the cagewash and autoclave.

  When the rabbits are housed individually, we furnish each cage with an old plastic mouse box. The animals often sit on top of the box; some turn it upside down and sit in the box instead. The rabbits can push the box around until it's in a spot they like.

- We use huts for our group-housed rabbits who seem to like them. We make the huts by slicing large, very thoroughly cleaned, recycled chemical barrels in half, and then cutting out a couple of entries.

- Gerson (2000) modified traditional rabbit cages by linking two cages vertically by means of a ramp and installing in each cage a 30-cm high platform that the pair-housed animals regularly used as a shelter or lookout.

enrichment for single-caged rabbits

How do you enrich the environment of single-caged rabbits?

- What my rabbits really like with great consistency is autoclaved hay. It serves them both as a foraging substrate and a hiding place. Sanitary paper rolls entertain them quite a bit. They play with them and chew them, but the material gets soiled quickly and the rabbits then lose interest in the rolls.

- Most of the time we give our rabbits toys that make noise, such as hollow objects containing one or several bells, or stainless washers inside of plastic balls; the rabbits can move the item—usually by nudging it with the nose or picking it up with the mouth—and make noise. Typically, not all rabbits in a room are ringing the bells at the same time, so the noise is not much of an issue.

- When we first started giving our rabbits items to manipulate, we used canning jar lids as they were inexpensive and, at the time, we had a very large number of rabbits but a very small budget. The rabbits loved to pick the lids up, drop them on the cage floor and push them around. If we went into the room and the rabbits were relatively inactive, all we had to do was drop a lid or tap it against a cage door to make the familiar tink sound and soon, most or all rabbits in the room were making quite a racket with their jar lids.

We have since expanded our enrichment toys to include small plastic barbells, and a variety of hanging toys such as metal chains with metal rings or bells attached to them. While inside the room the rabbits can be quite noisy with their toys, the noise level outside the room is not an issue.

Preference for the type of toy varies by rabbit but nearly all of them seem to enjoy any toy that makes a metal-against-metal noise.

- A little stainless steel bell, attached to a suspended foraging ball filled with hay, turned out to be a real hit for my rabbit at home. Both the hay and the bell exert an amazing attraction, but I must admit that the constant ringing can get on your nerves when you try to focus on something other than the cute rabbit.

- We used to fit to the front bars of all our rabbit cages large metal stainless steel rings, similar to a key ring. The noise of 40 rabbits, all playing with the rings was considerable, to say the least—the rabbits didn't mind it but it drove the staff crazy.

- Yes, rabbits love to make noise. We give them each a small stainless steel bowl. They pick it up and throw it around their pen. I love to see the effort and fun they have when the bowl turns upside down; they go to great lengths turning it around again and then flinging it across their cage!

- My favorite single housing set-up for rabbits was at a university in Canada. The rabbit room was subdivided by a series of baby gates that formed a grid. The animals had plenty of room for several hops across their floor space, could stand as tall as they wanted to, could hide in a big tube, and they could also touch noses with their neighbors and lay down on either side of the fence with direct body contact. The gates were too high for them to jump over.

When it was time to clean, the rabbits were temporarily placed in cages, the grid collapsed, the floor swept, and finally the grid and the bunnies replaced. Everyday the tech came in and fed them Cheerios; they would stand up to retrieve their treats. This served as enrichment but, additionally, the animals' reaction, or lack of reaction, was a reliable and early indicator of any illness.

- That's the way to do business with rabbits in the laboratory setting. So simple, but at the same time smart and rabbit-appropriate.

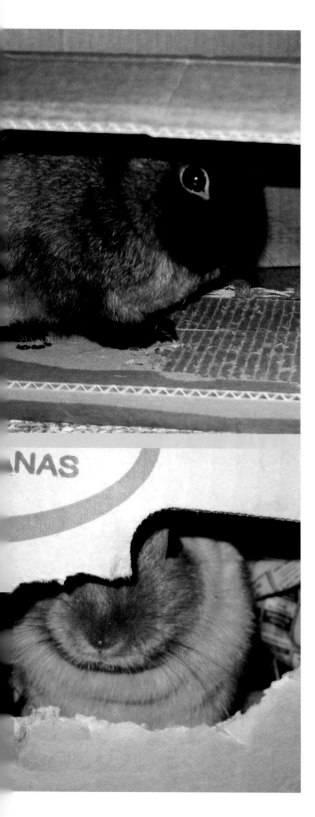

- Our rabbit banks have six cages, three rows of two. There are panels between the cages but they have a space at the top where neighbors can see each other and touch noses, if they so wish.

  All our rabbits get autoclaved hay daily. When distributing the hay, I pet each rabbit while talking to him or her gently.

  Each rabbit also gets a cardboard box. Some animals use it as a platform, some hide their toys or themselves in it while others use it as an outhouse. They all love to chew on them and tear them apart. We keep a steady supply of recycled cardboard boxes.

- We have no proof that the rabbits do not ingest any cardboard but have never had a problem. The cages are always full of the shredded cardboard but that is not to say they don't snack on it. We do take care to only use plain cardboard to avoid potential problems with ink from printing.

- Our single-caged rabbits also each get a small cardboard box, big enough for them to fit in or lie on top. We do not autoclave these boxes; we have been using them for many years without encountering any hygiene- or health-related problems. Nothing seems to make a bunny happier than a cardboard box to chew on! Our researchers do not raise objections that their rabbits have access to cardboard.

- If we single-cage rabbits, we arrange the cages in such a way that the animals can see one another. They are provided with hay on a daily basis including weekends, cardboard boxes—unprinted variety garnered from various sources and autoclaved—and a redundant plastic mouse cage that they can use as a platform. Cardboard boxes last an indeterminate time, some rabbits destroy them on a daily basis, and with other rabbits they may last a week. We have also tried metal rings fixed to the cage front which the animals can jingle—staff wear ear-protectors as noise can be deafening—but we found that these can cause problems as they become sharp; we had rabbits get legs stuck in these rings. We also supply food treats if protocols allow.

    Researchers are encouraged to visit the rabbits at least once a day.

- Our single-caged bucks also have visual contact with each other. For entertainment, we give them empty plastic bottles, which they enjoy pushing around and throwing against the cage walls, thereby creating some noise.

- All of our bunnies are singly housed for both research and safety reasons. I have noticed that the more attention they are given, the calmer they are and the easier they are to work with.

  We provide our rabbits with toys— jingle balls, plastic barbells, hay foraging balls and occasionally Kong™ toys. I've been trying to keep up a steady rotation as, like all other animals in labs, rabbits quickly become bored with the usual commercial toys.

- I have recently begun using large cardboard tubes—following investigators' approval of course—which the animals really seem to love. Some rabbits see how far they can fit into the tube, others knock it and roll it around the cage, and still others simply just chew the edges of the tube.

  Finally, I try to find the time to stop by each bunny's cage every day. During those visits I give the animals treats and, if they want, a gentle scratch. Our long-term bunnies have gotten quite accustomed to this little ritual; I now have several who will bang their toys around in the cage or try to climb the cage bars to get my attention. I have to say that I really enjoy my rabbit rounds and have become quite attached to this little routine. I find my day is just a little empty if I don't get a chance to visit my bunnies.

handling

Rabbits can be quite feisty at times when you handle them during procedures. Do you take any precautions when dealing with such animals?

- It is my experience that most rabbits like to have their eyes covered when you handle them and choose it when they have the opportunity. When we hold rabbits for blood collection, using the saphenous vein, we place them on a counter with one hand holding the scruff and the other hand holding the hind leg. The rabbit can rest her head on my forearm or, as most of them do, tuck it under my arm against my side and elbow.

- I had to deal with the occasional attack-bunny; our most problematic one was a charger, scratcher and biter. We found the best way to remove her from the cage was to use a rat box and scoop her out. This was easy, if all we needed to do was give her a clean cage. But getting her out for antibody bleeds became a bit more challenging. On those days, we would scoop her into a rat box, place the lid onto the box and move her down the hall into a quiet space. We would then—please note the use of *we* as it took more than one person—kind of pour her from the box into a towel or lab coat, quickly place the fabric over her face, firmly hold her by the scruff, and then move her front half into the crook of one person's arm—who would very gently bounce her while keeping her feet on the counter top or floor. This would, after a while, calm her to the point where the other person was able to inject her with some ace [acepromazine] to calm her further for the purpose of bleeding.

  So, long story short, I'm all for the use of a towel to calm a notorious "attack-rabbit."

- It seems to me that an animal—not only a rabbit but any animal—who is excessively intractable and, hence, suffers extreme distress when being handled and forcefully restrained, should be acclimated to the handling personnel and to the handling procedure especially thoroughly or be exempt from participating in that particular research protocol. After all, a distressed animal is not a good model for biomedical research. I also believe that we have an ethical obligation to avoid or alleviate suffering of the animals in our care whenever this is possible; and it is possible in almost all instances.

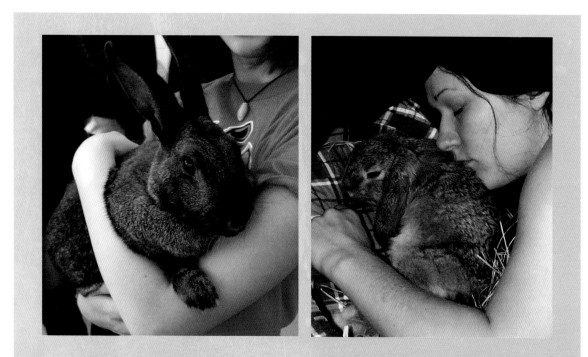

- I remember working with single-caged rabbits years ago at another facility. As soon as you entered the animals' holding area, all the rabbits freaked out because they were so frightened by people. To help them overcome their apprehension and fear, I developed the routine of brushing the fur of as many rabbits as I could during a week, clipping the animals' nails regularly and, most importantly, during my frequent visits, turning on a radio channel that played beautiful Gregorian chants and classical music in the rabbit room.

  When the animal facility supervisor entered the rabbit room after a few months of this routine, his jaw literally dropped. He couldn't believe how calm the rabbits were when he or even a stranger came into the room. I told him that I didn't consider the rabbits just a piece of meat.

  The rabbits came to appreciate me. They enticed me to pet them, whenever I came into their room, by tapping on the floor of their cages until I gave them a big body scrub. Needless to emphasize that any handling procedure I had to conduct with these bunnies was easy to accomplish because the animals had gained trust in me.

- Rabbits do have the potential of becoming attached to humans when they have learned through experience that they can trust them.

- We've been doing lots of rabbit studies lately during which the rabbits need to be removed from their cages and handled a great deal. One of our challenges is that they cannot be scruffed as one would do normally. At the start, we had several animals who were beyond feisty and would attack at the drop of a pin—I have the scars to prove it. In order to prevent further injury and hopefully reduce the animals' uneasiness, I started using a lab coat to remove them from their cages. I turn the coat around and put my arms through the sleeves in the opposite way in order to create a cover for my arms and a blanket-type cover under which I can scoop the rabbit up and which I can wrap around the animal, if need be. It works quite well.

I have now started to handle the rabbits upon arrival so that they get accustomed to being scooped up and subsequently manipulated, right from the beginning. I've found that taking the time to get the animals used to me and the handling procedure, prior to the actual testing, is much better for all involved. Petting them really helps with the handling process; I even had one buck recently who, when I opened the door to his bin, would butt my hand—much like a house cat—to ask for a gentle scratch.

By the time the study starts the rabbits are much more cooperative and we are able to do without the lab coat most of the time. However, we always keep a lab coat handy—just in case.

- When I used to look after rabbits, I always petted each animal daily while giving them their hay. I started with just gently placing my hand on the neck area and then gradually stroking them from the top of the head down to the rump. I always talked to them while doing this so that they get used to my voice as well. By starting out this way I have encountered only a few aggressive rabbits.

- I use a blanket to retrieve aggressive rabbits from their cages. For the rabbits, the large blanket functions like a barrier, so most of the time—but not always—they don't try to charge me when they come out of their cage. The blanket protects my side once the rabbit is scooped in a football fashion. A few rabbits have given me a bite or two when I tried to carry them. In these instances the blanket was very useful; the rabbit got a mouthful of the blanket instead of me!

- I keep forgetting that I may be in the minority when it comes to talking to the critters—some of my coworkers will catch me in the act and ask to whom I'm speaking! Regardless, I always talk to the bunnies as I'm getting them used to common handling procedures. I enter the room with a greeting and then speak in a soft voice throughout the process, so they might associate my voice with the fact that what they're going through isn't all that bad.

- It is also my experience that talking to animals—this includes also wild animals/birds—is an amazing tool to establish positive communication with another critter. Many people shake their heads when they hear you talking to animals, but they overlook the simple fact that words per se are meaningless—just symbols—but words are accompanied by certain emotional vibrations and those are beyond verbal language and, hence, can be properly interpreted by other people and animals.

- I talk the moment I walk into any animal room until I leave. It is my impression that the animals get calmer and less startled when I talk to them in a gentle tone.

- In my experience, animal "users" who don't talk to the animals need to be watched carefully, as I feel it's a sign that they are not seeing the animals as living beings but more as some sort of machines, and they will most likely treat the animals accordingly.

blood collection

What is the safest and, for the subject, the least distressing method to collect blood from conscious rabbits?

- We place a catheter in the auricular artery whenever we have a study where multiple blood samples are required. As long as the restraining person is gentle and firm and the individual placing the catheter is accurate, it is not really stressful for the rabbit. We burrito our rabbits in a lab coat. We then have the restrainer—usually me—hold the rabbit very securely and also cover the rabbit's eyes; this tends to have a relaxing effect. If the person placing the catheter is skillful, it takes only one prick and the rabbit usually does not even bat an eye.

- We apply an almost identical method. We never use restraining boxes but always restrain our rabbits by wrapping them in a towel and having someone hold them firmly but carefully while talking to them and stroking them between the ears.

- When we bleed our rabbits, we give them a small shot of ace and, once that has kicked in, place them into hard-sided restrainers. We use the restrainer rather than a lab coat because it allows the animal to be bled by one individual rather than two—we have a small staff, so we often need to fly solo on procedures such as this. We then insert a 21- or 23-gauge butterfly extension into the ear artery and collect directly into tubes.

- For once weekly blood draws, we first acclimatize the rabbit to being handled, then place the rabbit on a counter and hug him or her with one hand while inserting a butterfly in an ear vein and collect the blood sample. It is my experience that the animals get used to this procedure very quickly and basically stop flinching after a few times and sit there, while you hug them for insertion, and then the rabbits relax and quietly sit on the table while you finish. If clotting becomes an issue I use the 3-inch tubing butterflies with vacutainer; the speed of collection will prevent clotting.

  This method probably does not work for multiple blood collections per day. I think the rabbits would get fidgety.

- We normally sample from the saphenous vein. A 21-gauge needle without hub is inserted into the vein; the blood then drips from the needle into the collection container. If the rabbit dislikes this route, we use the ear vein with the same mode of collection.

  A good rabbit handler is the most important, stress-buffering factor. If the rabbit is held properly, then all are safe and hopefully the sample will be obtained with one try, which means less discomfort for the animal.

- It is probably not the blood collection technique per se that determines the welfare implications for the rabbit but the technical and manual skills of the person who performs the procedure and, above all, the empathy of the other person who restrains the rabbit.

inappetence

What do you do when your rabbits persistently refuse to eat with no other obvious clinical signs?

- At times, we have rabbits go off feed as well, even though they appear fine otherwise. We generally give them a product called Critical Care™; the rabbits love it! It comes in powder form and you mix it with water. We generally offer it together with five or six hay cubes, first two times per day then one time per day. This regimen helps in pretty much all cases—including post-surgical animals—and the rabbits gradually start eating again properly.

- It is my experience that allowing any rabbit showing signs of inappetence some additional exercise—such as running around the floor of the room for an hour—often helps.

- We also had this problem with our rabbits and found out that giving them hay every day as a supplement not only keeps their bowels working but also entices them to eat properly. We used to only give hay as enrichment a couple times a week. Adding hay daily to the rabbits' regular diet solved the problem of inappetence.

- Two years ago I adopted two dwarf bunnies. What I find very interesting is the differences between the diet of a lab rabbit and a house rabbit.

  I was always taught to feed lab rabbits ad lib pellets, and that's all; hay was regarded as an extra treat—if it was mentioned at all.

  After adopting my two bunnies and researching everything I could find on rabbit health and diet, I discovered that for house rabbits it is recommended that they are fed ad lib hay and restricted pellets. I have now learned that it is the hay that keeps things moving internally. The pellets are important, but given ad lib can lead to obesity and can, probably, also cause inappetence.

- At my laboratory, we feed our rabbits ad lib both hay and pellets. We met some initial resistance from investigators regarding the hay, but our veterinarian was firm and refused to allow any research to be done with rabbits unless they were given hay ad lib. The hay does keep the rabbits' digestive track working properly. Also, rabbits are hindgut digesters, meaning they use their cecum and large intestine for most of their digestion; the hay is a very important factor for cecum health and normal cecum functioning.

At my previous job, we did not feed hay, so we had constant problems with rabbits not eating, and once a rabbit stopped eating it was mostly downhill from there. Where I am working now, we have very little incidence of rabbits going off feed and I think that's largely due to the hay. Even after our rabbits have surgery, the first thing they do, once awake, is start eating their hay.

• Our rabbits are also fed ad lib pellets and hay. The group-housed animals do not have weight gain issues, presumably, because of the exercise they get. The single-caged ones receive the same food but are kinda chubby. The chubbiness has not been a concern as of yet; even though these guys get little exercise, their bowels still are kept quite regular due to the hay! We have had no loss of appetite problems since we started hay daily as routine food instead of occasionally, as part of the enrichment program.

• I'm really happy to see that there are facilities that do provide their rabbits ad lib hay. That's what the animals deserve and what they need.

How do you make sure that the hay is free from pathogens?

• We autoclave it for three minutes at 221°F (105°C).

• We do the same.

• Does the autoclaved hay have any nutritional benefit, or do you provide it simply for enrichment? Also, how do you autoclave the hay? We typically wrap it in surgical drape material, but that smells so bad; I imagine it could add a bad taste to the hay.

• I doubt if there is much in the way of vitamins left after autoclaving, but then isn't the main benefit of hay to keep the gut working properly by providing a lot of fibrous material? The fact that it provides a natural way of foraging is complementary. Our rabbits also get pelleted diet but only in small amounts.

We autoclave the hay either in strong paper sacks or autoclavable nylon bags that our sawdust is supplied in.

• At our institution the hay is autoclaved in cloth laundry bags and we always use the same ones over again. We no longer use the dry cycle after it burned the hay on occasion! We now dump it into big plastic bins and let it air dry. It works, and our rabbits seem to like the autoclaved hay.

• Since autoclaving destroys vitamins, we use irradiated hay at our facility.

pair formation of does

We will soon receive female Dutch Belted rabbits for an upcoming project. The PI would like to have these rabbits pair-housed. I have hardly any experience with rabbits, so I am wondering if anybody can share some practical advice on how to establish pairs of compatible does.

- We order our rabbits as early as possible and have them paired up already at the breeder station when they are still very young. This means, we get them at our facility as compatible pairs, so we don't need to worry about pairing them.

- When attempting rabbit pairing in the past, I found a children's plastic swimming pool very helpful. The floor area is much larger than the cage, and items such as toys and vegetables can be placed on it to give the two animals some distractions if they aren't very comfortable with one another in the beginning. Also, should the two rabbits decide that they don't care for one another's company, the pool provides much more space to thump and charge than the cage. It also has sufficient space for me if I have to grab and separate them.

  The rabbits I have paired in the past were mature NZW [New Zealand White] females; they are larger, slower and more docile than Dutch Belted rabbits who can move very fast and tend to be quite high strung.

- It has been my experience that female rabbits—including Dutch Belts—pair rather successfully when partners are introduced in the same cage as soon as they arrive at our facility, even if they are unfamiliar with each other. I think the transportation stress provides a bit of motivation to stick together with another conspecific. Most of our pairs are created in this way.

- It is not uncommon for paired does to groom each other; this suggests that they do enjoy the company of each other.

- In my experience, Dutch rabbits can be pretty aggressive both to each other and to humans, but it depends very much on whether or not the breeder has selected for relatively docile animals and has already socialized them.

When pairing NZW rabbits who haven't lived together before, we give them a sedative, just enough to make them sleep.

We then put the two partners side-by-side, touching each other, in a double cage. The important part of this pairing process is that the animals physically contact each other, thereby spreading recognizable smells, while they recover from sedation [Love & Hammond, 1991]. The front of the cage is covered with something to darken the interior—we use paper or black rubbish sacks so that we can easily lift a corner to observe without disturbing the occupants. We do not witness any overt aggression when we let them sleep the sedative off and slowly wake up together.

The new pair's cage is provisioned with an old mouse cage turned upside down that the two does can use as a lookout or refuge where they can quickly get out of each other's way in case things suddenly turn nasty. We also provide plenty of hay, which probably also fosters partner compatibility by distracting the animals a bit.

Chapter 3

Refinement and Enrichment for Primates

pair formation and pair housing of macaques

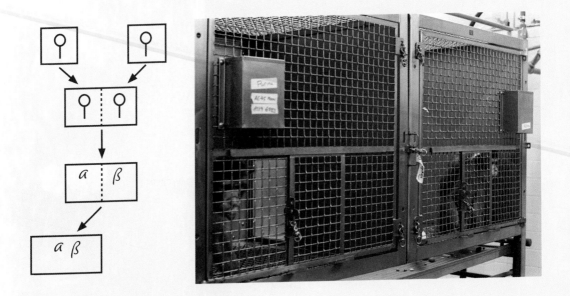

pair formation

How do you proceed when you want to establish a pair of adult macaques of the same gender who have lived most of their lives alone in single cages?

- In the past, we have pair-housed adult rhesus macaques with varying results. We are, therefore, in the process of changing our pair formation protocol hoping to increase our success rate. The biggest issue we have is pairing adult females who have lived alone for many years. In the past, we used to transfer a potential pair to a quad unit where the partners were separated from each other by transparent or steel-mesh cage dividers. We gave the two animals some time to get to know each other in this housing arrangement. When no overt aggressive gestures were witnessed in the course of several days, we pulled the cage dividers, thereby giving the two partners full access to each other.

  I believe that this method allows the macaques to develop territorial feelings, which decreases our chance of success when we pull the diving panel. This is how we plan to refine our pair formation procedure:

  (a) Pair potential partners in a new cage after their non-contact socialization period; this should eliminate territorial-related hostility.

  (b) Make systematic efforts to observe the animals during their non-contact familiarization, with the intent of determining if the two partners have established a dominance-subordinance relationship.

  (c) Form a new pair only if the two partners have established a clear rank relationship.

  (d) Give the new cage companions the option of breaking visual contact with each other, either by installing a privacy panel or by pairing them in a whole quad unit where one partner can be out of the other's sight in the top section and the other partner in the bottom section of the cage.

- It's true, pairing adult female rhesus macaques can be a big challenge; they are often quite crabby. I have worked with ten single-caged females and managed to match up only one compatible pair.

- I, too, had this problem with 15 female rhesus. Of 14 different pair combinations tested, only three turned out to be compatible.

- We had two adult male cynos [long-tailed macaques] who were housed side-by-side for about a week. No behavioral signs of incompatibility were reported during that time.

  On the day of pairing, the two sat at the divider beside each other and calmly took food treats that we offered them simultaneously. There was no social tension that we could notice, so we decided to pair them. Within five seconds of removing the divider the two males had inflicted substantial gashes on each other and had to be quickly separated.

- It is sometimes not possible to find out what triggered a fight between two animals who had given the impression of getting along well with each other. The case you are describing suggests that territorial competition triggered the instantaneous aggression between the two males.

  When I started pairing rhesus macaques 24 years ago, I also simply removed the transparent cage-dividing panel that had allowed two animals

to get familiarized with each other. After a few tests it became evident that being introduced to each other in their own home cages can trigger territorial antagonism, with one or both partners fiercely defending her or his home cage. After I learned my lesson, I made it a rule to transfer a new potential pair to another room and introduce them to each other in a double cage that is new for both of them. This required some extra time but solved the problem of initial aggression related to territorial feelings. Once the new pairs were settled and their compatibility was evident, I moved them back to their original, now interconnected home cages.

- It seems important to first allow two animals to establish a dominance-subordinance relationship, without risk of injury, in a double cage where they are separated by a transparent or steel mesh partition. It is my experience that most animals settle their relationships within a few hours; if I don't see clear signs of this within a week, I do not pair these animals but test them with other partners. Animals with a clear-cut rank relationship are then paired in a different double cage—to avoid possible territorial antagonism and interference by other familiar animals in the room. Since they have already established a dominance-subordinance relationship, they really don't have any good reason to fight over dominance again.

  I have tested in this manner several hundred same-sex dyads of adult rhesus and adult stump-tailed macaques without running into problems related to serious fighting (Reinhardt, 1989; Reinhardt, 1994a; Reinhardt & Reinhardt, 2008). Pairs were compatible in most cases:

-95 percent of 77 female rhesus macaque pairs tested;

-95 percent of 20 male rhesus macaque pairs tested;

-100 percent of 10 female stump-tailed macaque pairs tested; and

-100 percent of 6 male stump-tailed macaque pairs tested.

• I formed a pair of two adult male rhesus macaques who had lived, each by himself, in the same room for over ten years. I was very nervous because they were 13 and 16 years old animals, and at that time I had only paired juveniles and young adults.

I monitored their behavior on video for about a week during which I moved their cages closer and closer each day. They lived in ordinary baboon cages that allowed them to see each other only when they were up on the perch. I looked for unidirectional dominance or submissive behaviors.

Once I was sure that they figured out who is dominant and who is subordinate, I opened the doors so that they could visit each other. Initially, I left the doors open only during the day and separated them for the night. The two males did very well together, so I decided to leave the doors open permanently.

The two buddies got into a fight after several months, but we figured out what caused it, fixed the problem and allowed the two to stay together as a compatible pair.

Could you please tell us what the circumstance was that caused your pair to have a fight after several months?

- Big Guy and Theo, the two older males I had put together at that time, shared a room with two single-caged *teenagers*. One of the youngsters appeared to challenge the older guys; he was really a very wild fellow who made a lot of aggressive displays towards the two seniors. I had started to notice this behavior before the fight and, every once in a while, I would see Big Guy making intense visual contact with this teenager when he was strutting his stuff. I think Big Guy got fed up by the constant provocation of this young male and finally just snapped and took it out on Theo which then led to this pretty bad fight. I still have the big canine teeth that Theo lost during that fight! Even though Theo was the dominant male in this pair, he actually was injured the worst.

  I removed the two teenagers, with the thought that they had indirectly triggered the conflict, and replaced them with two single-caged seniors, Jay and Ross. This eliminated the problem, and Big Guy and Theo continued to live together as a compatible pair for about two years. Unfortunately, the two were then separated for husbandry-related reasons. When Big Guy started to engage in self-injurious biting, we got permission, fortunately, to pair-house him again with Theo. The self-biting stopped, and the two are still living together as a content pair.

- I think it's great that you took the risk of allowing Big Guy and Theo to continue living together after this extraordinary fight. It is more than fair to carefully assess the background that may have caused a spat between two animals who have been compatible for a long time and then consider leaving them together, if the cause of the conflict can be removed.

What tells you that two animals have established a dominance-subordinance relationship during the familiarization period?

- When the following behaviors are consistently shown by the same partner, I assume that a pair has established a rank relationship, with the animal showing these behaviors being subordinate and the other animal being dominant:

  (a) fear-grinning,

  (b) withdrawing,

  (c) looking/turning away when being looked at by the other partner,

  (d) yielding when the other partner comes very close, and

  (e) threatening the observer or other monkeys in the room and looking back over the shoulder to the partner—to make sure that the partner sees that he/she is *defended*.

  The rank relationship is ambivalent when both partners show these behaviors or when they both display threatening and aggressive gestures toward each other. In this case I will not attempt to pair them.

- I am looking for the same behaviors. In most cases the animals show clearly who is submissive and who is dominant. If they don't, I offer them food treats right next to the transparent partition. The dominant animal will take the treats directly, stay in front of the cage and beg for more, while the subordinate partner will hesitate, timidly watch the neighbor while taking the food, or not even dare to touch the food at all but retreat to the back corner of the cage.

- I have found this *treat competition test* the easiest way to check if two potential partners have sorted out their social rank relationship. You may have to test the pair several times, but you will then have the assurance that the risk of injurious, rank-determining aggression is minimal at the moment of pairing.

  Threatening the other partner is not a gesture that reliably reflects dominance. I have seen subordinate animals threaten dominant animals—who usually overlook such silly behavior.

- What seems to be crucial is that submissive behaviors are shown strictly only by one partner *before* you introduce the two as a pair in a cage without a dividing panel. If you cannot verify this, it's good advice to wait another day or two, continue observing the animals and test them with food treats. If you don't get a clear picture of the partners' rank relationship, it is better to give up and test another combination rather than take the risk of introducing them and possibly having them fight over dominance.

There are situations that I take as warning signals that two partners have not yet come to an agreement on who is the boss and who has to submit. Typical scenarios for such ambivalence are when:
(a) both partners threaten each other;
(b) both partners show fear-grinning after being looked at by the other, and
(c) both partners sit next to each other—with the familiarization panel between them—and calmly take treats from my finger tips.

- Consistency of rank-indicating behaviors is also the most important thing I am looking for before introducing two animals as a new pair. New partners are familiarized with a mesh/grid dividing panel. Only when I am pretty sure that the two have sorted out their rank relationship will I test them by drawing the panel just a bit so that they can touch and groom each other during a 30-minute and later during a 60-minute supervised session. When they pass these tests without noticeable antagonism, I remove the panel and allow full contact. This protocol has worked great for all my adult female rhesus macaques.

- It is my experience that potential cage partners often focus their attention on me rather than display gestures that could show me if they have established a rank relationship. I found it very helpful to set up a remote-controlled video camera in such cases to get a better picture of the animals' undisturbed behavior. Usually, I find out very quickly what the status of their rank relationship is.

Is sedation a safe option for the establishment of isosexual macaque pairs?

- There are no publications on establishing new pairs of macaques with the help of sedation; this strongly suggests that some people tried it, but the result was so disastrous that they did not publish the findings. Based on my own experience it would never cross my mind to sedate potential partners and have them gradually come to their senses in one and the same cage. Yes, perhaps juveniles, but not adults who would first have to establish a dominance-subordinance relationship in order to share a cage with each other in peace. Can you imagine two adult males, both groggy but regaining more and more consciousness, getting entangled in a dominance-determining interaction?!

- At my last facility, care personnel tried reintroducing paired rhesus macaques who were separated for a longer period of time, after first sedating the partners; it was assumed that, since the two companions had already been paired, they would have no problem waking up together. Wrong thinking! Monkeys wake up at different rates after being sedated; we learned the hard way that lower ranking monkeys will take advantage if they wake up faster than their higher-ranking counterparts.

We had two serious wounding incidents from using this method. After we had learned our lesson, we decided to no longer sedate adult monkeys in order to socialize or re-socialize them.

- By sedating potential cagemates, you are just delaying the inevitable. Two macaques have to figure out their respective rank relationship. This is their top priority when they meet each other for the first time. I would prefer to see their interactions while they are awake and have their wits about them. How does a groggy monkey accurately display signals of subordinance or dominance? If they cannot communicate clearly with each other, there is little chance that they will establish a clear rank relationship, but they may start fighting with each other even when they are not yet fully awake. At least with fully awake animals, you can watch for clear warning signs that a brawl is brewing and take action to prevent injury.

privacy panel and grooming-contact bars

What is the privacy panel good for?

- A privacy panel is a regular cage divider with a passage hole close to the back wall. Two animals can access the two feeders in the front of each cage section separately without having visual contact with each other. This makes food monopolization impossible, or I should say almost impossible. I remember one dominant guy who, during the first few days after pairing, tried to eat from both feeders kind of simultaneously, until he finally gave up this rushing around and allowed the subordinate partner to eat quietly. Fortunately, the subordinate didn't get depressed during the first days. He may have anticipated that the other guy would, one day, get so exhausted as to stop his silly racing back and forth. He was right; this pair also turned out compatible.

  Privacy panels have proven to be so useful in facilitating long-term pair compatibility that they were installed in all cages of the more than 300 pairs of macaques at our facility.

- We have two adult cynos who matched up very easily as a pair, but when they were fed for the first time in their new double cage, they tore each other up pretty badly; we have not been able to pair-house them since. Our cages don't have privacy panels. I wish they did, since the feeders are in the front of the cages and partners can watch each other eating and become competitive.

- In the journal *Animal Welfare* there is a great article by Basile et al. (2007). Based on their observations of 25 pairs, the authors conclude that the increase in proximity associated with the presence of the privacy dividers reflects an increase in social tolerance and/or attraction, and that a privacy divider may provide a safe haven and give monkeys the ability to diffuse hostile situations before they escalate.

  Encouraged by these results, we are now trying such privacy dividers for our adult macaque pairs to mitigate possible social tension.

Who can share experiences with the grooming-contact bars housing arrangement for monkeys?

- We tried the grooming-contact bars with duos of juvenile and adult cynomolgus macaques of both sexes and found that they caused more problems than benefits.

- It is my experience that paired rhesus macaques interact at lower levels and show fewer behavioral improvements when they are separated by grooming contact bars compared to when they have free access to each other [Baker et al., 2008]. However, it is clear that the welfare of the animals is improved in the grooming-contact bar housing arrangement relative to single housing.

- Crockett et al. (2001, 2006) tested adult same-sex pairs of several species by housing them in double cages in which partners were separated by widely spaced vertical bars that permitted grooming but not aggressive pursuit. The following pair compatibility was found:
  (a) female cynomolgus macaques, 89 percent,
  (b) male cynomolgus macaques, 67 percent,
  (c) female yellow baboons, 57 percent,
  (d) male yellow baboons, 64 percent,
  (e) female pig-tailed macaques, 53 percent,
  (f) male pig-tailed macaques, 57 percent, and
  (g) male rhesus macaques, 16 percent.

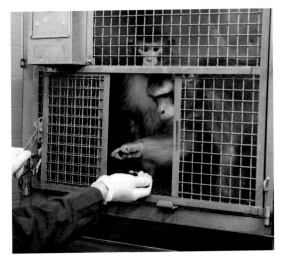

How do you know that two animals are reliably compatible after you have paired them without incidence of overt aggression?

- I check right from the beginning that the new pair clearly confirms its rank relationship; there must be no ambiguity about who is dominant and who is subordinate. I find that unidirectional yielding and unidirectional grinning are good signs for that. Threatening and mounting are by no means reliable indicators of a new pair's compatibility! The same is true, to a lesser extent, for grooming. Huddling with each other is a good indicator that the two companions are compatible.

- When I offer food treats to a new pair, and both partners retrieve a treat—first the dominant partner and then the subordinate partner—without being hindered by the other companion, I *know* that the two are reliably compatible, even in a potentially competitive situation.

males

Do you find that males are less tolerant of each other than females and, therefore, less suited for pair housing?

• In my own experience with rhesus and stumps, I can say that single-caged males are generally as readily transferred to compatible pair housing as females are. It's true, if two animals get into a fight, the consequence is usually more serious in males than in females, because of the long canines, but this does not mean that males are more aggressive or more intolerant of companions. They simply have more dangerous social weapons.

There is, however, one age group of rhesus males that causes me quite a headache. Many—not all—rhesus males turn into real rowdies shortly after they reach puberty; they can remain rather fierce and intolerant animals until the age of 6-7 years. When I have to deal with such monsters, I first try to find surplus infants as cage companions for them. It always amazes me how gentle and caring these big guys behave with little kids. When no surplus infants are available, I keep them alone. As time goes by, they settle down and become more mellow. I managed to establish compatible pairs with all of them that I can remember.

• I've found that a large proportion of the 6-7 years old, pair-housed rhesus males at my facility become intolerant of their companions at this age, resulting in injurious fighting and separation. I should add that the fights typically occur when a previously compatible pair has been separated for several weeks, and is then reunited after a brief familiarization period. Despite this, I've found that adult rhesus males are easier to socialize and keep in a social housing setting than adult rhesus females.

• From personal experience, I know that pair housing previously single-caged male rhesus macaques can be a highly successful procedure, if the exercise is well planned, executed, and the individual characteristics of the monkeys are considered.

I first test the rank relationship between two potential cagemates by arranging their home cages in such a way that they face each other and then offering a piece of food midway between the fronts of the two cages:

(a) The dominant monkey will take the food without any hesitation, while the subordinate monkey will not dare to pick up the food.

(b) The dominant animal will often redirect aggression towards the subordinate monkey when anyone is approaching them; the subordinate monkey will look away rather than retaliate with aggressive gestures.

If the two animals show no indication of a clear dominance relationship, we do not proceed with the pairing but test them with other partners until we find the right match of a clearly submissive and clearly dominant male.

Providing visual barriers and taking care that the males have no contact with receptive females has probably helped us to make the pair housing of our rhesus males a success in most cases. When we deal with a male for whom we have difficulties finding a suitable companion, we pair him with a juvenile male who always takes the role of a subordinate animal; these pairings always work well.

- This has also been my experience: even the most querulous adult rhesus male becomes friendly—even gentle—when you pair him with a little kid. Usually such pairs develop amazingly affectionate relationships that can last beyond the time when the kid has become sexually mature [Reinhardt, 1992].

- I do believe that male rhesus macaques are suitable for pair housing. It takes some time to match the pairs well and monitor their long-term compatibility, but it is worth the effort; to be housed with a compatible companion seems to be so important for these highly social animals.

- One of the LAREF members has recently co-authored an article that seems to be tailored for our discussion on pairing adult male rhesus macaques (Doyle et al., 2008). Behavioral and physiological data were collected on eight adult male rhesus macaques before, during, and after pair formation. Partners were first familiarized with each other during a 24-hour period via a panel consisting of bars spaced 2 cm apart. They were subsequently paired by removal of this panel. All four introductions were successful and subjects showed no physiological or behavioral signs of stress, such as increased heart rate, or psychological indices of distress. Aggression was minimal. Fecal cortisol levels were lower in the compatible pair housing situation than in the single housing situation. Obviously, living with each other as pairs was not a stressful housing arrangement for these adult males.

Do you have to keep male pairs away from receptive females to avoid aggression possibly resulting from sexual competition?

- In my experience, overt aggression among compatible cyno males is not provoked when they can see receptive females. Our cyno males live in isosexual groups who are frequently exposed to the sight and scent of mature females. When this happens, the males may perhaps get frustrated, but they show no abnormal behaviors, no injurious fighting, no conspicuous hair loss, nothing really alarming that would render it necessary to keep the sexes separated.

- It is also my experience with paired rhesus males that you can keep them in a room where mature females are housed, but there is a risk involved. Most male pairs will do just fine, but some will not. Those, who cannot cope with the challenge of facing females who are not accessible to them, can get so excited that they vent their frustration onto the other partner. The consequences can be devastating; nobody around, and two adult male macaques getting into a fight that is unlikely to end because the cause of the fight is still present! A very, very bad situation. I learned it the hard way and became strict in making it a *must* that all male pairs are housed in such a way that they cannot see mature females; a curtain between the cages of females and males will do the trick if there is not enough building space for male-only rooms.

- Male rhesus pairs with females in the same room can trigger serious animosities between compatible cage partners. I have seen females who would actually taunt the males.

- This is exactly what I have observed and it is the reason why I recommended, at our institution, to keep male pairs in male-only rooms.

- I have also worked with quite a number of male stump-tailed macaque pairs who had visual contact with receptive adult females; the males' compatibility was not noticeably affected by the females' presence.

There is published evidence that the blunting of canines of male vervets reduces the incident of serious trauma related to aggression (Knezevich & Fairbanks, 2004). Based on your own experience, would you recommend the blunting of canines of adult male macaques as a preventive procedure against serious laceration resulting from overt aggression?

- We don't blunt the canines of our males because we had some bad experience with males that we received from other facilities. Their canines were blunted and so badly infected that we had to remove them altogether. We want to avoid this with our own animals.

- There was a time when we blunted canines of subadult and adult male rhesus, hoping that this would reduce the incident of bite lacerations. We stopped this program after about a year because quite a number of males developed abscesses, which made it necessary to extract the roots of the amputated canines. On top of that, males with blunted canines will continue delivering bite lacerations that also require surgical treatment. Bite wounds inflicted with blunted teeth tend to be more tissue damaging than bite wounds inflicted with pointed, intact canines.

- The practice of blunting canines was stopped many years back at my facility. Some of the macaques who had the procedure done developed abscesses as well.

  I have also seen one case of a macaque who needed sutures after getting in a fight with another male with blunted canines.

- We have never blunted the teeth of our macaques. I believe the males could still do a great deal of damage even with blunted canines. I've also been taught that the removal or blunting of canines can affect species-typical behavior, as the males would normally use their canines to display dominance.

- I would recommend blunting the canines of rhesus in a group-housing situation. With blunted teeth there can still be serious injuries, and I have seen some. However, I think it helps to avoid life-threatening injury.

  Having said this, we pay for a veterinary dental specialist to blunt the canines. This way we minimize the chance of complications. Dental radiographs are taken, and can be retaken at a later date, to ensure the integrity of the teeth. I think this is one of the main points: if canine blunting is done, it has to be done correctly!

aged animals

How safe is it to try pairing old animals who have always lived alone?

- I have isosexually paired quite a number of over 25 years old rhesus males and females who have lived most of their lives alone. These animals created no special problems and I paired them in the same manner as younger animals. They must first show me that they have established a clear rank relationship during a non-contact familiarization period; they are then introduced to each other in a new double cage [Reinhardt, 1991a].

  Pairing aged animals was an especially positive experience, because these poor critters had spent so many years in single cages with nobody to groom and nobody to hug them. It was amazingly easy to establish compatible pairs, and you should have seen how new companions groomed each other! Finally they could be *true* monkeys; some of them reached the age of 35 years!

species differences

Do you notice a species difference in the readiness with which adult macaques can be matched up as compatible cage companions?

- I have found over the years that cynos can be paired much more easily than rhesus. They seem to be more tolerant, less suspicious when meeting a stranger. Sometimes I form pairs without any preliminary familiarization. I can do this with cynos from time to time without serious consequences, but I would not dare to do it with rhesus.

- Stump-tailed macaques are also easier to pair than rhesus macaques who, in my experience, are more quick-tempered and more readily instigate overt conflict.

SIV-infected animals

Do any of you pair-house SIV-infected (Simian Immunodeficiency Virus) nonhuman primates?

• Whenever possible, we keep nonhuman primates who are experimentally infected with SIV in pairs. The cagemates are assigned to the same experimental groups and receive the same infection and treatment regimen, thus minimizing the effect of cross-infection. The paired partners are also manipulated for treatment and other experimental needs on the same schedule to avoid temporary separation. Multiple experiments involving SIV infections have shown no adverse effects of pair housing. Indeed, stable pairing appears to prolong the life of a macaque with AIDS, presumably due to the support provided by the healthier companion animal (Murphey-Corb, personal communication).

• That's fantastic news! These findings could sway the opinion of those researchers who are still wary of addressing the social needs of SIV-positive animals despite published benefits of pair housing on the animals' behavioral and clinical health [Coe et al., 1982; Line et al., 1990b; Reinhardt, 1990; Eaton et al., 1994; Schapiro & Bushong, 1994; Schaprio et al., 2000; Weed et al., 2003; Steinbacher et al., 2006].

animals with cranial implants

Is it reasonably safe to house monkeys in pairs when they have head caps, eye coils or other appliances?

- It has often been argued that monkeys with cranial implants should not be caged with another companion because of perceived risks of damage of the implant and local infections.

- A colleague and I presented a poster at a National AALAS [American Association for Laboratory Animal Science] meeting regarding our experiences with housing two capuchin monkeys with cranial implants as a pair during a behavioral study (McDonald & Ratajeski, 2005). Neither of the two partners was injured, there was no damage to the implants and we encountered no chamber maintenance issues.

- We pair-house rhesus macaques with cranial implants and have not encountered any problems related to this housing system.

- For at least ten years rhesus macaques with cranial implants have been pair-housed at our facility. We have never had an incident involving an implant mishap or local infection that resulted from social interactions between cagemates.

- After initial resistance, our researchers are now more willing to house their cranial implanted rhesus macaques in pairs. There has been a shift away from thinking that this is not a possible option. We have worked with many pairs since and have not had any problems associated with the implants.

- We have paired rhesus males with cranial implants for several years. The monkeys tend to show no interest in their mates' implants and we have encountered no implant complications due to housing the animals in pairs.

- I have worked with a large number of pair-housed juvenile and adult female rhesus macaques assigned to neurophysiological studies requiring cranial implants. In the course of more than nine years, no report was made of partners damaging each other's implants or partners causing local infections when meticulously grooming each other's implantation margins. Yes, it is true, the principal investigator initially showed very strong resistance to the idea of having her head cap-implanted animals pair-housed. She finally became an ardent advocate of pair housing after having noticed for herself that her animals—especially the very young ones—were much more robust and able to withstand the challenge of the experiments when they had a companion.

- We keep our cranial implanted squirrel monkeys in social settings and encounter no specific problems.

- Many IACUCs accept the perceived risks as a legitimate excuse for single housing monkeys with cranial implants. While these risks are not founded in any documented or objective statistics, the burden of proof is left with those of us who successfully pair-house these animals. The more people make the effort to get this kind of info published, hopefully, the more the biomedical industry will be willing to move away from single caging to pair housing monkeys with cranial implants.

census

What is the prevailing caging arrangement for macaques, single or social?

- Six LAREF members responded to this question. They assessed the housing status of approximately 4,056 cynomolgus and rhesus macaques and found the following:
  –70 percent (2,828) of the animals lived alone, while only
  –30 percent (1,228) of the animals shared a cage with one or two companions.

- Baker et al. (2007) surveyed the housing status of 13,966 cynomolgus and rhesus macaques in 2003 and also found a prevalence of animals living alone without another companion (7,636 animals = 55 percent).

social housing of cynomolgus macaques

group formation

How do you establish a new group of cynos?

• Working with adult males, we first establish several compatible pairs, then a group of four and add pairs to this nucleus until there are 8-10 cynos per group. Each group is kept in a separate room and the appearance, appetite and body weight of each individual is monitored daily to make sure that the animals are compatible. This system works fine at our institution and we encounter no serious aggression-related problems with it.

- Asvestas & Reininger (1999) used a similar approach. They formed 12 compatible pairs of adult males and then brought all 24 animals, who had first been sedated with ketamine, into a new home enclosure where they regained consciousness and established a compatible group.

- Hartner et al. (2001) also started with compatible pairs. Five subadults were first paired with one another in all possible dyadic combinations and subsequently introduced as a group. No serious injuries occurred; the males transitioned through puberty and subadult stages and remained a compatible group as adults.

- Clarke et al. (1995) arranged the single cages of three adult males in such a way that the animals could have close visual contact with each other. After the animals were well familiarized in this manner, they were released into a new home cage. The trio established dominance-subordinance relationships mainly via submissive behaviors; no injurious fighting occurred. Relationships were primarily affiliative and the group lived peacefully together for more than two years.

- The best method I have found to establish a new group is to release all animals simultaneously into an unfamiliar pen. This puts them all on equal footing when figuring out the hierarchy and alliances. The most crucial detail for success seems to be visual barriers of some sort. You need to provide the option of visual escape for your subordinate animals. I use simple blinds behind which individual animals can hide, or open-ended tubes into which they can escape.

I would like to caution on grouping adult female cynos. In my experience, they have been some of the most difficult, violent animals I have ever dealt with. Initially, new group members may get along just fine, but then it is like a switch is flipped and the fighting begins. I would rather socialize adult males with intact canines than adult females. We have had so many problems with the females that we stopped socializing them in groups altogether. We do successfully establish small groups of juvenile females. They usually get along well with each other for one or two years before they become adults.

- In the laboratory adult female cynos often don't get along with each other in a group setting, but they readily match up as compatible pairs. I have had a lot of success pairing them; so if grouping them doesn't work out, all hope is not lost to socialize them. I once grouped 14 adult female cynos. This resulted in disaster after about a month and the group had to be disbanded. However, I was able to pair all 14 animals; each of the seven pairs turned out to be compatible and they remained compatible for a very long time.

- In their natural habitat, cynomolgus females are affectionate animals, but they have difficulties adjusting to enforced confinement conditions where they can become rather intolerant of one another.

group housing of males

How safe is it to keep adult male cynomolgus macaques in groups of three or more animals on a long-term basis?

- We keep our cyno males in small groups of up to six animals in male-only rooms without contact with females. These groups typically remain compatible for many, many years. We had groups who remained compatible for more than eight years. Problems may occasionally occur when individual group members are removed for research-related reasons and are no longer accepted by their group when they return.

- That some of your cyno male groups do remain compatible for eight years and longer is remarkable—unthinkable with rhesus males!

- Yes, we are also proud that we can keep the males together in compatible groups for so many years. Visitors are often surprised when they see our mature cynos sharing the same enclosure harmoniously. Our attending care personnel can take credit for this!

animals assigned to regulatory toxicology studies

Cynomolgus macaques have traditionally been single-caged when they were assigned to regulatory toxicology studies. I wonder, have new regulations and new published findings changed this situation over time?

- All cynomolgus macaques at my facility are pair-housed whenever possible. Pairs on tox studies are separated every day in the early morning for feeding, and put back together in the early afternoon after the food intake assessment for the day. Occasionally a tox study will have only one partner of a pair on study.

- Kelly (2008) illustrated in a recent article the implementation of group housing for cynos assigned to regulatory toxicology studies as standard accommodation at a contract research organization over the last ten years. The only occasion animals are temporarily housed individually is for collection of urine samples for a period of up to four hours. It turned out that study outcomes are positively impacted by the social housing arrangement of the macaques.

kindergarten

*What do you do with weaned macaque infants,
especially surplus infants from breeding troops?*

- It is my experience that an optimal
environment for these infants is a
kindergarten in which one adult animal
keeps order. The kids stay in these
kindergartens—spacious, well-structured
pens/rooms—until they are almost
prepubertal; they are then transferred to
compatible pair housing arrangements.

    I have established several
kindergartens. Follow-up observations over
a period of ten years have shown that the
youngsters develop very well and that the
adult supervisor does, indeed, keep order.

- I used to do something similar when we
weaned our rhesus and cyno infants. They
went into a pen with a big brother or big
sister to *teach them how to be adults*. These
were mixed-sex groups; as soon as we began
to see sexual swellings and/or any overt
aggression, we split the groups into same-
sex cohorts or into new breeding groups.

Before we got the idea of making use of aunts or uncles, we saw a lot of fighting between the kids. These prematurely weaned infants were extremely disturbed; idiopathic diarrhea was a constant problem. In their despair, some kids were clinging to one another pretty much all the time, even trying to walk while not letting loose from one another.

The kids started clinging to one another much less often once we added an adult animal to their group. The trick was finding good aunts or uncles for the kids. We ended up with a few who we re-used every year at weaning time. These adults were very tolerant of the kids but also taught them boundaries. When all of the kids were just weaned and missed the comforting presence of their moms, the aunts/uncles would allow them to cling to them; one very

tolerant male cyno even let the kids steal food from his cheek pouch. As time went on the adults became less lenient, but were still very tolerant of the young ones.

The kindergartens were a great way to socially house some of our older rhesus males who were retired from research but lived alone. Each of them adjusted very well to having a whole army of kids groom them—imagine one big male rhesus being groomed by five or six weanlings!

When we had aunts in the groups, we had to be careful and remove the older boys when they began to squabble over mounting their aunt when she was receptive. What is interesting is that we never saw the reverse, which means the uncles usually ignored the older girls in groups, even the ones who had begun to cycle. I figured the uncles knew it was a waste of time, as the girls were still too young to get pregnant. But who knows, they could have just been more careful and not done anything while I was around.

at a time and did a marvelous job with them. Not only would he allow them to be kids—jump on him, grab his ears and play with his tail—but he would also break up all kinds of disagreements, teach the little ones not to fight over food, and to wait their turn when the treats came around. It amazed us that, even without his sight, he was so wonderful with them. Every so often we would find everyone tucked away in a snuggle patch for an afternoon snooze; and once the little guys started to grow, we would always find them practicing their grooming skills on Grandpa.

- In the kindergartens I took care of, I often observed youngsters—not only females but also males—cradling and carrying new infants as if they were their moms.

- I had also observed aunts and uncles carrying the kids around.

- I have fond memories of a rhesus named Grandpa, a former alpha breeder who, sadly, lost his sight in his advanced age and was no longer able to breed in a harem setting. Because everyone loved him, and he had had several youngsters in his troop, our lab manager took it upon herself to see if Grandpa could be used for the weanlings. As it turned out, he was fabulous with them! After the height of breeding season, he would receive up to ten weanlings

foraging enrichment

foraging enrichment with standard food

Do any of you present the ordinary standard food to your animals in a way that promotes foraging activities?

- Foraging enrichment for monkeys often implies the provision of special food presented in foraging gadgets. It would be less labor intensive and less expensive to make the animals work, i.e. forage, for their standard food ration.

- I have tried using commercial 3-inch PVC [polyvinyl chloride] feeder cup puzzles for the daily chow ration. It didn't work out well with our rhesus macaques. The care staff wasn't able to see if the chow was eaten at each meal, so they would have to remove the puzzle and check the contents of the cups. Some monkeys made it difficult to load the cups when the puzzle was attached to the caging. You know how that is—it's either great fun to help or they don't want you taking their possessions. Also, some of our large males had difficulty getting their arms far enough through the mesh to properly manipulate the cups and retrieve biscuits.

Next, I tried using clear shoebox plastic containers. I cut a hole in the top of the container for loading the chow and attached the box vertically with cable ties to the outside cage front. The monkey now has to work each piece of chow through the cage mesh. Since the feeder is transparent, care staff can easily see how much chow has been eaten. Unfortunately, we have to remove these containers for cage wash and some animals do manage to break the cable ties.

- To make our permanently attached, stainless steel food boxes more puzzle-like, we simply added a bar in the access opening to make it more challenging for the monkeys to remove the chow.

- Murchison (1995) had a very similar idea when he modified the standard feeders by replacing the big access hole with several small holes. The time single-caged

pig-tailed macaques spent retrieving the daily biscuit ration increased and the number of biscuits falling on the cage floor decreased significantly when the food was distributed in the modified feeders versus the standard feeders.

- In a previous facility, we distributed the regular food rations of cynos on the top of the cage and have the animals manipulate the food through the bars; we also moved

the food hopper a short distance away from the feeding hole and made the animals work for their biscuits that way. Most of my monks seemed to prefer to work for the ration, even though they had biscuits in easy access locations.

- I also used the wire mesh ceiling of the cage as a food puzzle for pair-housed rhesus macaques on a routine basis. Retrieving their daily biscuit ration through the mesh rather than collecting it from ordinary food boxes resulted in a 80- to 290-fold increase in foraging time. Making the animals work for the daily food

ration did not jeopardize their general health status as reflected in body weight maintenance (Reinhardt, 1993a).

- Our upper-row caged macaques receive their daily biscuit rations in stainless steel boxes attached to the ceilings of their cages; this allows the monks to manipulate and pull biscuits through the mesh, while the box prevents biscuits from being pushed over the edges of the cage. Unfortunately, the box does not fit on the ceiling of the lower-row caged monkeys.

- A very similar system has been described by Bertrand et al. (1999) who found that single-caged rhesus macaques spent approximately 80 minutes retrieving their daily biscuit ration from foraging boxes fitted on the ceiling of their cages. Presenting the biscuits in this manner did not affect the animals' body weight.

- You may want to consider mounting the steel boxes right on to the front mesh wall rather than on the ceiling of the cage. I did this with the ordinary food boxes of several hundred rhesus and stump-tailed macaques and found that this little modification—moving the food box away from the big access hole—gives the animals a chance to spend some time foraging for the daily biscuit ration rather than simply collecting them from the food boxes (Reinhardt, 1993b,c). In fact, they will prefer working for most of their daily ration rather than collecting all their biscuits without effort from an open box or from the floor (O'Connor & Reinhardt, 1994; Reinhardt, 1994b).

When you mount the food box on the front mesh panel of the cages, the animals will not create a mess. They will work for the biscuits and actually eat them rather than drop some of them on the on the feces-contaminated cage floor (Reinhardt & Garza-Schmidt, 2000).

- Bertrand et al. (1999) noticed that single-caged rhesus macaques spent about 60 minutes foraging when their daily biscuit ration was distributed in boxes mounted over the mesh front walls of their cages. The amount of food wasted was 17 times lower when the animals had to work for their food than when they could collect it from traditional, freely accessible food boxes.

- We throw the daily chow ration of our group-housed rhesus macaques on top of the wire mesh ceiling of their enclosures. The enclosures are nine feet tall, which means the primates must climb to the top to access the chow and manipulate it through the mesh.

Do your animals push many of the biscuits over the edge of the top of the pen, thereby wasting food and creating a mess?

- I can see how that would create trouble, but in my case the pens are actually reinforced with a metal edging, which makes it impossible for the primates to push the chow over the edge. If pieces of chow fall down, they drop to the wood shavings of the pen floor.

- We throw the daily biscuit ration on the large chain-link fence ceilings of our two rhesus breeding troops to promote skillful foraging behaviors. The animals do push some of the biscuits over the edge, but this does not really create a mess. When you throw the biscuits directly on the floor, food wastage is probably much higher because of contamination with fecal material and urine. When the animals have to retrieve their food through the chain-link barrier, they eat it rather than drop it on the floor, so there is hardly any food wastage in the pens.

foraging devices made of cardboard

If we could give caged monkeys simple foraging devices made of cardboard tubes/boxes, we could provide them not only with foraging opportunities but also with entertainment, as they could shred the material. Has anybody tried this?

- When I worked at a zoo, our main method of delivering diets for primates was in cardboard boxes, tubes, egg cartons and anything the animals could tear apart. Tubes were a special hit; we'd stuff shredded paper on top of the food to make the foraging more interesting for the animals. Besides their chow, we would put in frozen mixed veggies, goldfish crackers, chopped fruit, grapes, raisins, nuts and seeds. It was always fun, as a caretaker, to be creative and come up with new ideas. Of course it made the cleaning up at the end of the day more time consuming, but it was worth it.

  The trouble in the lab setting is the cleaning up. The enrichment crew and the cleanup crew are different people, so the cleanup crew isn't very willing to clean up the enrichment crew's mess. The main problem seems to be that cardboard pieces

get stuck in the drains. At the zoo, we would hose debris to the drains, leave the drain covers on, and just pick them with tongs and empty them into buckets at the end of the day. But in the lab setting, the drain cover is often removed, so stuff gets down in there and can create clogging problems.

I think a great idea would be to get the cleanup crew involved in giving enrichment so that they could see for themselves that the animals benefit from the enrichment so much that it is worth making an extra effort to clean up the mess.

• We routinely give all of our primates cardboard treat-packs. We stuff large boxes, paper towel and toilet paper rolls with dry treats and crunched-up magazine paper. Our labs regularly save glove and mask boxes for this monkey foraging program.

To make the treat harder to obtain, I sometimes roll the dry treats inside magazine paper and use painter's tape to secure it and then stuff it in the boxes with other crunched-up paper, making the monkeys work their way through a variety of materials to get their treats. Often I spread jam or peanut butter on the magazine paper and sprinkle it with small seeds and nuts before adding them to the boxes.

Cardboard is a huge part of our enrichment program and the primates seem to really enjoy ripping into it, especially large boxes with a variety of treats inside. It is probably not so much the treats that hold the value for the animals but the actual job of ripping open the boxes and magazine paper.

• Your animals are pretty lucky. Obviously, species-adequate environmental enrichment does not necessarily need to be complicated, let alone expensive. A bit of imagination and good will can make a big difference! It is true, some of the enrichment ideas will require some extra work to clean up the mess or—as I have experienced myself many, many times—get the drain pipes unclogged with this darn heavy and long snake. But it is worth the extra effort and time when you see how the animals benefit from your ideas.

- I work with rhesus monkeys and use almost every type of recyclable paper item from home and from the lab, such as cardboard boxes, paper towel rolls, toilet paper rolls, magazines, shredded paper, glove boxes, and surgical mask boxes.

  The cardboard boxes get stuffed with dried treats and then taped. The animals seem to enjoy trying to get into the boxes and often, if the boxes are taped firmly, they simply rip enough to get an arm into the box and grab treats. By the end of the day the boxes are torn to shreds!

  I often fill the larger boxes with a bunch of loose treats so that, when the most dominant group member gets hold of it, climbs up on a perch and rips the box open, the submissive animals can scramble at the bottom of the pen for the falling treats.

  We do not autoclave any of these paper products. Over the years, we have encountered no problems with this kind of inexpensive enrichment.

- It's true, providing extra enrichment can prove to be time-consuming on the clean-up end of things. We are fortunate in our facility, however, to be able to house all our primates in large pen-like enclosures in which the floor is covered with shavings, and the enrichment, such as shredded cardboard boxes, simply gets scooped out.

- For our cynos we use toilet paper and paper towel rolls for enrichment. They are first autoclaved, then rolled in honey, and afterwards in granola, and finally refrigerated. The monkeys enjoy the extra enrichment and then shred the paper. We have not encountered any problems with this inexpensive enrichment.

food scattered on the drop pan

Can you use the cage floor as a kind of food puzzle and have the animals retrieve treats scattered on the drop pan?

- I remember a rhesus male who used his tail to retrieve a liquid food treat from the drop pan. He did this regularly when his aged neighbor spilled some of the daily Ensure™ ration, and this delicious liquid slowly flowed on the surface of the drop pan under the male's cage floor (Reinhardt, 1991b).

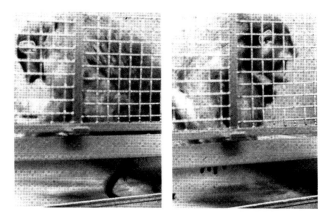

- We've had cynos use their tails to scoop up hard-to-reach pieces off the floor several inches below the bottom of the cage, but a rhesus using his tail is impressive!

    As a standard for our caged primates, we scatter peanuts, sunflower seeds and cracked corn on the clean woodchips or paper-pelleted bedding of the drop pan at the time of daily cleaning. It only takes a minute to dump the old bedding into garbage cans and spread new bedding along with foraging mix in each pan.

    We don't hose the caging while it is in use, so there is no danger of clogging drains. The cages either have a wide-grid flooring or a small hole cut in the center through which the monkeys reach down to retrieve the foraging mix. This simple arrangement allows for a great deal of time spent sifting through the clean bedding and finding the food.

Since you don't hose cages with animals in them—but rather use bedding— how often do you change cages?

- The cages are completely changed every two weeks; they aren't excessively dirty at that time.

Have you ever considered using the standard food ration rather than treats?

- Yes, we do occasionally distribute the animals' standard food ration onto the clean bedding of the drop pans, but the monkeys take their time eating, so there is always a risk that they continue to forage in the pan when the bedding is soiled.

- Allowing your animals to forage for their biscuit ration in the bedding of the drop pan provides almost ideal foraging enrichment but the hygienic implications are too serious to implement it as a standard operating procedure.

colored food

Commercial food treats for nonhuman primates are usually quite colorful. I am wondering why do we add artificial colors to the treats? If we do it for the benefit of the animals, do they show preferences for specific colors?

- From my personal experience, I believe the animals do have a color preference.

  I give our rhesus macaques Fruit Loops cereal as food treats. When I was a kid, I used to eat them with my eyes closed to guess the flavor. I later found out that the Fruit Loops have all one flavor despite their different coloration. When I give monkeys the cereal, some actually do selectively pick out loops of the same color; for instance they would consistently first choose all the loops that are red before taking others of a different color.

- We had a female rhesus macaque who, for a period of more than a year, would only eat green items. She had no interest in food treats unless they were green.

- I have worked with a capuchin who thought all red food was scary; he persistently refused red food treats or simply threw them out of the cage.

- There was a female cyno in my care who loved red things in general, not just food treats. This conspicuous color preference came in handy when I had to administer some of the study compounds; when these were red, she promptly accepted them. When relocating her to a different cage, a red toy made her quickly feel at home in the new cage.

- I did a little experiment with my ten rhesus girls. Over a 22-week period, I presented them five freezies of different colors and recorded which color they chose first. During the first 11 weeks, the five freezie colors were presented once a week strictly in the same order. During the remaining 11 weeks, the five colors were again presented once a week, but now in random order. Two of my girls showed a strong preference for the color purple, that they both chose 91 percent of the time in these 11 trials.

- Barbiers (1985) tested juvenile orangutans and noticed that the animals' consumption of chow biscuits increased when they were colored and that one juvenile had a significant preference for red biscuits over green, blue or orange biscuits.

foraging substrate for new world monkeys

Does anyone have suggestions for a good foraging substrate for New World monkeys?

- We use sani-chips and alfalfa, oat or timothy hay for our squirrel monkeys. We also place treats in the clean bedding when we change the drop pans.

- We place beta-chips, shredded paper and dry oats in the drop pans—right after pan change—and add foraging mix to this substrate for our New World monkeys. The owl and squirrel monkeys really like this, and even the galagos get into foraging from the pans.

- Our group-housed squirrel monkeys
  have access to high quality hay on
  which small food items are scattered
  at least once a day. The animals
  seem to be fascinated by this natural
  foraging opportunity of which they
  do not get tired over time.

popcorn

Does popcorn provide a suitable foraging enrichment option for caged monkeys?

- We air-pop corn several times a week in the rooms of our cynos and distribute the popcorn directly to the animals. The whole process is perhaps a bit time consuming, but the animals' enthusiastic response makes it pay off. They attentively sniff the air and stare at the popping machine when the kernels pop and eagerly first investigate each popcorn they get, then nibble at it, and finally eat it. Popping and distributing popcorn in the animals' room provides great entertainment not only to the animals but also to the attending personnel.

- Our macaques get air-popped corn once a week in their rooms; sometimes it coincides with movie time, but not always. Most of the monks like the popcorn; some don't care much about it. However, all of them like to watch the air popper in action. The squirrel monkeys also get popcorn popped in their rooms and they go crazy for it; I think squirrel monkeys love anything that smells and makes noise. They are not very keen on the popcorn but their response leaves no doubt that they enjoy watching when it is created by this noise-making gadget in their room.

- We have "melted" one air-popper, so we have all learned to unplug/turn off the poppers when you stop hearing it pop, even if it isn't your responsibility that day.

- I will sometimes get the popcorn popper out for our rhesus macaques on Saturday afternoons and make a big display in the middle the room. They go nuts! My facility manager and care staff will come down to help distribute the popcorn, and it's a fabulous time for all. Occasionally, I'll pop extra and then use it during the week by putting a measured amount into a bag or box. I'll then drizzle a tiny bit of honey over the top and give it all a good shake. It's low in caloric value. The monkeys have a blast eating the popcorn and then picking or licking the honey off the sides of the paper.

- Wouldn't it polish the image of our company/facility/laboratory if we shared with the public in animal welfare-oriented magazines or newsletters that we provide our animals quality produce/fruit on a daily basis, that our animals get their favored treats when we visit them, and that we entertain them by popping corn right in front of them, give them mirrors to secretly watch us, and entertain them with videos, if they want? Some of us even take the trouble to spend much time and patience to train the animals in our charge to work with, rather than against us, when we handle them during experimental procedures.

- The public often "knows" through hearsay that we do bad things with the animals in our charge. Why should we not let the public know that we actually do care for the welfare of our animals? It takes some effort to write such stories but it certainly can pay off for everybody involved in the biomedical research process.

fruits and vegetables

What is a reasonable serving size of fruits and/or vegetables for a macaque as part of the environmental enhancement program?

- Each of our adult rhesus macaques gets the equivalent of half an apple or comparable sized fruit and a vegetable, like a stalk of celery or a quarter of a green pepper every day. Immature animals get about half of that daily portion. These supplemental food items do not interfere in any noticeable manner with the animals' normal consumption of their daily biscuit ration.

- We give our group-housed rhesus macaques fresh produce twice a day. Each animal gets at least one piece of fruit or vegetable the size of an apple. We feed a great variety of produce of the season such as apples, oranges, bananas, yams (favorite of all the monkeys!), pumpkin, lychee fruit, grapes, cranberries, lettuce, bok choy, cabbage, lemons, limes, onions, potatoes, garlic, carrots, beans, peas, corn on the cob, peaches, nectarines and apricots.

- Based on species/age/weight, our monkeys receive quarters, halves or whole oranges on a daily basis. In addition we feed them fresh vegetables and fruits based on seasonal availability—such as bok choy, tomatillos, banana leaves, celery, kiwi, lettuce (all varieties), cabbage, kale, mustard greens, herbs, turnips, onions, bell peppers, fresh corn, cucumbers, cauliflower,

broccoli, carrots, pears, melons, apples, bananas and grapes—three times a week. Our animals also get a variety of herbs— such as basil, chives, oregano, rosemary, tarragon, mint and thyme—that we grow ourselves throughout the year.

- We distribute whole fresh fruits and veggies to our rhesus and cynomolgus macaques, in the morning and in the late afternoon, every day.

- Each of our 700 pair- or single-housed rhesus and stump-tailed macaques receives one whole apple, orange or banana each day—including weekends and holidays. Group-housed animals in pens receive daily more whole fruits than there are adults in the group so that low-ranking animals can also get their share.

  Rather than wasting time chopping the fruits, our caretakers are encouraged to take their time distributing whole fruits to each caged animal and check the compatibility of groups while distributing the fruits to them.

- Your phrase "caretakers were encouraged to take their time distributing whole fruits to each caged animal" warms my heart. Time is what the staff needs, to establish important bonds with the animals in their charge; this time should always be available. Unfortunately, some facilities regard time as money, so animal care staff is often overworked with too little or no time to spend in *nonproductive* friendly interaction with their animals.

- Our rhesus macaques also receive fruit or veggies twice a day, every day, as a supplement to their standard diet. We give them pretty much anything you can find in the produce department of a grocery store.

When you provide fruit and vegatables to primates on toxicology studies, are there any precautions you need to take?

- Suitable for human consumption is the requirement at our facility. We stick to a standard list of fruits/veggies though; this applies to GLP [Good Laboratory Practices] and non-GLP studies.

- I work at a CRO [Contract Research Organization] with primarily GLP tox studies and the thinking here is that, if the produce has been purchased through an approved vendor—one that sells for human consumption—it is acceptable for the monkeys. Of course, the produce is washed and most of the fruits are peeled as well. Our clients are aware of our guidelines and if there is any concern on their part we will modify our feedings to accommodate the study. As of yet I have not had anyone raise objections to the feeding of fruits or vegetables.

- I have recently found that our monkeys love red beets. They look adorable with the red lipstick; so the only time we don't give them the beets is when we collect urine for a one-week study, as we do not think the investigator would appreciate the purple pee.

- I would certainly have to send out word to all technicians and study directors, if I was to give red beets to our monkeys; red lips, black feces, and purple pee—I would have people going crazy!

- We're also a CRO; about 90 percent of our primate work is GLP. We have an IACUC-approved standard section in all our primate protocols that states: "Certified Primatreats and fruit and food suitable for human consumption are also given as a supplement at least once each day and documented." If clients want to opt out, they must present written scientific justification to the IACUC. In 13 years I've had this questioned only one time and, when told what must be done to opt out, the client said "never mind."

- The majority of our work is GLP and we do supplement feed our monkeys with fruits, vegetables and foraging mix. We have a list of seven fruits and veggies and foraging mix that we can choose from; the amount to offer the monkeys is predetermined. A fruit or veggie is offered on Monday, Wednesday, Friday, and Sunday; foraging mix is offered on the other days. The animals do not receive the same fruit or veggie more than once a week.

- The fruits and veggies are considered fit for human consumption and we do not wash or peel them before giving them to the monkeys. During a study, the technicians document what is given to assigned monkeys every day.

    It is rare for an investigator to express concerns about our supplemental food program. The only time that I recall us modifying the amount or kind of food supplement offered during a study was for monkeys who were having GI [gastrointestinal] issues. If an investigator wants his or her animals excluded from the supplemental food program, he or she would have to submit a written explanation to our IACUC and get the committee's approval.

foraging balls

Does anyone bait plastic foraging balls with fresh produce?

- I have used grapes, baby carrots and slices of sweet potato with great success for many of our long-term rhesus and cynos. The grapes are a great motivator, but are relatively easy to retrieve. The slices of sweet potato are harder to manipulate through the little holes, but the monkeys love it anyway!

- Our monks—rhesus and bonnets—seem to like pretty much anything edible we put into the balls, such as all sorts of treats, popcorn, fresh or dried fruits, and vegetables. We sometimes make it more challenging for the animals to retrieve the food items by chopping them into relatively large pieces. One of our fabulous techs had the great idea of attaching the baited balls with a short chain on top of the animals' cages so that they can forage either through the bars of the ceiling or, when the ball rolls over the edge, forage through the bars of the side wall of the cage.

- Frozen red globe grapes are my favorite baits for the foraging balls. The monks have to figure out the one hole through which the big grapes fit, or they wait until the grapes are thawed and then retrievable by squishing them through any hole; either way, it is quite a time consuming process for the monks to get these big grapes.

- I wrap peanuts, dried fruit, and pieces of fresh fruit in paper and stuff this package into the balls. It makes the foraging a bit more challenging for the monkeys, who first have to rip the paper to get to the treats.

- I fill the balls with peanuts in the bottom half with no holes, and shredded paper in the top half. The shredded paper helps prevent the peanuts from falling out and makes it harder for the monkeys to get them.

- Rather than paper, I use hay to stuff the top part of the balls; the bottom part is baited with treats. The rhesus and stump-tailed monkeys spend quite some time fiddling with the hay in order to finally get hold of a peanut, raisin or piece of apple.

- You can easily make inexpensive foraging balls from coconuts that you suspend in the animals' home enclosure. Squirrel monkeys love such natural food puzzles when they are filled with their favored treats. Coconut puzzles are probably not so suitable for larger primates; I am sure macaques would destroy them rather quickly but, on the other hand, to replace them with new ones is not so expensive.

inanimate
enrichment objects

toys

How do we know if a monkey likes a toy?

- I don't know if a monkey *likes* a particular toy, but I think a toy fulfills its function if the monkey interacts with it on a regular basis. If the monkey plays with the toy on one or two days and then loses interest in it altogether, then I would say that the toy is not enriching the monkey's environment, maybe because it does not trigger species-typical activities.

- We recently validated the Flexi-Keys™ with juvenile and adult cynos. Some of the animals would manipulate the toy a lot, and finally push it out of the cage through the food hopper and drop it on the floor. Some people could interpret this as the animal not liking the toy.

- I have seen some of our monkeys maneuver all kinds of toys through the feeder, until they drop out of the cage, and then try to reach out to get them back again; it's probably an entertaining game for them.

- We had quite a number of individuals in our rhesus colony who used their biscuits as a toy substitute, and with great perseverance kicked one biscuit after the other out of the food box. Not only that, but the monkeys would attentively look out of the cage and check where the biscuits had landed on the floor. For them, it was all fun, albeit a waste of food.

- Our monkeys seem to love the Flexi-Keys™. We use a chain to attach these to cage fronts, and the monkeys manipulate and chew them through the cage bars more than most other toys attached this way. When we place the keys on the top of the cage, the monkeys will pull individual keys through the bars to have them hang down. They often shake or carry these toys when we place them on the cage floor. Some will push them through the feeder and then try to get them back inside. When they do this maneuver, they sometimes lose their grip and the keys end up on the floor. Others seem to drop the keys on the floor on purpose so that they get the attention of the personnel who will fetch the toy and return it.

- I assume that your monkeys find this little game quite entertaining, especially when the attending person is cooperative and picks up the keys over and over again, to the delight of the critter. Throwing something out of the cage does not necessarily mean that the monkey does not like the object. It's just another way of doing something other than being bored.

- Toddlers do that also: they may throw their favorite toy out of the crib, and they are so happy if you pick it up and return it to them. This can go on for some time until you get tired of it. The child may then try to keep you playing the game by throwing all the toys out of the crib. If nobody comes by to return the toys, the child may get frustrated and cry because the toys are now out of reach.

safety issues

Based on your experience, what specific safety issues have to be taken into consideration when supplying monkeys with enrichment objects?

- When we design and evaluate new enrichment ideas for our animals, we try to make them simple in design, durable and easy to clean. Most of our devices are made from PVC. This material is very durable and can withstand severe treatment from the animals; some of our devices are several years old and still in reasonably good condition. We also do not use small parts that the animals can get loose and possibly swallow. For manipulable enrichment we use solid rubber toys that can be thoroughly sanitized. We replace them before they have been worn/chewed down so much that the animals could swallow them.

- We have used small branches for enrichment with our monkeys and it has been really good for them as natural objects for gnawing.

    We did encounter problems when we gave the gnawing sticks to diabetic monkeys; these animals often have a real craving for food and eat everything they can get hold of. We had one diabetic monkey who swallowed so much of the shredded branch material that she bloated and died. Needless to say, we no longer give branch segments to any diabetic monkeys.

- We had a bad outcome when one of our monkeys got strangled by a chain that suspended a toy from the wall of the cage. We now put a short piece of PVC pipe over these chains; this simple modification has made all our chain-suspended toys safeproof.

- A lot of times I purchased dog toys for primates. They have these hollow cubes where you put the treats inside, and dogs roll them around on the ground and eventually a treat falls out. I thought these would be great toys for the monkeys. When we came in one morning, we found one of the girls got her hand stuck in the hole. We had to anesthetize her and cut the cube off her hand. Her hand was pretty swollen, but she recovered completely. All those toys went straight into the garbage after this incident!

- Monkeys can be extremely inquisitive and possessive. I remember a young rhesus male of a breeding troop who managed to get hold of a padlock that was not properly locked. The top ranking male immediately stole the trophy, examined it, and being encircled by many curious monkey faces, stuffed the padlock into his mouth and pushed it right into a cheek pouch! When he was alone, he wanted to retrieve this hard and edgy, apparently not edible thing but didn't succeed. He tried very hard—perhaps even regretting his hasty mistake!—but failed. After a half-hour, I had no choice but to catch the fellow, give him a ketamine injection and carefully remove the large padlock from the small cheek pouch. The lesson I learned from this incident was, not to give the animals play things that are small enough to fit into a cheek pouch.

mirrors

Based on your own experience, do you find mirrors useful enrichment devices for monkeys?

- The cages of our baboons are each furnished with a mirror. The animals do not seem to lose interest in their mirrors but use them with consistency to kind of secretly observe people and activity going on in the room without directly looking at people.

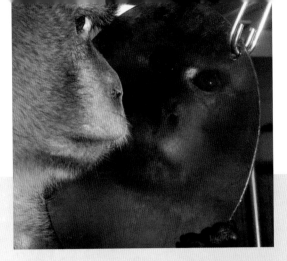

- We use round stainless steel mirrors for rhesus, baboons and vervets. They are hung on the outside of the cages. The animals use them very frequently to see other animals who are not in their field of vision, as well as people who are entering the room. Some monkeys prefer to manipulate the mirror while others constantly hold it up to their face as they look around the room and appear fascinated by the multitude of reflections they see.

    Since the animals' interest in their mirrors decreases over time, we give them access to the mirrors not permanently but always only for a few days on a rotating basis.

- I cut rectangular mirrors from clear, mirrored acrylic sheets for our rhesus macaques, and either hand them directly to the animals or suspend them with zip ties from the cage tops. The monkeys seem to prefer their *own* mirror that they can carry around and use to look at us without having to make direct eye contact. I work with my primates daily and see them using the mirrors with great consistency. They do not seem to lose interest in their mirrors but handle them more often than any other enrichment device we have at our facility.

- For our cynos, we use three different mirrors: two disposable polycarbonate types, one rectangular (76 x 127 mm/3 x 5 in) and the other circular (152 mm/6 in diameter). The third type is two-sided enclosed in a frame (102 x 152 mm/4 x 6 in). We attach the mirrors outside to the front panel of the cage, and rotate them often to avoid habituation. The animals can manipulate the mirror, changing its angle and pulling it into their cage an inch or two.

  When the mirror is placed on the cage, the monkeys typically respond to it as if they were encountering another monkey by displaying dominant or subordinate gestures toward the mirror reflection. This interaction takes about five minutes before they simmer down and start manipulating the mirror and changing the angle in order to see other reflections.

- Our cynos mainly use the mirrors to watch us while we are in the room. Some of them like to watch themselves in the mirror and will lip smack or study their reflection. They use the mirrors far more often and for longer periods of time than any other, also frequently rotated, enrichment device.

  The mirrors are particularly useful for adult feral males, who take little notice of other enrichment gadgets.

- I use 3-inch stainless steel mirrors for my marmosets; initially they seem to like them. When I leave the mirrors attached to the cage all the time, most marmosets give the impression of getting a bit bored, but some will sit in front of their mirrors for hours, obviously really enjoying them. Once, I handed a small plastic-backed mirror to one animal who picked it up, then moved from one side to the other, back and forth, as if to look for the other members of the group—very cute!

television and videos

We have been using television for visual enrichment of our macaques for years. I was wondering what you all do at your facilities for visual stimuli for your animals?

- TV time is written into our Enrichment SOP [Standard Operating Procedure]. Each primate room will receive a minimum of one hour per week of undisturbed TV time. We are in the process of exchanging all cartoons with primate videos.

- Our capuchins can watch TV in the afternoon and on the weekends. We train them to help disabled people, so we actually teach them how to use a regular TV. They use the buttons on the front of the TV; they can go up or down the dial until we either ask them to stop (training) or they find something they like (free time). It appears to me that the animals like some programs more than others. These animals are smart and need something to at least think about. I figure it is like being at car repair garages: all have a TV to amuse us while we wait.

- We have a TV that rotates through the rooms; it really seems to be great for the animals in restraint chairs, even if they just listen to the sounds. Our chair-restrained macaques are always with others whom they know very well; there are four animals per study group and we place the TV in such a way that each animal can watch the screen. Generally our animal rooms get between one and two hours of TV per week; sometimes monkeys get popcorn along with their movie.

160

I am not kidding when I ask you: do your animals prefer eating popcorn or watching TV?

- I'm not sure. I think they enjoy the sounds sometimes more than the pictures on the TV, but many animals will watch at least part of the TV session. They certainly love the popcorn, and it doesn't last long!

Why are you switching from cartoons to primate videos? Did you find evidence that the animals respond in a more appropriate/interested way to primate videos than to cartoons?

- We are making the transition to nature videos based on an in-house study documenting that the animals paid more attention to other monkeys compared to cartoons.

- We used to show our indoor rhesus macaques nature films or even cartoons like *The Little Mermaid*. The monkeys couldn't care less most of the time.

- Our enrichment team took several videos of the outdoor monkeys. The indoor monkeys are now fascinated when they can view this material. They watch intently, sometimes lip smacking, grunting or threatening. These videos are much more engaging and elicit sustained interest in the macaques.

- Our rhesus macaques also love videos of other macaques, but show no interest in watching cartoons.

- We occasionally show videos of outdoor macaques to our indoor macaques. Some, but not all, of the animals orient themselves in their cages so they can get a good view, and they are quiet and attentive during the viewing. I observed a similar response when I worked with baboons, who gave the impression they enjoyed watching the movie *Babe*.

- Videos are regularly played for our rhesus macaques who also seem to have a preference for movies with animals.

- One of my concerns here is that when nonhuman animals view movies, they might not be perceiving what we think they are; therefore it is difficult to know whether TVs and videos are really enriching.

- People have for many years studied object recognition in birds. It appears that birds are unable to recognize images shown on conventional TV screens. It has now been demonstrated that the likely reason is a basic physiological difference: their higher critical flicker fusion frequency makes birds perceive a film on the screen as images flashing on and off, whereas we humans see a continuous flow of images. I accept that the difference between humans and other primates is likely to be less dramatic than the difference between humans and birds, but before saying that we entertain our animals by showing them particular films on TV screens, we must ask ourselves, do we actually know what the animals are perceiving?

- I studied the preference for movie contents in caged male Japanese macaques; these movies had no sound tracks, so the animals could only see but not hear the contents. A touch-sensitive monitor was attached at the animals' cages and the monkeys could select movies by touching the monitor.

    In this setting, the monkeys showed a clear preference for human and animation movies, although they could chose movies with Japanese macaques, rhesus macaques, and chimpanzees [Ogura & Tanaka, 2008].

Were the animals familiar with the people in the human movies, and in what kind of activities did the people and the animals shown in the movies engage?

- In human movies, the monkeys had a preference for strange people rather than familiar people such as caretakers and me. Yes, this finding was a bit surprising for us. Interestingly, one of the male monkeys had a clear preference for movies with women.

  People in the movies were just walking, cleaning a room, reading a book, using a computer, or talking (no sound track!) with another person. No movies included people eating something. Chimps and macaques were resting, feeding, walking or interacting with other animals. Animations included a moving human or a moving object such as a cube or a ball. The monkeys showed a preference for human animations.

- Your findings are particularly important because they provide data-supported evidence that monkeys not only can perceive the contents of movies, but also can identify different species and, as shown by one of your males, distinguish the gender of the human shown on the screen. I guess your findings are a good example of how easily we humans underestimate the cognitive capabilities of animals, in this case, monkeys.

We will be purchasing televisions for our NHP (nonhuman primate) rooms, and I am wondering if anyone can share their experience of which types of televisions have or have not worked for you. While we have a number of older TVs on carts that we can bring into the rooms for short periods, this is the first time we will be purchasing new TVs and permanently mounting them in the rooms. With the advent of flat screen TVs, does anyone have any advice for us?

- At this time we still have our TVs in enclosed carts. We had a flat panel TV mounted in one room. The screen was installed in a box that was closed when the TV was not in use. This allowed us to protect the television from water, especially when the room was sanitized. It fortunately never happened that a monkey got loose while the TV box was open.

- Our TVs are on carts inside plastic boxes; they are removed when the room is cleaned.

behavioral problems

poo-painting

Has anyone encountered monkeys who repeatedly smear feces on the side of their cages?

• Oh yes, we have a lot of macaques who do that. We call them Picassos!

• We have quite a few rhesus Picassos—or poop-painters—as well. Some of our original painters have inspired others in the room, so now we have a room of juveniles who paint their cage walls with feces almost daily—unfortunately. We have tried various enrichments in an attempt to stop them from making such a mess; it works for a while, however, once they are done with whatever foraging-type of enrichment we give them that day, they resume the painting. Oddly enough, all these animals are pair-housed. It is very difficult to deal with this strange behavioral habit. Our cages are hosed daily—twice during the week, once during weekends and holidays—and I sometimes wonder if this circumstance might encourage them to repaint their walls over and over again after they have been washed and the familiar odor removed from their cages.

- For many of our capuchins poo-painting seems to be a favorite past time.

- Poo-painting is perhaps a kind of creative behavior that helps the subject cope with abnormal living quarters. Extreme boredom and frustration resulting from enforced confinement can trigger an array of behavioral coping strategies, feces smearing is probably one of them, just like hair-pulling and self-biting.

    Choi (1993) noticed in single-caged baboons that feces smearing was dramatically reduced once the animals received more attention from the attending personnel.

hair-pulling

Can you cure single-housed nonhuman primates from hair-pulling through environmental modifications such as foraging enrichment, inanimate enrichment, or social enrichment?

- This is one of the most frustrating behaviors to deal with, in my opinion. Despite having little success in treating it, we do spend a lot of time enriching the cages of our rhesus macaques who persistently engage in hair-pulling. It seems hopeless but we keep trying anyway. Even pairing them with compatible companions does not stop the compulsive hair-pulling, which is now often redirected toward the cagemate.

- It is my personal experience with caged macaques that alopecia resulting from hair-pulling-and-eating is impossible to treat effectively with inanimate environmental modifications. It is true, you can temporarily distract a subject from hair-pulling, for example with enrichment devices, but this is not a cure. Once the distraction gets weak or stops, the hair-pulling appears again just as before.

- I have the impression that hair-pulling in rhesus macaques and marmosets is often triggered by watching another monk showing this behavior in the cage across the aisle. Once an animal gets the hang of it, the compulsive hair-pulling is very difficult, if not impossible, to eradicate.

- Social facilitation probably explains the overall progressive increase of hair-pulling behavior in primate research facilities. After all, nobody will argue that it must be extremely boring to sit alone in a cage every day all year round; so why not imitate the behavior of the neighbor across from you? This is probably true not only for hair-pulling but also for all other compulsive behavior patterns and stereotypical movement patterns.

- Our cynos stop pulling their hair within two weeks when they are moved from individual housing to social housing. I have had quite a few single-caged bald girls who grew back beautiful coats in the company of another cagemate.

- At a previous institution we had a cyno—Grandpa—who suffered from severe hair-pulling. He had removed practically all hair from his body. Grandpa was not shy about his idiosyncratic behavior and would contort into strange positions to remove the hair from his body; all that was left was a patch in the middle of his back! He was not an active animal and gave the impression of being a bit depressed. The veterinarians tried various treatments to alleviate the problem to no avail. We gave him various enrichment devices; they would only keep him occupied for a day or so. We pulled all the dividers from his quad cage to give him more space; no luck. We were reluctant to pair him as he was an older male who had been singly housed for so long; he didn't seem to be a promising candidate, but we saw no other option to address his behavioral problem.

  The first two pairing attempts with two other adult males were not successful. We finally settled on a newly acquired juvenile who was very rowdy and active. This was the little guy's second pairing attempt; during the first attempt with a young male, all he did was start a fight. We were a bit surprised and so relieved, when his pairing with Grandpa turned out to be a success. This truly odd couple got along great right from the start. Grandpa responded correctly, brought the little guy in line, and he actually perked up. The most surprising part, however, was that Grandpa stopped hair-pulling—completely! He didn't even over-groom the little guy; we were monitoring them closely, just in case.

- A few years ago, a bachelor trio of gorillas was transferred into the zoo where I was working. One of the males pulled the hair from his forearms and legs to baldness. The new exhibit was twice the size and far more complex than the previous exhibit. The male's hair-pulling decreased in the new, more species-appropriate environment by approximately 90 percent, and most of the hair grew back in a few weeks. We did notice that the hair-pulling did not stop completely, and when this male gorilla was disturbed by personnel or by surrounding changes, he always started pulling his hair again.

- I find it very surprising that hair-pulling in single-caged monkeys and apes has been largely overlooked in the published literature. In humans this behavior [trichotillomonia] is classified as a mental disorder, causing clinically significant distress (American Psychiatric Association, 1987), and occurring in the context of depression, frustration, boredom, or other emotional turmoil (Christenson and Mansueto, 1999). If hair-pulling is associated with similar mind states in nonhuman primates, it seems reasonable to conclude that the cause of this behavior deserves more attention and potential cures explored.

- Hair-pulling, or obsessive grooming, just screams mental distress arising from being denied full contact with a compatible companion. Plenty of things can be done to help curb this behavioral pathology, but unless the animals' social needs are addressed it is probably impossible to effectively deal with this problem. I have seen hair-pulling very often in rhesus and cynos and in marmosets who have lived alone in single cages, but never in animals living in pairs or groups.

- Being imprisoned in a small, barren cage, without the possibility to touch and interact with another companion may well constitute a stressor significant enough to trigger and promote behavioral pathologies such as hair-pulling in any social animal, including monkeys.

- Trichotillomania in people is generally thought to occur during stressful situations. From personal experience, I know this was true for my sister, who struggled with trichotillomania in high school. She was diagnosed with obsessive-compulsive disorder and the hair-pulling was a symptom of the mental problem, not the problem itself. So my understanding is that she had an underlying mental disorder, which made her more sensitive to stressful situations, and when faced with stress, resulted in compulsive hair-pulling almost to the point of baldness.

stereotypical locomotion and self-injurious behaviors

It seems that nobody can share a successs story on ways to stop—I mean stop for good—hair-pulling in nonhuman primates. How do you deal with other behavioral problems such as stereotypical movement patterns and self-injurious behaviors?

- I can think of two cases where pacing and rocking were nearly extinguished in two single-caged adult female rhesus by pairing them with compatible isosexual partners. The stereotypies disappeared, but popped up again when the pairs were separated for research-related reasons. The separation stress was probably too much to cope with for these animals.

- I had a similar case where a locomotor stereotypy was almost extinguished. We had a back flipping, backward pacing adult rhesus female who pretty much stopped this idiosyncratic behavior once she was group-housed with juvenile males in a kind of kindergarten situation. The stereotypy only reoccurred whenever the vet staff showed up for TB testing twice a year.

- It is my experience that alarming situations, such as a white-gowned vet with heavy gloves entering the room, very often triggers unusual behavioral reactions in any behaviorally healthy macaque.

- Animals who have been cured of behavioral pathologies typically have an acute relapse and resort to pacing, self-biting, ear-pulling or whatever their behavioral pathology was. I take this as an exception for an animal who exhibits normal, species-typical behavior patterns under undisturbed conditions.

- Isn't that true also for humans, at least some of us? Our little habits pop up during stressful times. I know mine do: USDA is here and I have chewed my lips all week and picked off most of my nail polish.

- I had two male rhesus here at our facility who lived in the same room together, but each one alone in a separate cage. Since Big Guy suffered from self-injurious biting I decided to try pairing him with Theo, hoping that this would stop Big Guy's behavioral pathology.

    The two turned out to be a compatible pair. Once Big Guy lived with a social companion he stopped the self-biting. Unfortunately, the two were separated many months later. Not surprisingly, Big Guy resumed his old habit of self-biting after he was kind of condemned to live alone again.

- When dealing with behavioral problems, I am primarily interested in finding the cause so that I can prevent their development in other animals and, perhaps, cure the already affected subjects.

    For example, I had to deal with seven rhesus macaques who engaged in self-biting. The animals were all housed alone in barren cages. In an attempt to treat them, I first provisioned their cages, each with a perch so that the monkey could at least access the arboreal dimension of the enclosure. The perch did not change the self-biting behavior in any way. I then gave each monkey a food puzzle to allow for more foraging related activities. While the monkey was engaged with these gadgets he or she did not self-bite, but the self-biting was resumed once all the food was retrieved and eaten. Environmental enrichment, obviously, was not what the animals needed to stop the self-biting. After some hesitation, because of the potential consequences, I decided to try pairing each of the seven monkeys with another behaviorally healthy partner of the same sex. To my great relief all new pairs turned out compatible with no incident of injurious aggression. The new social housing arrangement cured all seven subjects from self-injurious behavior within the first four months after the transfer to pair housing (Reinhardt, 1999).

I concluded from this intervention that lack of social companionship is a cause of self-biting and, therefore, committed myself to transfer as many as possible—several hundred—single-caged rhesus macaques to compatible pair housing arrangements in order to prevent the development of this serious behavioral pathology in any other animals. During the remaining four years I worked with this rhesus colony, no new case of self-biting was recorded.

- I would hope that our primary goal, when dealing with behavioral problems, is to reverse the underlying cause, not just distract the animal. That may be difficult to do but it has to be the goal.

- That goal is very noble, but it seems difficult to achieve at the same time. Do we not know the underlying causes for most behavioral pathologies, but keep treating the symptoms rather than preventing the development of behavioral problems in the first place?

For example, if we would allow infant macaques to stay with their mothers until the biologically normal age of weaning and house them then, either in the maternal group or in other compatible social settings, the animals would have no reason to resort to self-injurious biting. Well, do we reverse the underlying cause of self-injurious biting? Presently the majority of macaques—who make up the bulk of nonhuman primates in research labs—continue living in single cages [Baker et al., 2007], and self-injurious biting continues to be a common behavioral problem [Dellinger-Ness & Handel, 2006; Lutz et al., 2007; Davenport et al., 2008; Novak et al., 2008; Major et al., 2009].

Rather than trying to reduce the incidence of certain behavioral pathologies, we should perhaps take these conspicuous activities as silent but clear messages from the animals that our design of their living quarters is inadequate, and act accordingly, for example by making it a standard practice to house all social primates in compatible social settings. This would probably be the best preventive against self-injurious biting and there would no longer be a need to deal with it as a problem.

husbandry-related stressors

double-tier caging

When primates are housed in a double-tier caging system, are they affected by the level of their cage's position?

- If I had to guess, I would imagine that monkeys on lower tiers feel safer because they are out of direct view.

- Given the fact that these guys are arboreal animals who avoid ground predators—such as humans—by spending all night and most of the day at elevated sites, and who flee from ground predators by climbing up into trees, it is unlikely that they feel particularly safe in bottom-tier cages. Based on my own experience, I would even argue that the majority of bottom-tier caged monkeys feel cornered when a person whom they do not trust approaches their cage. Some rhesus males get so frustrated in such a situation—they can neither flee nor can they attack—that they bite themselves to the point of self-laceration.

- When I managed a colony of macaques, I hung my hat on the generalization that the animals are arboreal, and I still feel that most prefer high places. However, I would imagine that there are a few out there who break the mold. If they don't have the possibility to flee upward, a relatively dark area farther away from human eye level is perhaps the lesser of two evils. I imagine it would be like covering a rabbit's eyes during a fear-provoking handling procedure.

- Working in primate facilities for quite a number of years and visiting numerous primate facilities in different countries, I got the impression that personnel tend to give more attention to animals in the top rows than to animals in the bottom rows of the cage racks.

    If this is correct, the two-tier caging system—the prevailing caging arrangement in the United States [Bentson et al., 2004]—would be an important variable that could affect not only the health status of the animals and the hygienic conditions of their living quarters, but also their stress response to being handled by personnel.

- I would agree with your observation. Unless there is an animal in the lower tier who is particularly outgoing, the same amount of attention is not given.

- Underlining the inadequacy of the two-tiered caging system, the International Primatological Society (2007) also points out that "animals in the lower cages tend to receive less attention from attending personnel."

- I have witnessed more than once that bottom-caged primates with health problems did much better when we transferred them up to a top-row cage.

    Cages in the top row do provide much more light; this gives the occupants a better chance to be checked and monitored more thoroughly by the attending technicians.

    The only reason I might purposely place an animal into a bottom cage would be if it were a very dominant, feisty one who is scheduled to be pair-housed with another partner. I think living in a bottom cage would mellow such a potentially difficult animal.

- Unlike the cages in the upper tier those in the lower tier have very little direct light. This makes health observations more of a challenge. I agree that bottom-caged animals do have a disadvantage when it comes to the daily health checks by the attending staff or vet.

- Being permanently confined in shady, crepuscular lower-tier cages is probably also not conducive to the monkeys' general well-being.

- Personally I feel that the outdated two-tier turkey caging system—dating back to the time when very large numbers of monkeys had to be quickly accommodated in laboratories for polio vaccine research [Kelley & Hall, 1995]—is counterproductive both in terms of animal welfare and scientific methodology. It's time to get this caging system phased out not only in Europe [Council of Europe, 2002] but also in other countries, especially the United States.

- It is my experience that males and heavy females tend to end up in lower-row cages for obvious reasons: it is not so hard on your back when you remove a heavy animal from a bottom row, plus it is easier to force a big animal to exit the cage into a transfer box when the animal is housed in the bottom row. Animals in the upper tier tend to flee from you upwards—not into the transfer box—while animals in the lower tier tend to escape from you right into the transfer box; that's their only route of escape.

- It may be difficult to completely phase this caging system out, as space is at a premium, especially in a country like the U.S. that keeps large numbers of monkeys in research labs. Researchers defend the prevailing two-tier caging system not for scientific but for economic reasons; it certainly is cheaper to keep 100 monkeys in a two-tier system than in a single-tier system.

  As a compromise solution, we rotate the animals from top to bottom during cage transfers. There are times when a dominant male, moved into a top location, agitates everyone in the room, so he stays on the bottom tier, but for the most part it works well. When we first implemented the rotation schedule, there was a lot of push back from the techs, so we had our facility department fashion a mobile tunnel connection between lower and upper cages to make the rotation process less strenuous for the personnel.

- Rotating the animals does not solve the problem; it literally "rotates" it. Even if you take the trouble to rotate your 100 animals on a regular basis, there will always be 50 of them who have to live in dark bottom-row cages. This is not a satisfactory solution.

- When I worked at a preclinical toxicology facility, flashlights were a necessary component to daily health checks for the cynomolgus macaques. Those lower-row cages were very dark. I am not sure what is more stressful for a monkey, being pulled forward with the squeeze-back to have the ID tattoo read by a person at very close quarters, or having a light shine in your face by a human once a day. I think this circumstance provides evidence against the use of double-tier caging.

- It is not uncommon that attending care personnel make use of squeeze-backs to push monkeys in dark bottom rows to the front of the cage to facilitate routine health checks and correct reading of the tattoos. With flashlights the animals can be monitored easily, making it unnecessary to forcibly restrain them with the squeeze-backs [Savane, 2008].

- We use flashlights but have a policy in place, and strongly enforced, to create a positive relationship with our animals.

Most of them are calm and come to the front of the cage to receive a treat while you can check the tattoo.

- We don't use flashlights in our facilities; most rooms have sufficient light at the floor level so that we can read tattoos and identify individual monkeys correctly.

changing housing arrangement

How important is it to keep a particular housing arrangement of caged macaques?

- At my current institution, our rhesus macaques get shifted quite frequently, and, much to my chagrin, folks tend to never think twice about where to put them. Animals sometimes end up in different positions during the cage-jump process, or are shifted by the research group for ease in handling. Additionally, we move animals in and out of the rooms frequently due to new animals entering or leaving the colony. The monks go through a short period of adjustment, but amazingly, things always seem to work out fine.

- I have no data to back this, but I feel that keeping the room arrangements consistent helps to minimize stress in the primates. We do our best to keep things the same in our monkey rooms. If animals need to be moved around, we closely monitor the events.

- Based on my own experience, I don't think it is critical for the well-being of primates to keep a particular room arrangement. In fact, changing the arrangement may even be a kind of enrichment under the condition that the animals are properly monitored. If new neighbors don't settle down peacefully—this happens occasionally—it would not be fair to force the issue.

  I remember several instances where the residents of a rhesus room staged quite a havoc after a new animal was transferred into *their* room. This can cause distress if the animals don't settle down within the day of the transfer. When I noticed that a particular transfer gives rise to conspicuous displays of aggression and threats, I always found a way to move the newcomer to another room where he or she was accepted without much ado.

  Moving macaques around is usually not a welfare issue, but you have to take some time to carefully check that the animals do get along well with the new neighbors.

training to obtain cooperation during procedures

working with macaques

Injection and venipunture can be a rather distressing event for caged macaques. The distress results not so much from the needle prick but from anxiety (not knowing how it will work out this time) and fear (knowing that it will be disturbing or painful). Based on your own experience, what technique is the least distressing for caged macaques?

- We had several groups of adult male rhesus who had been donated to us for plasma production. The males were bled once a month. This entailed first catching them with a net, then physically restraining them with gloved hands for ketamine injection; blood was drawn when the animals were sedated. After only two or three months, we had several boys in each group present their rears when our vet entered their enclosure, so they didn't have to be restrained for the ketamine injection; obviously, they did not like this part of the procedure at all and figured out by themselves how they can avoid it.

- I have experienced with single-caged female and male rhesus macaques, who have been squeeze-back restrained in their home for routine blood collection, or have been transferred to a squeeze apparatus for this procedure, that some animals learn over time that they do not need to resist and finally cooperate. These animals will come to the front of the cage, when you talk to them and partially open the cage door, and present for saphenous or femoral blood collection without the need for being physically restrained. I reinforce this kind of *spontaneous cooperation* always with a little food reward at the end of the procedure.

The response of an animal during a common procedure, such as blood collection, injection and nasogastric intubation, is predetermined by his or her relationship with the handling person. If the relationship is based on fear, enforced restraint or a formal training program will be necessary. If the relationship is based on mutual trust, the disturbing element of fear is absent, and there is a good chance that the animal gradually learns through positive experience to cooperate rather than resist during the procedure; restraint then becomes unnecessary.

The problem in the lab setting is often that we do not find the time to allow the animals to learn through experience that simple procedures such as venipuncture or injection are not a big deal, and that it is not our intention to do them any harm.

- It seems to me that we are coming into a new age of training options that are based on truly voluntary cooperation by the trainee rather than forced acclimation. Positive reinforcement training gives us that opportunity, and I do believe that mutual trust—the cornerstone of successful training—can be built even faster and stronger with positive reinforcement training than with forced acclimation.

- I would like to respectfully state that I am uncomfortable with the term "forced acclimation." I worked with a group of rhesus macaques and used strictly positive reinforcement for the chair training process. It took quite a bit of time before the animals started coming to the front of the cage and allowing me to touch them with the pole. Then, after the first time you actually catch them, there is a tremendous regression, and they no longer want to come to the front.

  I found that a combination of acclimation, desensitization and PRT [Positive Reinforcement Training] works best:

  (a) *Acclimation* is a step-by-step process where animals are gradually exposed to something, and reinforced with a reward for appropriate responses. The goal is to progress without fear.

  (b) *Desensitization* is placing animals repeatedly in a situation and expecting them to become used to it—like buying a house next to a highway; eventually you don't even hear the cars.

  I acclimated macaques to being pushed forward by a squeeze-back to make it easier to catch them on the pole. It's true that by pushing the animal even a tiny bit, you are forcing him/her to move forward, but when this process is done patiently with *gentle firmness*, it will develop a trusting relationship between you and the animal who, although the squeeze-back is carefully employed, will come to the front of the cage without any ado, allow you to attach the pole to the collar, come out of the cage readily and accept a reward for being cooperative.

- In a research setting, there are so many reasons for squeezing up a monkey, so most animals are used to the squeeze-back; it's nothing new to them.

  I have trained animals to cooperate with injections without using a squeeze-back. In the biomedical laboratory, there just isn't the time to do this on a larger scale. And what I mean by that is, there isn't time to take an entirely positive approach to training. If you use the squeeze-back to move your animal to the front of the cage, you are no longer using positive reinforcement to train the animal. My intent is not to debate terminology, but rather to say, desensitizing an animal to a procedure, using equipment that speeds the process, can get you the results faster, and without detriment to the animal.

• It is fair and realistic to point out here that, unless you are working with a completely naïve animal, chances are that a macaque has experience with being restrained with a squeeze-back *before* you start your training program. Therefore, you will not be making use of a new technique that will scare the animal up front. When you then allow the animal to gradually learn that being gently coaxed with the squeeze-back and subsequently rewarded [either with a treat or by you gently touching/grooming the animal] is not at all a fear- or anxiety-inducing exercise, you desensitize the monkey in just a few sessions to a formerly distressing apparatus. Personally, I feel that this initial desensitization has nothing to do with forced acclimation or negative reinforcement training, but some of you may have a different opinion. I should perhaps add that a harsh person can nullify all your desensitizing effort by subjecting the animal to a traditional, brutal squeeze-back experience. When you train your animals, everybody who works with them will have to collaborate with you; it's teamwork that benefits everybody involved in it.

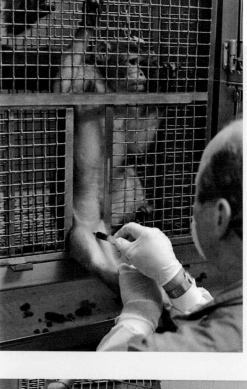

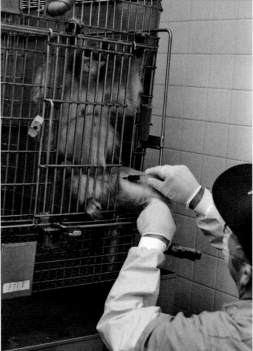

- It is my experience with more than 50 adult rhesus macaques of both sexes that gently desensitizing a monkey to the squeeze-back will strengthen the animal's trust in you and shorten the cumulative time needed to achieve the final goal of the training. A well-acclimated monkey will come to the front of the cage *without* being pushed by the squeeze-back when you approach his/her cage and ask him or her to come forward. The subsequent training for injection or venipuncture is no big deal because the animal trusts you and is willing to work *with* rather than against you. These training sessions were one of the most uplifting experiences for me when working with macaques.

- The situation is totally different when you work with a naïve animal who has never been exposed to being pushed against his/her will with a squeeze-back. In this case it is more than fair to first target-train the animal so that he/she comes voluntarily to the front of the cage and, only then, continue with a formal training program to achieve cooperation during blood collection or injection.

- We also use the squeeze-back during pole-and-collar training sessions. Even after the animals are trained, we still will pull the squeeze-back up about halfway—the animal is in control of the situation and has the ability to present his collar or not. We do this for safety reasons; the squeeze-back is released completely and pushed back into place only after the second person has clipped onto the collar. The monkey is then rewarded with a food treat, removed from the cage and walked to the chair where another reward is in store.

- I work with both single- and pair-housed rhesus macaques who are fully pole-and-collar and chair trained prior to going on PK [pharmacokinetics] studies where multiple blood samples are collected. Successfully trained animals get an IV [intravenous] catheter placed. We then take blood samples using needleless syringes, so the only needle the animals feel is the initial one for the catheter placement.

  The monkeys are quiet and calm when we take the samples, and I have the impression that they are not at all disturbed, let alone distressed.

It has traditionally been claimed that adult rhesus males are very aggressive, intractable animals who must be physically restrained during procedures to protect the handling person from scratches and bites (Gisler et al., 1960; Ackerley & Stones, 1969; Valerio et al., 1969; Altman, 1970; Henrickson, 1976; Wickings & Nieschlag, 1980; Wolfensohn & Lloyd, 1994; Johns Hopkins University and Health System, 2001; Panneton et al., 2001; IACUC Certification Coordinator, 2008).

Is it your experience that adult rhesus males are less tractable, more difficult to train to cooperate during procedures than adult females?

- It seems to me that adult male rhesus are very often big bluffers. They have learned over time that they can get our attention whenever they want by acting up like little devils; children sometimes do the same when they are desperate to get their parents' attention. It's just bluff, nothing to be taken seriously.

- I have only done training as enrichment, not for actual husbandry procedures, but it hasn't been my experience that the males are more aggressive. I've had just as many sweet males as I had sweet females, if not more.

- Some of our adult males are amazingly cooperative; they will present a leg even before I ask them to do so and will allow me to draw a blood sample without showing any sign of resistance, let alone aggression.

- Adult males always gave me fewer problems than adult females or juveniles, provided I had a very good relationship with them. Granted, I have met very calm and submissive females, but my males have always been very willing to work with me and learn how to cooperate during various procedures. I've found that most males have a keen interest in food treats and in

me being around; I use this as positive reinforcement when training them but also afterwards when they have cooperated during a procedure.

I've worked with large, over 18-kg-heavy males who could have overpowered me during chairing activities, or while I was prepping them for training, but as long as they had a very clear understanding of what I was asking of them, they never gave me any trouble.

Are there circumstances that justify using aversive stimuli when you want an animal to learn something, for example to cooperate during a procedure?

- When one of our cyno girls won't come and sit next to the cage door to allow poling for the chair, we just pretend to pull the squeeze-back. This kind of warning gesture is always enough to get her butt in motion to come sit by the door. We very rarely need to actually squeeze such an animal.

• Given the fact that the animals we are working with are confined, it seems important to make sure that they trust me. They should feel at ease when I am present; only then will I have a chance that they will understand what I want them to do. Yelling at them or threatening them with a broom, when they do not respond properly to my training cues, would not only scare them and make them confused, but they would also lose trust in me and resist my attempts to train them any further. A losing battle!

On the other hand, however, I do believe that while gentle coaxing with the squeeze-back is not essential, it shortens the time necessary to achieve the goal of the training *without losing the subject's trust*. The point is that the coaxing is not used as a kind of punishment to enforce a certain response, for example extending a leg through an opening in the cage.

Is it safe to train macaques to cooperate during blood collection in their home cages?

• I've been met with opposition about training the monks for blood draws in the cage for safety reasons; instead, our monks are sedated in the restraint chair to facilitate blood collection. I would love to get them to cooperate in their home cage rather than sedating them so often.

• Any hands-on interaction with a monkey bears a potential risk regardless of the environment in which the interaction takes place. What I have learned over the years is that the risk of being scratched or bitten by a monkey can practically be eliminated when you have first allowed the animal to establish a relationship with you that is absolutely based on trust, mutual trust. The animal knows through direct experience that you do not intend to harm him or her in any way, and you know through direct experience that there is no reason to be afraid of the animal. In order to establish such a safe relationship that is free of any traces of fear, some extra time is required in which you offer the animal your undivided attention and affection during encounters that are pleasant for the animal and enjoyable for you.

- I personally feel that we should make attempts, whenever this is possible, to train our animals for cooperation during procedures in their familiar home cages. You don't really have to make a study to demonstrate that animals, just like humans, are less stressed by a potentially distressing procedure, such as injection or venipuncture, when the procedure is done *at home* [Phoenix & Chambers, 1984; Reinhardt et al., 1991c; Schapiro et al., 1997].

  Sedating animals for blood collection introduces stress as an extraneous variable [Aidara et al., 1981; Line et al., 1991; Crockett et al., 2000; Mori et al., 2006], unless the animal has been trained to cooperate during drug injection. Again, why not train the animals to cooperate during such a simple but common procedure in their familiar home environment?

  When people argue that training monkeys for blood draws in the cage is dangerous, they cannot have much first-hand experience with monkeys. When you train a monkey, you are creating a predictable, safe environment for the animal; so there is no need for aggression. Many people ignore the fact that personal safety is markedly increased when the handling person works *with* an animal who feels no need to defend himself or herself.

I am observing increased self-directed aggression in a few individually housed rhesus—mostly males—after positive reinforcement training sessions and wonder why they do this.

- I've also seen this in some of our single-housed males. For every training session, the males come out of their cages on a pole-and-collar system to sit in a primate chair. They then perform various tasks at a computer with either touchscreens or joysticks. Correct responses earn reinforcements, usually water or juice, and occasionally other treats.

  The training sessions are probably so much liked—the subjects get generous doses of positive reinforcement during those sessions—that a return to the home cage is perceived in a negative manner. We've found that making the return to the home cage a more pleasurable experience helps to decrease self-directed aggression upon returning. We carefully avoid forcing the males to stop their training, and return them only when they show indications that they are finished. We consistently reinforce instances when returning to the cage is done in a calm and willing manner. Having a surprise novel toy or foraging task waiting for them when they come home has also helped to make the return more enjoyable and hence give the animals less reason to engage in self-injurious behavior.

Do you find it more effective to schedule training sessions at short intervals (e.g. two sessions per day) or at relatively long intervals (e.g. one session per week)?

• Based on my experience with rhesus macaques and baboons, I definitively find frequent but short training sessions most effective. The more training you can get in, the faster the trainees learn, but you can't do it all at once, otherwise the animals get frustrated or bored.

• I have found with rhesus and stump-tailed macaques that frequent, short training sessions—two or three approximately 5-minute sessions per day—are very helpful in the beginning to develop a good work relationship with the individual animal. Once this relationship has been established and the animal has gained full trust in me, I space longer, up to 30-minute sessions according to my work schedule; two sessions per week can be just enough with a monkey who has settled into the training program. These sessions are now a form of environmental enrichment for the animal, who seems to look forward to them. When you approach the cage, the animal will now attentively come to the front of the cage, ready to interact with you and eager to get raisins after accomplishing the first training step of the day.

By the way, the training sessions are a kind of environmental enrichment not only for the trainee but also for me; they break the monotony of my routine husbandry work and challenge me to make a creative, and at the same time useful, contribution to scientific methodology.

• Two brief, 5 to 10-minute sessions per day seem to work best with the monks I have worked with, namely rhesus, cynos, bonnets, marms, owls, galagos and squirrel monkeys.

• It is my experience with male rhesus that the animals work best with me when I keep the training sessions short; the males are more attentive and learn better during two 5-minute or shorter sessions per day than during one 10-minute session per day.

working with marmosets

Marmosets often give the impression of being distressed when they are caught with heavy gloves for oral dosing. Has anyone of you come up with a refinement technique that makes this common procedure less traumatic for these little guys?

- I have worked almost exclusively with common marmosets for the past four years and have developed a refinement technique for oral dosing.

  First, I interact with the animals individually to establish very close bonds with them. Mutual trust is the key for successful training. Some marmosets feel so much at ease when I am with them that they allow me to pick them up without gloves, pet their backs and bellies—wouldn't recommend this unless you *really* know that animal very well and know that the animal trusts you without reservation.

  I have been able to successfully train 42 marmosets to accept dosing via 3 cc blunt-tip syringes through the bars of their home cage. We generally mask the flavor of the drug, depending on the individual animals' likes and dislikes, with maple syrup, blueberry or raspberry syrup; none of the marmosets I have worked with cared for the flavor of cherry syrup. Occasionally I have to reach my arm into the cage to coax an animal. Once they taste the flavored dose, they usually ingest it without being hand-caught.

  Oral dosing of trained marmosets has become incredibly faster—about three animals per minute—and so much less stressful than the traditional procedure where you first have to chase the animals in their cage, catch them and position them for involuntary oral drug application.

  With trained marmosets we are able to conduct studies requiring one or two acute doses, one dose for pharmacokinetics, and up to 28 daily doses. The only problem we encounter is that with repeated doses, the marmosets seem to get tired of the flavor mask after about a week; when this happens we have to switch flavors. We have tested several flavors, so we know in advance which flavors each of the marms would accept; we actually charted each individual's likes and dislikes, so we are always prepared if a study requires daily dosing over an extended period of time.

- I have used this syringe technique with rhesus, cynos and baboons with great success.

It is my experience that marmosets are scared when they are caught by the dreaded human gloved hand(s) in order to be subjected to an uncomfortable or life-threatening procedure. What can we do to make the capture procedure less stressful or distressing for these little animals?

- I use deer skin gloves; they are fairly thin, allowing me to firmly but gently feel the animal's body. They are bite resistant yet soft enough so that the animals cannot break off teeth if they do bite the glove. Marmosets do become upset when you start training them, but they adjust quickly and accept the catch procedure if the training is broken into small steps [Donnelly, 2008]:

  (a) Before handling marmosets, I habituate them first to the sight of these catch gloves. For this purpose, I place the gloves on a cart in the middle of the room and move it to the front of each cage several times in the course of one week, so each animal can see the gloves on different occasions at close quarters.

  (b) After this week of habituation, I offer the animals favorite treats from the glove from the outside of the cage, then reach inside and allow the marmoset to take more treats from the gloved hand if they choose.

  (c) Next, I catch the animals with the gloved hand but do not remove them from their cage; usually I grab them around their waist while they hang on the bars of the cage.

  (d) I then progress to catching the marmosets, briefly remove them from their cage and promptly release them back home; this is followed by offering them a reward from the gloved hand.

  (e) Finally, I will catch the trained animal for a procedure. Upon returning to the home cage, the animal always receives a food reward.

  This training program requires some time investment in the beginning, but it pays off quickly in the long run because you don't have to spend time chasing monkeys around; it is also so much better for the animals' welfare! The hard part is convincing people who have done it the conventional way for so long that this refined approach is so much better!

- In our facility, we don't use gloves anymore. Our marmosets are pair-housed, each pair in two single cages on top of each other with removable bottom between both cages. When catching the animals, we insert the bottom. Inevitably, the marmosets will retreat into the upper half of the cage. We then insert a small Perspex cylinder, catch one marmoset at a time, and put a lid on it.

  This exercise is initially a bit frightening for the animals, and you have to slowly drive them into a corner to trap them, but since we use this method routinely each time we need to move the animals, and most procedures are actually quite nice—behavioral tests with marshmallow rewards—our marmosets quickly get used to it. Many of them walk into the cylinder without any coaxing.

- We also capture our mamosets in a Perspex box. The animals are very used to us and come to the front of the cage when we approach them. This means we do not actually need to catch them because they are not running away from us.

  There are small openings, with sliding doors, at the front of our cages; we hold the carrying box up to those. In the beginning, we just encourage the marmosets to come into the box where we reward them with treats that we pass through little holes. Then we close the box for a short while, still giving treats, before letting the marmoset return back into the home cage. The animals learn that entering into the box is not a frightening experience, so eventually they cooperate and we can carry them to another area. The problem is always to get only one partner exiting into the box at a time.

- We have several marmosets who will spontaneously jump in their nest boxes, which then allows for easy transfer to a clean cage or on the scale for body weights.

- Our marmosets were all trained to enter a jump box for cage change. We were lucky and had a great grad student working with them and really caring for his animals. He would come in and jump the animals on cage change days for the animal care staff. We found that the socially housed animals shift much quicker when allowed to shift together instead of one at a time, which is

understandable. The training itself really didn't take all that long, and once the grad student's behavioral portion of the study was over, the training was transferred to the animal care staff. I am pretty sure they all preferred the jump box to hand-catching, as marms can be quick and feisty, but they are pretty delicate and easily hurt by a gloved hand that is not careful enough.

- I had a colony of marmosets for over seven years and never once had to use gloves. In that time I was only bitten once and that was from an unruly male who got loose in the room. Even then, I feel, the bite was accidental. He almost looked at me apologetically after he did it and immediately calmed down. I think the biggest key is trust between the caretaker and the animals.

For cage transfer we had a caging system that used industrial tubing attached to the cage doors so that the marmosets could run into the next cage. I had tried to get them to go into the nest box and transfer them that way but there was always one who would stay out to keep watch over the others, or they were all just so curious to see what I was doing that they wouldn't go in. I should also state that my colony had extensive interaction with people and the families were almost exclusively made up from hand-reared infants over a long period of time. While hand-rearing can have it's own drawbacks, I feel it really created a colony of very cooperative animals with very low stress. The time and effort that was invested in the program rewarded us very well.

What are the options of bringing procedures such as weighing, injection or blood collection into the marms' home cages?

- I haven't done blood collection in the cage, and I am not sure I would. I place the animals in restraint tubes in a separate quiet room and take femoral blood samples. They are never alone. There are always three or four buddies present who provide psychological support. After taking a sample, you need to hold the vessel off very well, as marmosets are prone to hematomas—even days after the bleed; we had two animals who needed surgical removal of a clot resulting from venipuncture. Bleeding in the cage would scare me, because the animals could struggle before you are certain that the bleeding has stopped completely. We have tried to acquire blood samples from other veins, but it hasn't worked well; so we only bleed via femoral vein.

- McKinley et al. (2003) successfully trained marmosets to step one at a time on a platform for weighing in their familiar home cages.

- Cross et al. (2004) describe a training method that allows saliva collection from unrestrained marmosets in their familiar home cages.

How do you feel about the restraint tube? Do the animals get so desensitized to blood collection that being restrained in the tube is no longer a source of stress/distress for them?

- We condition and train each and every animal for the restraint tube by first catching and then placing them in the tube. The time being restrained in the tube is gradually increased and the individual animal returned back to the home cage after each session and rewarded with a food treat. This training exercise is done with each marmoset over and over again. I spent many, many hours working with these guys and have finally trained them

enough that I don't have to constantly give them refresher sessions for the restraint tube. They now have no problem being placed into restraint tubes, and they do not seem to be stressed in the tube, as long as nothing is done with them.

When blood collection starts, many marmosets are still somewhat stressed; they have never gotten completely over the blood collection part; many seem to tolerate it, maybe because a marshmallow is waiting for them as soon as they are done.

We always do the blood collection procedure on all four animals of a group at the same time, assuming that the presence of friends exerts a stress buffering effect.

I'm not sure if you can ever have these rather flighty animals really *accept* being restrained and subjected to blood collection. It seems to me that in general, marmosets do get stressed to some extent when it comes to blood collection in the tube.

institutional support of training program

When you train your animals, how do you find the time for this? Does your institution support your efforts to achieve cooperation of the animals during procedures?

- At our facility, training animals to cooperate during procedures is an integral part of our daily work.

- I have to sell a cost benefit analysis of training animals in my charge to the management of our laboratory. This brings out the salesman in me.

- In order to implement a training program, I first had to train my staff to re-think their routine. No real time difference, just a change in the way everyday tasks are performed. For example, to train macaques for transfer or injections, we teach the animals what the clicker is by using it during regular morning feedings. Click means biscuit as a reward. Any animal who naturally presents during that time will receive a click along with a biscuit and raisins as a reward. Whatever desirable behaviors we can catch will be rewarded throughout the day. Once the clicker has a meaning for the animals, the tech starts using a simple target—this can be the mirror already on the cage, or the plastic cage tag—to reward animals during regular feedings when they touch the target. Now we can begin targeting individual animals where we need them to move and station.

  This training program does not require an extra time investment, so it is endorsed by our facility.

- My institution is very supportive of training our macaques to cooperate during routine husbandry procedures such as shifting animals. Unfortunately, however, our animals are not trained to cooperate during specific procedures such as injection and blood collection.

- I work at a facility where we have to do certain chores and must complete them in the allotted time. If we have a slow day—which is rare—we can spend as much time as we want training the animals or simply visiting them; this inconsistency is of no real value. If necessary, I spend lunchtime training animals in my charge so that they overcome their apprehension and fear during handling procedures.

- It will be great when all investigators understand the importance of training. Research does show that working with animals who have been taught to cooperate during procedures is very beneficial, but it's odd how that research gets often dismissed so easily with the presumption that there is no extra time for conducting training sessions with the animals.

- Not only that, but also many investigators are kind of stuck in the inertia of tradition. They interpret any attempt to change their traditional practices as a personal critique, so they have the tendency to stubbornly defend the *status quo* even if it implies a resistance to well-documented progress.

- All involved, the researchers as well as management of facilities, have to look more closely and give more attention to efforts to train animals in order to minimize or avoid stress reactions. It is not only a welfare issue but it is also a scientific issue.

No animal should fear his or her caretaker or any procedure if there are training techniques available that can avoid this.

- My staff has the training/conditioning of animals built into the care schedule and, if things take longer than planned, someone else will pick up some of their chores so that the animals don't lose out.

  All research benefits if animals are trained to some extent, even if it's only to prevent them from stressing out when someone approaches them. Investigators and administrators at our facility understand that training helps produce better science, so I get very little opposition from the research team. Occasionally there are investigators who, used to working overseas, dismiss our ideas in the beginning. However they don't have a choice and in the long run will actually admit that our "quaint British ways" are progressive and provide a better research methodology.

spontaneous cooperation

Does it occasionally happen that a monkey, or any other animal, spontaneously cooperates during a procedure that used to entail enforced restraint, for example injection, venipuncture or replacing a bandage?

- Because I am a Vet Tech, I often see animals who are in distress. I find it amazing how cooperative many of these animals become. It is almost as if they want to help you take care of them. I have worked with animals who had the reputation of being very aggressive, especially some of my male cynos; but when they get a little finger injury, they would just turn into big babies. They often say that a hurt animal is more dangerous and more likely to act out, but I have found quite the opposite in most cases.

- I would argue that animals, even potentially dangerous ones, cooperate and allow you to help them only if they know, kind of intuitively, that you have good intentions and that they can trust you fully. If they don't trust you, then the situation can become extremely dangerous, because the injured/hurt/distressed animal will feel cornered and resort to self defense.

- It is my experience that macaques who are being pushed forward with a squeeze-back for routine injection sometimes start cooperating without any formal training, making the squeeze-back unnecessary in the future. I think such animals learn from the repeated experience that being squeezed is very unpleasant, but that the injection itself is not really painful, and that they can avoid the squeeze-back by voluntarily coming to the front of the cage and presenting a specific body part for injection. I have encountered quite a number of such animals, especially, but not exclusively, animals assigned to diabetes studies.

- I work with 12 rhesus who behaved just as you describe: being approached by me, the monkey comes forward without me even touching the bars of the squeeze-back; I encouragingly say "come" and then "hold" and give the injection without triggering any fear or aversive reaction. These animals have not received any formal training other than receiving a food treat reward after the injection. They have learned on their own to avoid being squeezed by voluntarily coming to the front of the cage and accepting the injection.

- I cannot think of an example from the laboratory at the moment, but I remember several incidents of spontaneous cooperation during my time working as a humane society officer, in particular dealing with wildlife. A common call to attend to was skunks getting themselves tangled in hockey nets—as I live in Canada, a frequent encounter for skunks. Skunks are fairly gentle creatures, but of course have their secret weapon, and can still spray even in compromised positions. Yet, on the calls that I attended, after approaching the animals slowly, and gently restraining them, they were quiet as could be while they were cut free from the net. Then, once free, they would waddle off.

  Though shock is obviously a factor when dealing with wildlife, I have memories of skunks who truly seemed to connect with me during that moment, and surrendered themselves to the task at hand, allowing me to free them quickly; these were always rewarding experiences.

• I had a similar experience with a wild animal. We share our property with a large family of mule deer, and over the years cared for a number of leg-injured animals. It happened last year that we noticed a yearling limping, but we could not see any signs of injury. Observing this kid for a few days, I finally saw that she had a kind of bandage around her right front leg right above the hooves. It took me a few days to get close enough to realize that the bandage was not a bandage but a 3.5-cm-long section of white PVC pipe. Obviously, the animal hadn't managed to get the pipe pushed back over the toes after she had got trapped in it. In the meantime the skin had started to react and was slightly swollen, making the scenario pretty hopeless for this young deer. After much pondering I decided not to ask for help from the Wildlife Service but work with this little creature myself.

Next morning, I was sitting at a nice spot with a gorgeous view of the rising sun behind a bank of clouds when out of the blue Elli, the yearling's mother, and the patient turned up right in front of me. This was a big surprise! I gave Elli some raisins and groomed her while attentively getting a very close look of the yearling's leg. Having no other choice, I finally moved my right hand in the direction of the leg—the kid did not seem to take any notice of my endeavor—and then very, very gently but

at the same time with great resolution got hold of the leg, held it very firmly, while carefully turning the PVC section with my left hand and pushing it slowly to the rims of the hooves—and off the leg. To my utter amazement, neither the kid (who got the name Lilly) nor the mother budged during the whole procedure, which took about two minutes. The two gave the impression that they didn't even notice what had been going on. Somehow, we three communicated on a non-verbal level to make this happen to save Lilly from painful and serious consequences. Not surprisingly, Lilly got very affectionate and she is now just like her mother, one of those deer who gets kind of blissed-out when you groom her just at the right spots.

touching
monkeys

Working with the monkeys in your charge on a daily basis, it is almost unavoidable that you develop affectionate relationships with them and that some of the animals get to like you and trust you so much that they want to be groomed by you. Does it sometimes happen that you groom some of your monkeys?

- We have a few female and male rhesus macaques who give the impression that they really enjoy it when I groom them through the bars. They approach the front of their cage and present themselves in such a way that I can easily reach all the body parts that they would like to have scratched. While I groom them, they relax completely and get this typical glazed, blissed-out look—eyes at half mast. Some of the animals like to be scratched on their heads/necks while they are sitting in their chairs, and again they show blissed-out faces while they are groomed.

- I am working with several female and male macaques who regularly extend their arms out of their cages, while others press their chests or hips against the cage bars and then let me groom them for several minutes. I have no doubts that these animals really like it when I follow their invitations and groom them.

- Some monkeys don't like people for legitimate reasons; they will use the grooming invitation to tease you. Our Holly is such a brat. She's clever and will lure her victim by deception to get close enough to accomplish her mission. Once you are in her reach, she will perform that lightening fast turn, pinch you and give you some attitude. I am sure Holly enjoys these little attacks and the victims' surprise reactions.

  But we also have a few monkeys who genuinely beg to be groomed. Some of these individuals arrived with serious behavioral disorders. They had been singly housed for years. The touch they routinely received from our seasoned staff made a tremendous difference in their emotional well-being and many neurotic behaviors all but disappeared in a short time. These animals pose in different positions to receive their *therapy* in just the right spot and they will fall asleep while we groom them.

- I have worked with cynos, rhesus, pigtails and boons of all ages and both genders who presented themselves regularly for a good butt scratch. For instance, currently there are two aged rhesus males who tend to "fight" for my attention when I am in their room. First, the more dominant partner will put his rear end up against the cage bars and, when I approach, will settle down so I can groom his entire back. The other partner will then saddle up to the front of the cage and present his body so that I can scratch his chest/belly/face and other parts of his body—he's even presented his tongue to me. When either of them is really happy, they'll go into that trance-like state and have a glazed look; the less dominant guy has even sighed a couple of times while I groomed him. There are days that, once I get done with these two, the rest of the room—all aged rhesus males—start presenting body parts for grooming.

- I remember a female pigtail on a viral tox study who wouldn't show friendly behavior towards people and would lash out from time to time, but for some reason she really liked me. I never figured out why, but whenever I entered the room, she would stand, hoot, and duckbill in my direction until she got my attention. Then, when I would walk to her cage, she would calmly settle and present her hips to me for grooming. We got to a point where she would reach out of her cage and attempt to groom me. I really don't know why she has only taken a "shine" to me and not to other staff members.

primates in labs versus primates in homes

It was recently written in an article published in the Journal of the American Veterinary Medical Association that pet primates are better off than primates in labs. Is this a valid comparison?

- It would probably be more realistic to assess each case separately rather than making a categorical statement.

- My own impression is that pet owners are more variable in their adequacy as caretakers with most being worse than a typical lab and a few being better. Unfortunately, as primate-owning is not illegal in the United States, we seem to have decided to let people own primates without any oversight, sell them online, and generally continue unregulated in any aspect other than interstate transport.

- I really worry about the primates in the care of individuals who may have bought them on impulse, lack understanding of the species-typical behavioral and psychological needs of their new pets, and are not ready to make a long-term commitment. What happens if the monkey bites a child? That poor monk could end up being shoved from one home to the other. I lean on the side of the labs as generally offering more suitable housing and better care for these animals.

I'm sure that there are a few people who go out of their way to learn all they can about the species-specific needs of the monkey they intend to adopt and are committed to providing the best possible care for their pet. The majority of monkey pet owners, however, are probably getting tired of trying to diaper and keep a cage clean with a monk; or the monkey is going to get frustrated and then aggressive towards people who treat the animal like a human kid—monkeys aren't meant to be dressed up and carried around like dolls. Just look at how many adorable puppies go home only to end up abandoned in a shelter! Monkeys are also cute and adorable when they are young, but it's their nature to grow into adults who have their own personalities and the means to defend themselves if needed.

- The following comment doesn't really fit, but I still have the urge to post it, given the fact that we are all so particularly concerned about nonhuman primates as pets:

  > In the United States there are approximately 1,000,000 pets—mainly dogs and cats—abandoned by their owners for convenience reasons, for example pets dumped in rest areas of highways.

  Now talking of *human* primates:
  > In the United States there are approximately 750,000 homeless children, most of them too scared to go home for good reasons of which we are all aware.

- That's terribly sad.

- We have a long way to go to make this world a more compassionate place.

Do you think that nonhuman primates in research are better off in general than rodents?

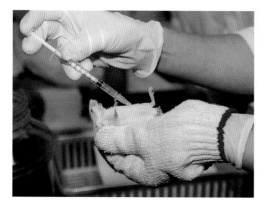

- I would say that currently—at least in the United States—nonhuman primates are better off in that there are more explicit regulations and considerations addressing their psychological well-being and their perception of pain and distress. While there are certainly exceptions—including many or all members in this discussion forum—people often consider rodents to be "just mice" used for research in much larger numbers and for much more distressful experiments.

- Recent changes to primate housing focus on providing more space, increased social interactions, and increased complexity of the primary enclosure, while changes to mice and rat housing focus more on containment and isolation of biohazards. While some administrators and investigators make efforts to go beyond minimum requirements for these species as well, there are still many in the field who are willing to provide only the very minimum that is required in order to get their research proposal funded.

  The situation for nonhuman primates in research facilities is still not beyond further improvement—far from it—but I think the efforts thus far have been more effective and better accepted by the research community than those efforts made for their rodent counterparts.

- Nonhuman primates are better off in research labs; this may be related to the fact that they share many more similarities with humans than mice and rats.

- And when you compare the strong concern that humans display for the well-being of chimpanzees who have been used for research, with their rather shallow concern for monkeys, you are also tempted to make this inference.

- When looking into the mirror, a human sees more similarities with a chimpanzee face than with a monkey face and, therefore, feels more sympathy with a distressed chimpanzee than with a distressed monkey. This does not imply that the monkey suffers less than the chimpanzee; the opposite may be true, but our reaction will still be biased by the unrealistic, emotional interpretation of our visual perception of the chimpanzee face versus the monkey face.

- Money may be another factor that determines the attention given to the well-being of a specific group of animals used for research.

Compared with rodents, primates are pretty costly animals, so you try to assign as few subjects to your research protocol as possible. Good care translates into fewer animals—hence less grant money—needed to achieve statistically significant results.

When you check the literature, it becomes obvious that the number of animals used in research protocols is relatively low for chimpanzees, higher for baboons, much higher for macaques and marmosets, and much, much higher for mice, rats and hamsters. When you lose a monkey because of poor housing conditions you lose a lot more money than when you lose a rodent for the same reason. Ultimately you will save more money when you take good care of nonhuman primates than when you take good care of rodents. This is perhaps one reason why primates tend to be better off in labs than rats, mice and hamsters.

Chapter 4

Refinement and Enrichment for Other Animals

barking

Has anyone used music in dog rooms? I would like to see if exposing the dogs to music, radio talk or nature sounds can help keep the barking down to a dull roar whenever anyone enters the room or when the elevator goes by (classically conditioned to "elevator" means tech with food).

The dogs are used to me, and get quiet very quickly once they have recognized that it's me who entered their room. The problem starts when someone else comes into the quiet room and sets everyone off. I have been working with the barking ringleader to remain calm when others enter the room, but he is really stubborn; unfortunately, we have kind of trained him to bark by giving him attention whenever he gets all riled up. I am now wondering if some background noise/music might help to buffer the barking noise when people are entering the dog room.

- We provide music in many of our dog rooms. Personally, I don't think the radio (music) will keep the barking noise level down. When we want a short break from the barking, we make a tone: all ears are pricked and eyes focused on the person making the sound. But this is only a momentary effect and the barking continues unabated.

  We have found that the only way to get the barking to settle down is to stay in the room and *not* interact with the dogs but go about the work that needs to be done. If the work involves some of the dogs then, for sure, take them out but ignore the others. In time, the barking will only last for the initial entrance into the room, and then you will be quietly but very attentively watched. Once quiet, say "hi!" at your own risk.

- Wells et al. (2002) found that exposure to classical music encouraged sheltered dogs to spend less time barking and more time resting.

- When we had a kennel of dogs that loved to bark, we set up some basic rules for people entering the building. It is a bit tedious at first, but if most people can stick to it, there will be positive results by the end of a week:

  (a) Walk up to the door and start to open it—but first make sure you have plenty of time to train!

  (b) As soon as the dogs start barking, shut the door—if you have an automatically locking door, shut it almost all the way, so you don't have to re-unlock each time you do this little exercise.

  (c) Wait until the dogs are silent again, and then open the door. Make sure you are opening and closing it normally, not inching it open or slamming it shut.

  (d) Once the barking starts again, shut the door.

  (e) Keep doing this until you are able to open the door completely and take a step in. Then go about your business calmly in the room.

  (f) Each time you do this, it will be quicker and quicker to get back in that hallway with no barks. It takes some time to condition the dogs, but it is definitely worth the effort. Don't get discouraged! We used to double check that our earplugs were in place before going near the door of a dog room; we are now able to walk into the room with quiet but happy animals.

toys

Do commercial toys provide long-term enrichment for single- or group-housed dogs when no person is around to entice them to play with the toys?

- In my experience, it very much depends on the dog. Some dogs will readily play with the toys whether a human is involved or not while others aren't the least bit interested even if a human is there. This holds true for play toys as well as chew toys.

- This has been my experience as well: the attractiveness of a toy depends greatly on the individual dog. However, the dogs in general make it overwhelmingly clear by the behavior they show when people enter their room that they much prefer the human contact and interaction to any other environmental enrichment. Often, this makes them pay attention to the toys even less, as they are far too busy trying to get attention from the human. I've secretly watched the same dogs, who seemed to have no interest at all in a toy, pick up the toy and play with it when they thought no humans were near or watching.

- We tried different commercial toys at our facilities. Some dogs like certain toys while others have no interest in them. It seems to be the individual dog, not the breed, who enjoys certain toys. We rotate the toys weekly or more frequently. I have the impression that the more often we exchange a certain toy, the more attractive it becomes for the dogs.

Many of the dogs enjoy a tennis ball, but we don't leave it in the pen overnight since nothing would be left of the ball the

next morning. This automatically enhances the attractiveness of the tennis ball: it's always new again the next day.

We have an elderly beagle who loves his blue hard plastic ball. He noses that around and flips it in the air all the while barking up a storm. It is really fun to watch. He does it on his own, no one is rolling the ball to him. Most of the other dogs show no interest in this type of ball, but this particular dog just loves it.

• The majority of our dogs like the dumbbells. They show more wear than any other hard plastic or hard rubber toys they have in their kennels. Unfortunately, we cannot give any rubber items softer than a Kong™ toy because of protocol issues; this is a shame because the dogs all loved them. We had a big dog who actually snuggled with his squeeze-and-toss football; it broke my heart when I had to take it away from him.

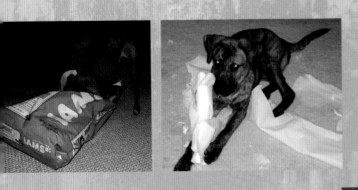

Healthy dogs love toys that they can tear apart. Is it reasonably practicable to give caged/kenneled dogs recycled cardboard or other paper-based material every few days as enrichment gadgets?

- I give our dogs small cardboard boxes stuffed with shredded paper and goodies. They also receive paper towel rolls with treats; the ends are stuffed with paper towel to keep the treats from falling out, so the dogs have to rip the rolls open to get the rewards. I also use food or bedding paper bags stuffed with shredded paper and treats.

- We have been giving our dogs in pens whole bags of shavings so that they can rip them open themselves. By the end of the day, the entire bag is ripped up, partly shredded and the bedding is spread. The other day I was watching one of the dogs digging his way into the bag, kicking out bedding as he went. It is a fantastic enrichment item.

- Paper-based toys are great for dogs, but you have to be willing to cleanup the unavoidable mess.

In your own experience, are there real safety issues—such as injuries or gastrointestinal obstruction—associated with certain dog toys?

- From my experience, it seems that for every toy given there will be one animal who succeeds in having a safety issue with it:

  (a) Latex/soft vinyl toys: I have used these toys for years. Some dogs would completely devour them; others would be conspicuously gentle with them. I had dogs eat these soft toys with no problem, but one dog did suffer from an intestinal obstruction caused by a piece of one of these toys.

  (b) Rope tugs/bones: Most dogs do fine with these toys, but one dog also got an obstruction caused by a string of the rope.

  (c) Hard rubber/plastic toys: These toys are pretty indestructible, so most dogs need a little extra encouragement to actually play with them. Even though these toys are so hard, we had one dog who managed to break a tooth while playing with a dumbbell.

  What I have learned from this is, to carefully evaluate any new toy for at least one week and to make sure it doesn't become a problem. After that, I inspect every item in the enclosure on a daily basis, but first verify that no toy is missing. You never know what a dog may choose to do with a toy!

- When they are very hungry or when they compete with each other over access to

food, dogs have the tendency to directly swallow the food, this means they don't take the time to first chew and find out if it actually is edible stuff. Obviously, this can make it a bit risky to give dogs any kind of toy that they are not supposed to swallow. We evaluate whether a dog tends to be a chewer or a swallower and give soft toys to the chewer and hard toys to the swallower.

This problem does not exist with rodents, rabbits, pigs, goats and cattle who all are strict chewers/grinders. They do not swallow large pieces, and if they happen to destroy a toy, they chew it into small segments that, if swallowed, pass through the gastrointestinal tract without ill effects.

- I have worked with quite a number of dogs who were pretty trouble-free with toys, but I remember one exception. We had one dog who chewed a rubber bone and the knuckle end got stuck in the duodenum. "Small" operation, and he was all right, but he was not given such bones again!!

oral gavage

In your experience, what is the least stressful oral gavage technique for a dog?

- I am the lead positive reinforcement trainer at my facility; my team and I have spent so much time training our dogs that they really seem to be willing participants for all of the experimental procedures we ask of them. I am sure it helps that I am the oral gavage doser for almost all of the PK studies we perform, and my restrainer is our *dog whisperer*.

  We have a solid trust relationship with our dogs. We place them on the exam table, and the restrainer simply hugs his arm around the dog so he/she is comfortably snug against the restrainer's body. The restrainer then has his hand placed gently on the dog's chest while his other hand is scratching the dog's head and ears. We always speak reassuringly to our dogs throughout the procedure, to keep them calm. The gavager then opens the dog's mouth and feeds in the gavage tube. I have to say, whenever I gavage our dogs, they seem to be very focused on me, relaxed but focused on my face while I speak to them in a reassuring and calm tone. We don't have any of our dogs squirm or try to get away at all; they literally don't move. They simply lean into the body of the restrainer and cooperate. Some even close their eyes as if they are going to fall asleep.

  It has taken a lot of training sessions, but the trust the dogs have in us is key for their cooperation. I think they almost look forward to being on study because of the tremendous amount of attention they receive. The individual who is taking the role of the restrainer has been doing husbandry for these dogs since they came to our facility many years ago. These dogs have known us since their first day at the facility; I am sure that helps us greatly in our training.

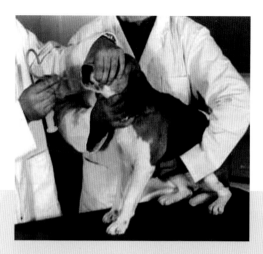

- That's the kind of comment I had hoped for. Thank you so much for sharing your experience and expertise. Yes, it certainly is mutual trust and patience that are the keys to working with animals!

    Just to clarify, you do not make use of a bite bar?

- We do not use a bite bar to aid in placing the gavage tube. I simply open the dog's mouth using my free hand. I keep my hand over the top of the muzzle—always making sure my fingers do not cover the nose—and slide the tube in while the dog is swallowing. We have never had a dog bite down on the tube, but I know that it could happen.

- I have observed some of our dogs during the oral dosing and can attest that the animals are really calm and amazingly cooperative. Some of the dogs were wagging their tails with great excitement because they got our attention, so it was sometimes difficult to keep them still during the procedure. Many of them actually raised their necks when you got ready to intubate them; it was amazing the first time I observed this.

    The procedure is very fast and the dogs are apparently comfortable with it; they certainly do not appear disturbed, let alone distressed. To me, they give the impression of being very happy to be on study as they are receiving so much attention.

socialization with personnel

What is the most practical and effective approach for socializing dogs with attending personnel so that the animals overcome their anxiety prior to, and fear during experimental procedures?

- We preferably order dogs from a vendor who has an extensive socializing program and will train the puppies beforehand to the specific procedures they will undergo in our facility. This makes the task of socializing the animals at our facility very easy.

- We receive our dogs from the same vendor. It's really amazing; some dogs even begin to lift their neck when you are getting ready to take a blood sample. The dogs seem to enjoy going on study as they get so much affectionate attention from the vet staff.

- Walking our dogs on a leash every day is the basis of our socialization program. It seems to me that these outings are highlights for the dogs, fostering a very positive relationship with their caregivers.

We are in the process of putting together an environmental enrichment program for our broodstock canines. Concern has been voiced over the males becoming perhaps too socialized, preferring human contact and not being interested in breeding. Does anyone have any comments on this?

- I honestly can't imagine bringing a female dog in heat around a male dog and having that male be more interested in the human than the female; those hormones kick in and create very strong urges, so much so that your well-trained pet may not listen to you, escape from your yard, urinate indoors—I know some people where the dog began to actually urinate on the people—and get into all kinds of trouble; all this is just from male hormones going into action even without a receptive female around. I can't see the dog losing his interest in the girls because he prefers human contact.

- Not to be trite—but Mother Nature will trump human contact every time. Intact, healthy male dogs, in my experience, never loose interest in making puppies.

- We have a group of very socialized breeders; they all have no problems breeding when in a room with a female in heat. These dogs are given supervised exercise as well as interaction with humans *every* day, and yet we have puppies all the time.

purpose-bred dogs for research

Should researchers only be allowed to use purpose-bred dogs for their projects?

- I personally would use dogs who have been purposely bred for research protocols. If I didn't know exactly a dog's medical and health history, I would have no assurance that the results obtained from such a dog are actually caused by the test drug and not by extraneous variables I don't know, because the dog comes from a shelter.

- In The Netherlands we are obliged by law to only use dogs who are purpose-bred; it is illegal to obtain dogs from shelters for research. Personally, I endorse this for several reasons:
  (a) Purpose-bred dogs are specifically bred for research; they all have a well-defined history.

(b) Purpose-bred dogs can be prepared for research already at the certified breeders. Good breeders—and there are some—will train the puppies to undergo several common procedures without stress. You can even ask some breeders to train the puppies for specific procedures prior to sending them to your lab. These animals will already be acclimated to laboratory conditions when they arrive at the lab. For them, the laboratory environment will not be distressing.

(c) Dogs from shelters have an unknown history. They may have had diseases, were medically treated and had all kinds of experiences that can interact with your research; you may never find out. Having to take unknown variables into account in your experimental group, you are likely to need more animals than when working with purpose-bred dogs.

(d) Unlike purpose-bred dogs, dogs from shelters are not at all used to the laboratory environment and, having to go through experimental procedures, however mild, is probably extremely stressful for them.

- I also feel that purpose-bred dogs, unlike dogs from shelters, are raised for and hence are familiar with laboratory-type living conditions. Dogs from shelters are not at all used to this, and they are probably extremely upset when brought into a research laboratory and subjected to procedures that evoke intense fear.

  Their greater variability, however, makes random source dogs probably *better* research subjects than purpose-bred dogs because they resemble much more an intrinsically variable human population.

- I sometimes consider laboratory animals, in this case purpose-bred dogs, to be like Formula 1 racing cars. They are very good at what they do on the race track with a nice flat surface and well-designed curves, but you could not drive one down the street to go shopping.

cats

environmental enrichment

What kind of enrichment is effective and practical for cats kept (a) alone or (b) in groups in the laboratory?

• We allow most of our cats to play together outside of their cages most of the day. If a cat doesn't get along with others, we give her some time out alone at least once every day. All cats are returned to their cages at the afternoon feeding.

   All of our cats have sanitizable toys such as fleece ropes or jingle balls. They also have access to scratching posts. We had "cat trees" at one time, but because we could not effectively sanitize them, they were removed from our program.

• Working with group-housed cats, I can recommend the following enrichment options as practical and effective:

   (a) Cardboard boxes with or without a hole cut for hide and seek.

   (b) Airline crates left open (the same ones the cats probably came in; the crates are cage-washable).

   (c) Fast-Trac™ (all plastic, chemically sanitizable); this commercial toy has never lost popularity—neither with the lab-housed cats nor with my cats at home; the round design makes it enticing to nap in, and one swat of the ball, or even a slight bump, and the fun begins anew.

(d) Access to a window looking onto the hallway; we have a shelf installed on the door so the cats can sit on it and look out of the window.

(e) Feeder puzzle toys; these are commercially available or easy to make from food storage containers with random paw-sized holes cut in it; add cat treats or even kibble and the cats have to paw or bat out the treats.

(f) Laser pointer (we hang the laser pointer outside the room so that technicians passing by can play with the cats through the window for a few minutes without having to enter the room).

(g) Time with people (brushing, petting, playing with ordinary cat toys).

- Our cats also make constant use of the Fast-Trac™ toy. Singly housed animals curl in the center to sleep; if startled, the ball moves, and the game begins. Group-housed kitties line up around the outside edge—with one sitting in the middle—and don't get tired trying to somehow get the ball out. Now, my cat at home has no interest in this toy at all.

- My cats at home also have no interest in this device.

- They are probably less bored than cats in laboratories.

- Paper towel cardboard tubes can easily be turned into sham rodent burrows by connecting a few of them to a length of 2-4 feet, closing one end with packing tape and baiting the device with dry cat food pellets. Cats will first attentively check the entrance of the burrow, smell its contents and then bat and paw its wall. Moving the cardboard around will inevitably trigger a rustling noise created by the pellets tumbling at the far end of the burrow. The cats will now eagerly try to get hold of their prey by reaching into the burrow as far as they can while vigorously shaking it. Our house cat receives all her food in this manner; it takes her more than a half-hour every day to retrieve her pellet ration from these tubes.

- Access to a window is one of the most attractive enrichment options for cats. They love to watch what's going on outside their room.

- We have a cat at our facility who made her own enrichment. She was kept alone in one of our cat rooms for about three weeks and finally decided to get out for a walk. After everybody leaves in the late afternoon she does jumping exercise at the door, pulls down the lever handle, allows the door to swing open, and out she goes, roaming the hallway all night until we come back to work in the morning. We have found her like this every weekend, and now she has also started to go for a stroll during the week. Pretty smart kitty!

We finally decided to intervene and changed the door handle so that she can no longer open the door. As a compromise, we added two other kittens in the room so that our escaper is less bored.

- I remember a similar story of mice, leaving their cages during the night, hoarding food from other mice and returning back home before personnel can witness the escapade.

- I strongly believe that the most effective enrichment for single-cage cats is contact with humans. Time is one thing that is in short supply in most facilities, but I do feel it can be worked around.

We don't have cats at our facility anymore but when we did, anyone who had even a few minutes would drop in to spend a few minutes with them. A good brushing, if desired, a play with a toy or just a lap to sit on was so much appreciated by these felines. The cats were visited quite a bit daily and therefore were not lonely. We did supply toys for them, including tinfoil balls, Fast-Tracs™, cardboard boxes for scratching, dried catnip, pieces of medium sized rope suspended or loose on the floor, small cat balls, plus many food treats. We tried to give them something new each day and eventually came back to the first toy which, by then, was a brand new, interesting toy to them. All cats were usually given free run of a room and never caged unless absolutely necessary. I think we did a pretty good job of keeping the cats—and us—entertained!

handling

Cats can be quite feisty when you have to treat them for whatever reason. What is your trick to get the job done without being scratched or bitten and without unduly distressing the cat? Using the very least restraint possible is probably the basic condition to do hands-on work with cats without distressing them and without taking chances of being scratched or bitten by them. A cat who feels forcefully restrained can turn into a fiercely self-defending creature who will show no inhibition to swiftly strike out at you even if you think you can trust her.

- From my experience at a small vet clinic, the least restraint possible with cats is best. Encircling them with your arms and body rather than holding them down usually works.

  Another trick that I find very effective is the *kitty burrito*:
  (a) place the cat on a towel,
  (b) flip the two sides over the cat,
  (c) flip the back end up, and
  (d) leave the cat's head sticking out of the front opening.

  This maneuver has the advantage of holding the cat's limbs in, without cranking down on the cat. It is useful for administering pills as well as collecting blood.

  When the burrito is impractical and the cat is squirmy, holding a bit of scruff can work. Some cats react to this as they did when they were kittens; they go limp. It depends on the cat; stressful to some, helpful to others. Watch their reaction!

- Yes this is a very good trick also in my experience; it works with almost all cats.

- If cooperation has gone out the window, I agree that the towel roll helps get things done with a minimum of wrestling.

- To take the temperature of a cat with a rectal thermometer, getting an assistant to gently tap on the cat's nose between her/his eyes tends to take the cat's mind off what is happening around the back, so that there is no objection, unless perhaps the cat is already very upset. We routinely tap or stroke the area between the eyes towards the nose to calm many cats down in order to facilitate lots of procedures. Some of the cats definitely go into a calm, almost trance-like state.

Cats tend to be more skittish when you want to take a blood sample than dogs. Are there practical ways to train cats so that they relax and perhaps even cooperate rather than resist and struggle during blood collection?

- When I first started at my facility 24 years ago, we used bags to restrain most cats. What a struggle that was! We no longer use that system thank heavens; but what we discovered over the years is that cats respond much better to mild restraint rather than being strongly subdued.

  The cat must be able to trust the person who is holding her; and the person must be able to read the cat's emotions properly and respond accordingly. *Cat people* hold this key! I myself am a dog/pig person and respond to their behavioral signals much quicker and more accurately than I do with cats; and of course cats sense this. I believe that we all have our niche in the animal care field and it should be nurtured and called upon at all times to ensure that the animals we look after receive the best quality care possible!

- A long time ago, I worked with a vet who had her own unique way of calming fidgety cats during jugular blood sampling. She used to get a third person to rhythmically and gently tap the cat on the head during blood sampling. Almost invariably blood sampling would be a lot easier and the cats did not appear unduly stressed by this procedure.

pigs

socialization with personnel

Do you make attempts to socialize pigs so that anxiety and fear do not become uncontrolled variables during experimental procedures?

• Absolutely! It helps calm the researchers as well as the pigs. Our work would be impossible if we did not spend the time getting our pigs really well used to people and to being handled.

• We receive our pigs from a vendor who has a really nice socialization program, so the pigs come to us with great behavior and we are, therefore, able to handle them fairly easily, especially while offering yummy prima treats, fruity gems and other treats.

- The caregivers at our facility socialize the pigs who are in their charge. Young pigs are quite easy to get familiarized with humans because they have not yet learned, through aversive experience, to associate them with fear and anxiety.

On arrival, mature adults seem quite indifferent to me once settled in and at home. They are primarily concerned with their food supply; they tolerate being petted and scratched and are quite easy to handle for their size. Once they tolerate my presence and contact has been made, it is all downhill from there. They love to be scratched and have their bellies rubbed; they can't resist it. Good hard pats to injection sites will prepare them for those later. I use jam, peanut butter and large marshmallows for treats; medications can easily be hidden in there.

The one thing I have learned over the years is not to try playing with them. Pigs bite each other during play, but also when something is not going their way. They will do the same to you if they have not learned that you are *not* one of them but a provider of all good things, and that a bit of respect will gain them some excellent treats; they are extremely fast learners!

- I believe, first and foremost, socializing pigs is a welfare issue, it *must* be done; not only the pigs, but also the research will benefit from it. I strongly believe an animal who is less stressed or not stressed at all will make the best research model.

blood collection

What is the least distressing way to collect blood from pigs on a regular basis? I am sure these intelligent animals can readily be trained to cooperate during this procedure; what are the training steps that work best?

- I dealt with a highly food-motivated boar of about 200 kg. His kind nature made him popular with people, so he got a lot of attention. This is probably one of the main reasons why I could train him successfully.

  Training took place daily for 5-10 minutes. I used juice in a squirt bottle as positive reinforcement and a fruit as a bonus at the end of each session. It took about a week to shape his behavior to allow for his first jugular bleed with no restraint.

- We frequently bleed pigs and usually apply a numbing cream to their ears, then while one person distracts the animal with petting, food or treats, the other person obtains a blood sample from the ear. The pig has to be very well-acclimated to humans in order to cooperate during this procedure. Since most of our pigs are very friendly, we've even been able to take blood samples from other peripheral vessels like the cephalic, using the same handling technique.

- We sedate our pigs for blood sampling. This does not seem to be a big issue, but I would love some day to have the time with a pig to really concentrate on training for sampling with no sedation. I am sure this is possible.

- Having a good, that means trust-based, relationship with the person in charge is probably the key factor to making the blood collection procedure stress-free for the pig and stress-free for yourself. I don't think that the venipuncture per se is a big deal for the pig, provided you know what you are doing and how to do it swiftly and correctly. When you have a good relationship with your pigs, the animals will, over time, start to cooperate during blood collection without any formal training.

- Socialization is the most important first step when trying to manipulate a pig in any way. An intramuscular injection can be administered without any ado if the pig is well-socialized. Even injections that sting a little—for example ketamine—can be given without the pig really associating the sting with the handling person.

I think it is important to acknowledge that pigs are very easily spooked and, once their trust is broken, it takes a lot to earn it back!

• I find that farm animals, like pigs, are not looked at the same way as companion animals. Since they are still treated a certain way on the farm, some people in the biomedical industry feel that this should be good enough in research. I think this is hogwash and I strongly disagree. No animal used in research should fear the caregiver, the environment or any procedure. Pigs are very easily stressed and a stressed animal cannot be a good research model. I have found in most cases with pigs that major stress can be avoided, but it takes time. Unfortunately, in a lot of facilities time means money and that seems to be more important than compassionate animal care.

• We did not train for blood collection, but we had a project with daily bandage changes for 14-21 days. At first this required injectable anesthesia and a prolonged recovery. This was unpleasant

for the pigs and for the technicians. So we taught the pigs to walk down the hallway to the OR [Operations Room] and allow us to mask them down.

Pigs are food-oriented animals so we used favored treats as enticement to make them move in the right direction and as reward for cooperation during inhalation of the anesthetic. We worked with each pig twice a day for a total of about 30 minutes. It took four days for the smartest pig and nine days for the dumbest to get successfully trained before the actual research project started. The training shortened recovery and made the pigs and techs much happier and, in the end, saved time and money.

• That's the way to do business with animals in the research lab setting. When you have some first-hand experience with animals and are a bit concerned about their feelings such as fear, anxiety and despair, you must come to the conclusion that animals like pigs, cows, rats, rabbits, monkeys and dogs are too intelligent and trustworthy to be treated with force rather than taught to cooperate during procedures and work *with* rather than against you. This kind of working together is, by the way, also a valuable mental enrichment not only for the animal but also for yourself.

social enrichment

Pigs have a very strong social disposition and suffer in a similar manner as primates and sheep do when they are kept without a social partner. How do you address the need for companionship when the pig is housed alone during an experiment or test?

- When they find out that you are nice to them, pigs readily socialize with you and, if single-housed, will value any time you can spare to be with them. I visit each of our pigs at least once a day, talk to them, groom them a bit, and distribute food treats.

- Our single-housed pigs are well-socialized with humans; I spend a certain amount of time with each one of them every day, scratching, petting and giving them lots of attention. A good scratch with a toilet brush and lots of petting goes a long way!

  While I am cleaning their pens, I let two pigs out at a time so that they can interact with each other and play if they feel up to it.

  It is my experience that socialized pigs very quickly adjust to being housed in individual pens; they don't appear to be distressed. I can go into a pen with a socialized pig and give a pre-med with little or no stress to the animal. In a group setting this is harder and, once the group is disturbed, the pigs don't settle easily and are spooked for quite a while. They are harder to socialize in a group since they rely on each other for comfort instead of me.

- We use mesh-sided pens so that pigs can maintain contact with each other even if they can't mix. They also get lots of human contact and I do mean contact: lots of scratching, brushing and rubbing, and playing. On the odd occasion we only have one pig in the room, the human contact is increased even to the extent of just sitting in the bed alongside the animal for 10-15 minutes several times a day; pigs do seem to like lying, so they will typically lean up against you. I think we humans can provide—and should provide—highly valued companionship for pigs who have to be kept alone.

How do you go about establishing new pairs or groups of unfamiliar pigs? Does it help to sedate the animals first and then allow them to wake up together?

- It certainly works both in agricultural pig units as well as in the lab situation.

  It does seem to be important that future pen mates have body contact while they recover from sedation. They will stir and stumble over other pigs, settle back amongst the others and by the time they are fully recovered, all the pigs will have the same smell mix, distinguishing each one as a member of the *same* group. Our pigs wake up and just get on with things as if they've always been housed together. We have gilts, but my pig technician who is from a commercial background says that this technique also works with adult females, young intact males as well as adult castrated males.

environmental enrichment

Pigs are intelligent, highly inquisitive social animals. What can we do to mitigate boredom when they are kept in laboratories and assigned to research?

- We provide our pigs with balls and hanging soft nylon tug toys, which they chew up and destroy very quickly. We have tried several different types of scratchboards with limited success. The animals keep chewing them up. My ideal enrichment for our swine would be increased floor space and more human-animal contact.

- All of our pigs get basketballs, cardboard boxes stuffed with hay and treats, or empty, relatively large boxes in which piglets often sleep. Empty glove or hat cardboard boxes stuffed with hay and treats entertain our pigs quite a bit. They love shredded paper; I put a huge pile on the floor and sprinkle cereal on it; this simple trick promotes a lot of rooting. We have the large rubber feeders and I will place treats under stainless cat bowls, usually four or five bowls will fit in upside down. I then add shredded paper on top of the bowls to fill the feeder. The pigs have a blast rooting and trying to lift up the bowls to get their rewards underneath!

These delights are rotated so there is a new treat each day! The pigs also have chains hanging from the fencing as well as long strings of old rubber sipper tube stoppers; they love to chew and pull on these. They also like blankets to sleep on as well as play tug of war with. When possible a good hosing with water is much enjoyed! I would love to have a playroom for them with a children's swimming pool! Something to work on for the future!

Dry leaves or straw provide attractive substrate for rooting, especially when you sprinkle small food particles on it. The pigs will flip the substrate around and happily oink while rooting through it for goodies.

- All our mini-pigs have a Jolly Apple™ hanging from the ceiling, as well as a bowling ball or Boomer Ball™ on the floor of the cage. We give them produce occasionally. I have tried the Scratching Pads™ but the pigs always manage to break them and pull them down.

- Pigs have a very strong urge for scratching themselves and love rubbing their bodies against sturdy objects.

Plastic broom heads can easily be turned into scratching pads. We attach them to the wire mesh of the pens with plastic strapping. The pigs will chew them on occasions, but they last a reasonable time and are cheap enough to be replaced as needed. Mind you, our pigs are large White x Landrace hybrids who, in my experience, are much less destructive than the mini-pigs.

- We give our pigs the following:

  (a) A large wad of wheat straw every day so that they can make a bed; we leave the wad in a slice as it comes from the bale so that the pigs can work it up. They get enough straw to completely bury themselves in it.

  (b) Cardboard boxes that the pigs can tear up.

  (c) Old rubber boots that the pigs can toss around the pen; admittedly, this can prove to be a problem as they don't differentiate between these boots and the ones full of leg!

  (d) Water; pigs love to play with running water; but again this can create a problem as they may pick up the hose and stuff it down the top of your boot, if you aren't quick enough.

  (e) Stiff broom heads fastened to pen walls at just below back/shoulder height. The pigs use them for scratching themselves at great length.

  (f) Lots and lots of human companionship for at least a week before any procedures and again for at least one week afterwards. Pigs love to have their bellies, but also their ears, rubbed and scratched.

  Animals who are used to regular human contact are relatively easy to handle during research-related procedures.

Your comments clearly suggest that your pigs receive the attention and care they deserve. That's the way to go!

- Thanks for the appreciation, but I'm lucky in that I have a first class technician, superb staff in general and pretty much a free hand—any experimental reasons for not providing enrichment have to be justified in the appropriate project license.

  Probably the best aid to pig welfare are our rather progressive researchers who appreciate that contented pigs are so much easier to work with and, in addition, yield better results.

When a research protocol requires single caging of a pig, what are practical options for housing arrangements so that the subject can keep contact with one or several non-experimental pigs to help buffer fear, anxiety and boredom?

- We house pigs on a regular basis individually due to surgical procedures. Individual housing makes it easier on each pig when the others are used terminally. Our pigs are kept in dog runs or pens and can hear, see and smell their fellow swine. I keep them side-by-side and they always lay beside each other even though there is wire between them.

  They have a conditioning period to become comfortable with human contact. Once a pig likes you, she *really* likes you and social time or playtime with you then becomes a must. I spend a certain amount of time every day with each pig, scratching, petting and giving the animal lots of attention.

  Often we let our pigs out in the hallway to interact with their neighbors while the pens are being cleaned. Once accustomed to being kept alone, our pigs make no fuss going back to their home runs.

- Pigs love any amount of human contact, especially if that involves food, petting or playing in water. We try to do as much of that as possible at cage cleaning. I believe that regular interaction with a human friend provides valuable social enrichment for our single-housed pigs.

- I've started to play a CD with digitally recorded pig grunting in a room where a specific pig had to remain in isolation. Her activity, positive interactions with human caretakers, and appetite immediately improved after the CD was introduced.

- Even though it is our default to house pigs in pairs or groups, there is often a need to keep some individually. We utilize every method available to provide the single-housed animal visual, olfactory, and/or auditory contact with other conspecifics.

coprophagy

Can anyone confirm that coprophagy is a normal behavior in pigs?

- I have never noted this behavior in swine. In fact, pigs stay as far away from their feces as possible and are very specific to defecate away from where they eat. We house our pigs on sawdust bedding; they will definitely snack on it, but not where there is any fecal material. So I would say this is not a normal behavior in swine.

- In Yorkshires, housed in solid bottom pens with aspen chip, I have not seen coprophagy either. They will eat walls, toes, rodent chow and all kinds of other stuff, but not feces.

- I've spoken to my deputy who managed a 200-sow research herd of pigs for many years and who also has extensive experience in commercial piggeries, and our current pig supplier; both have never seen coprophagy in pigs and their response was the same, "there is something wrong if they do." My experience has also always been that pigs dung in a discrete area and avoid contact with their feces as much as possible unless they are stressed, in which case they will soil their sleeping area or roll in feces—usually an indication that they are too hot.

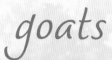

goats

There is a rumor that we are going to get goats at our facility. I have no experience with goats other than petting zoos or friends' farms. Can anybody share advice on enrichment?

- You are in for quite a treat: goats are fabulous animals. Depending on where you source them from, they may be quite skittish or already humanized to chew all your clothes.

  Big males can be intimidating, but if you have ever worked with cows or horses, it is the same working style.

  Goats do best on solid flooring with bedding and fed hay twice a day; grain makes them fat if they don't get enough exercise. Since they do chew everything and can stand on their back legs, you may always want to check what is in reach for them over the top edge of their pens.

- If they have to be kept alone, interaction with humans is the best enrichment for goats. They love people to talk to them, scratch them and hand out treats such as yogurt drops, alfalfa cubes, Cheerios and ginger snaps.

- I used to manage a research herd of over 300 goats; they are fantastic animals to work with and I still miss them.

  Goats investigate everything with their mouths and can be *very* destructive if bored. They are browsers rather than grazers, so if you can provide woody material for them to browse on, it's the best form of enrichment, but obviously you need to be careful about toxic trees and herbicides. If you can't get browse, then red clover hay, Lucerne hay (alfalfa) or straw will keep them busy; they prefer rough hay to good quality meadow hay. Mineral licks are also popular.

Goats like things they can climb on; if you have the space, old wooden packing cases or concrete blocks—as long as they are sturdy and won't topple—provide great enrichment. They will happily stand on their back legs for long periods; if you can suspend browse or hay at a good height, it will make them work. An adult Saanen-type goat can easily reach up to six feet when standing like this; this means any fittings in the room need to be made goat-proof even at this height.

Plenty of rubbing posts will be welcomed; goats are a bit like pigs in this respect and enjoy a good scratch. If they are housed in groups, the lead animal will start the rub and then the rest of the group will take their turns; so posts, gates and other vertical structures need to be quite robust. A daily brush, just like you'd groom a horse, is usually enjoyed and helps keep the goats clean.

Space is quite important to goats; if you can provide plenty, it will act as enrichment.

Goats love to be outdoors. If group-housed they will play *Follow The Leader*. This activity doesn't seem to be a stereotypy as the goats will play this game in a variety of ways out in the field.

I don't think footballs or similar toys would last five minutes, but a large puzzle ball might be enjoyed by goats, providing it is made of very tough material; goats don't have a particularly strong mouth but they are very, very persistent; same effect as dripping water on stone, but quicker!

If you have intact males, you will need separate clothing for use just with them, as once contaminated with their smell the odor does not wash out.

- Goats love to climb. Ordinary fences, usually, have only symbolic value for them; they are experts in climbing over them just to get out. If you have a good relationship with them—which is really not difficult—you will easily get them back in.

Structures onto which they can climb provide great enrichment for goats.

poultry

- The simplest method is probably autoshaping. Stick a piece of food to the key of the apparatus, stand back and wait! The broiler will quickly make the association between pecking the key and the food presentation. The birds learn remarkably quickly when they can watch each other; so once you have got one broiler trained, let the others watch. You should get close to a 100 percent success rate.

- I started at Waikato University where the operant animal of choice is a chicken. They autoshape much like any animal. A good-sized key with some positive contrast will make it harder to get them to stop pecking than to get them to start pecking.

- Thanks for the encouraging responses. It looks like it will be easier than I thought. It is my intention to work with a breed that can be (a) non-food restricted and (b) re-homed after termination of the study.

- You will almost certainly *not* be able to ethically re-home a broiler chicken! These animals have been artificially selected to put on massive amounts of weight, very quickly. As a consequence, by six weeks of age, most birds have difficulty walking, and many will have become so lame that they will no longer be able to walk to get food and water. This limited mobility might also confound your study—as the bird gets older, its motivation to eat might be increasing, but its physical ability to actually peck the key might decrease, thereby giving misleading results. I'm not entirely sure of the aim of your work, but the broiler hen is a difficult animal to work with because of these inherent problems. Layers are much more robust and agile. We often keep them for a year or two and then re-home them.

- Our hens had the lab as their true home where they were allowed to retire.

Is it customary to keep trained hens in retirement or re-home them, or are they used in repeated studies?

- I am not sure if that lab is still running. When I was there in the late 90's, trained birds tended to be kept on as long as they would last. New birds would be named and trained by undergrads and then assigned to research projects. When one study ended, healthy birds would move to another study. Respect for the animal was implicit in the way things were run. Culling for other than health reasons was very rare. I went back and visited my birds—Glady, Slim, Roadrunner, Scats, Struggle and Spooky— many years after I graduated.

- To re-home your animals after the studies, they need to be signed off by your named vet. We regularly do this with layer hens, sometimes sending hundreds to free-range farms after termination of studies.

{Chapter 5}

Miscellaneous

professional stigma

When you work as a technician, caretaker or veterinarian in a biomedical laboratory you are bearing the risk of getting stigmatized by outsiders as a vivisectionist who does not care about animals. How do you deal with this often rather frustrating situation?

• It is my opinion that we need to inform outsiders what actually does go on in research facilities. They should be able to form their opinions based on facts, not on some stories that contain only half-truths. I tell critics that I wish animals would not have to be used in research, but since they are being used I feel an obligation to give them all the care, respect and humane treatment they deserve. I am not hiding the fact that I am pro-research but I am also not hiding that I am pro-animal; both positions can complement each other when you work in a biomedical research lab.

- I talk about what I do fairly freely, stressing the controls we have in the U.K., the fact that I very much care about the well-being of the animals in my charge, and the benefits that medical research, using animals, gives to everyone. There are sometimes sharp intakes of breath when I first tell people that I look after research animals but, generally, I am given a fair hearing and most people will accept what I do as being necessary. Of course you'll never convert the hardened *anti*.

- In my experience here in Italy, speaking with people about my work and discussing with them honestly the pros and cons of animal experimentation is the best way to respond to the allegation that we torture animals in secret labs.

- Yes, I also speak to people openly about my work in a research lab. I first began with my family and close friends who know that I have loved animals since I could talk and wanted to be a vet since I was five years old. These discussions helped me to openly speak with other people, such as my neighbors, who don't know me as well as my family and close friends do. I hold myself back at certain places such as the local vet clinic, where I know that the vet techs are very much against animal experimentation.

- It is my experience as a clinical vet that some people have the unshakable belief that everybody working in animal research labs is a bad person. Such individuals are usually misinformed but very attached to their opinion. They are not willing and not ready to listen. There is not much you can do but keep your mouth shut and go. After all, you have no reason to defend yourself. Other people may have the same belief, but they are more open-minded and will listen. When you tell them the truth, they no longer have a good reason to insult you but will respect your commitment to making life as easy as possible for the animals in your charge.

   Sometimes people argue that my commitment is rather naïve because there are millions of animals in research laboratories; I am wasting my time when I try to help a few of them. Telling the following story of the man and the starfish serves as a gentle but effective way to counter this way of thinking:

   A man is picking up starfish on a beach and throws them, one at a time, back into the sea. Another man comes along and wonders what he is doing. The first man explains that the starfish are above the high tide line and will die if they don't get back into the water. The second man is incredulous and says "but there are hundreds of starfish on the beach; you can't possibly make a difference!" The first man calmly picks up another starfish, throws it back to the sea, and says, "made a difference to that one."

- I used to hide what I did for a living from folks but then one day wondered, "why am

I hiding?" After all, I care for animals and do what I possibly can to make life easier for them. Nowadays, I have no problem talking with interested people and critics alike about my work in the research lab.

I always start by making it clear that, as far back as I can remember, I always wanted to work with animals and to make a positive difference in their lives. When I first came into the animal research environment, I didn't know how long I would stay, but it didn't take me long to realize that here was the place where I could make a big difference; that was 23 years ago. I explain to people that, while I do find research interesting, it is the animals that brought me here and keep me here. I have been fortunate enough to have been able to bring about positive changes in the way they are kept and treated. This has been, and still is, very rewarding!

I once was asked how an animal lover, such as myself, could ever do what I do. My reply was, "would you rather have someone who doesn't love and respect animals work with them?" This was not rude, but it ended the conversation about my job.

- I have had people leave parties when they found out what I do. Fortunately, that is rare; most people listen, and I will explain to them that my job as an animal technician is to love animals, make sure they get the best care, use them well and, unfortunately, kill them well.

- I don't say a lot about my job unless I can trust the other person, and even then I do not go into details. The few people with whom I have discussed my work were at first rather critical, even judgmental, but after listening to me changed their view and told me that they do understand that research laboratories need caring technicians who do the daily work with and for the animals.

- It is no problem for me to talk about my job without fear everywhere I go here in the U.S. I tell people truthfully what I do, and how my job is precisely where I should be because of the level of concern I have for the welfare of animals in general and those in laboratories in particular.

- It is my personal experience that most people—not all!—quickly stop their accusations when you tell them honestly what you are actually doing, and how your presence alleviates rather than causes suffering to animals in research labs.

Many people think that working as a caretaker, technician or veterinarian in a research laboratory implies that you condone the research that is done, even if it may cause suffering and death to animals. How do you respond to this assumption?

- When I am drawn into a discussion on biomedical research and testing, I do my part to steer away from the question of pro or con animal experimentation. Yes, I do have a personal opinion on that issue but it is of no relevance, simply because I do not perform invasive experiments with animals myself. My mission is to care for animals assigned to such experiments, so I do my best to make sure that the animals are, at least, properly housed and handled.

- If you come across as not agreeing that the research being conducted on the animals in your care is beneficial, you are going to send a negative message to the public about research in general. I can hear comments like, "she is actually working in the lab and does not even believe that the research is necessary." That can hurt all of us in the field. I cannot imagine being able to justify to myself the use of animals for projects that I don't believe in.

- Exactly! That's the reason why I categorically refuse to be actively involved in a project in which I don't believe, either:
  (a) because of its adverse implications for animals, or
  (b) because of its scientific weakness.

- For me, the answer to the question if I believe that research is necessary is neither a *yes* nor a *no*. Based on my own experience and based on the literature that I have read, my answer would be that it all depends on the particular research protocol:
  (a) yes, there are certain invasive research projects that have significant scientific merit and, hence, are justifiable because no alternatives are available;
  (b) yes, there may be certain invasive research/testing projects that are necessary or legally mandated, but I am not in the position to argue for them because I am not an expert in that particular area of scientific research;
  (c) no, there are certain invasive research projects that have insufficient scientific merit and, hence, are not justifiable;
  (d) no, there are certain invasive research projects that are repetitive, hence are not justifiable because they are likely to cause unnecessary animal suffering; and
  (e) no, there are certain invasive research projects for which alternatives are available; they are not justifiable because they are likely to cause avoidable animal suffering.

It seems important to me to be very honest and factual when addressing this question, otherwise you can lose credibility and get labeled as a vivisectionist or an animal rights activist.

- I have always been frank about what I do at work with people I know very well; with strangers I tend to be reserved, more cautious. I learned that the hard way on a flight to Sacramento to attend an AZA [American Zoo and Aquarium Association] course on Enrichment & Training, when I struck up a conversation with the lady seated next to me. We started discussing what we did and I was a bit evasive until she said she was a pharmaceutical representative; I thought, "hey, a comrade, why not tell her more of what I do for a living?" She freaked, and I was shocked; how can a pharma rep be against animal/ drug testing?! In the end, we decided not to speak anymore and then had to sit next to one another for two more hours, very tense.

Fortunately, this was an exception; most people I talk to about what I do are very understanding. I find very few people who haven't had their lives touched by cancer or other diseases we are all working really hard to treat. I think, once people get over the "ick" factor and hear how regulated the field is and how much we all care for our animals, they calm down.

- All of us have probably found ourselves in sticky situations, from time to time, when it comes to our work. Yes, we're all very passionate about what we do, and care deeply about the animals we work with on a daily basis; but there are other persons/ organizations out there that feel very differently than we do.

I am very open to speaking about what I do even though I've had an active hand in several of the more ugly things that occur in this line of work. No, I'm not about to wear a t-shirt prominently displaying a head-capped monkey, but if I'm asked what I do, I tell the truth. What I try to remember is that there are several views about this field out there and that what we do isn't for everyone. Thus, if some people feel strongly against what I do, I allow them to voice their opinions, and then try my best to make it very clear that we do more than experimentation. I explain that we have government animal welfare regulations [that negate the status of "animals" to the great majority of animals found in research labs] as well as voluntary regulations that we use along with everything in our power to ensure that the animals we are working with are not only healthy but also happy. If the subject of euthanasia presents itself, I let people know why terminal work is sometimes necessary, that we utilize the most painless and peaceful method of euthanasia possible, and that it's hard on us as well. Once people hear this, and find that a majority of folks in biomedical research are indeed *animal people*, it usually lessens the tension.

job interview

Imagine, I am applying for a position at your Animal Care unit. What qualifications would give me the best chance to be hired by you? As part of the job interview would you give me a tour through the animal quarters?

- I would want someone who can communicate well with others, is able to work independently, has pride in a job well done, likes animals, has an open mind about research, and has a good level of patience. I would only take you on a tour if you passed the first level of interviews, and I would watch you during the tour to see how you react to the animals and how the animals react to you.

- Rather than focusing on diplomas, I check if the job applicant has a positive connection with animals. For this purpose, I do make the necessary arrangements so that I can take the candidate on a tour of the animal holding areas.

- Job applicants should be calm and not afraid of animals; this should, in my opinion, be a basic condition for considering a candidate to work with animals.

- If I have any doubt about an applicant's relationship with animals, I take her or him to a rabbit room and keep asking questions about his/her background. If the rabbits stampede or thump, the person does not get the job. The animals are the best judges of a good or bad team player and animal welfare enthusiast.

- Rabbits may stomp when any unfamiliar person enters their territory, so I am not sure I would hold it against an applicant initially.

- It seems important to me not to take the animals' initial reaction to the presence of a strange accompanying person, but wait and see how quickly they settle down and how they react when the person tries to communicate with them. I take it as:
    (a) a good sign when monkeys come to the front of the cage to get a better view of the stranger, and the stranger can look at the monkeys without scaring them away, and
    (b) a bad sign when monkeys kind of freeze in the back of their cage while the stranger talks to them.

- When I interviewed potential candidates, I first spoke with them on the phone and then brought them in; I needed to see them around some animals. I actually had them walk rounds with me; it helped a lot! Especially when you are dealing with primates, many people think they really want to work with them until they come face to face with them in the laboratory setting and reality sets in. It is very frustrating when people look so good on paper and in person, and then you get them around the animals and notice that something is missing—you don't see that sparkle in their eyes that says "WOW! This is awesome, when can I start?"

- What is true for monkeys holds true also for any other animal species found in the research lab. If a person applies to work with rodents, rabbits, dogs, cats, frogs, fishes, birds or farm animals, she has to convey her fascination with these animals in some spontaneous manner, otherwise there is a risk that she regards animals as *things* and will interact with them accordingly.

role on the
animal care committee

How many of you on this forum serve on the Institutional Animal Care and Use Committee (IACUC) at your particular facility?

- I am a behavior technician and serve as the chairperson of our IACUC. It is important for me to be actively involved in meetings so that I can present and discuss ideas, techniques and protocols that best address the physical and behavioral needs of the animals and the needs of the research scientists.

- As part of our post-doctoral training, we rotate on the IACUC as a veterinarian for six months and then serve as ad-hoc members for the remaining time in the program. During my rotation, I performed designated reviews and site visits. I learned a great deal and feel I made a significant contribution during my rotation; I still attend as many of the meetings as possible.

- My title is Enrichment Specialist; my duties include the management of our enrichment program and the behavioral health of our animals. I am an ad-hoc, nonvoting member of our IACUC, and serve to keep the rest of the Committee informed of the state of our enrichment program. I review all protocols involving nonhuman primates and exemptions from any aspect of our enrichment program for all animal species during the approval process.

- Your situation is a fair compromise, even though it is my personal opinion that a qualified animal caregiver or animal technician should be a voting member of any Animal Care and Use Committee. This person would quasi-represent the animals who, after all, are in most cases at the mercy of people who have very little understanding of their research subjects' biological needs.

  It is my experience that most animal caretakers and most animal technicians are better qualified to assess "their" animals' needs to be free of stress and distress prior to and during experiments/tests than principal investigators and chief veterinarians.

- I think your idea makes a lot of sense since we, the animal care technicians, are the ones who are in direct contact with *our* animals every day. I could tell you specific behavior/personality traits of each monkey in my room and in a lot of the other rooms I work in.

- I feel the same; no one knows these animals like the folks who care for them daily but, sadly, in many places they are not yet recognized for the important jobs they perform. They often feel overlooked and insignificant in the big picture.

- The question then is, how do we get the scientists, veterinarians and administrators to bend down and acknowledge that practical animal care-experience is at least as valuable as academic degrees when it comes to deciding how to control husbandry-related and handling-related variables that may skew scientific data collected from the animals? A professor who knows his/her animals only as computer data is certainly in a much less qualified position to assess the impact of the housing conditions and the actual data-collection procedure on the animals' well-being and stress status than the caregiver and technician who work with the animals on a daily basis and collect the data directly from them.

- One way to convince scientists of their dependency on animal care staff to produce reliable scientific data is for the people who do the hands-on work with research animals to take the time—even free time—to publish their refinement ideas in the professional literature.

- Here in Canada, the Animal Care Committee (ACC) is similar to the IACUC in the United States. I am the lab animal technician who looks after all animals listed in our research protocols. I review the protocols prior to the ACC meetings and discuss any issues that I may have with the committee members before they vote. I am a non-voting member but like to attend the ACC meetings, as it gives me a chance to find out what's going on with the protocols under review and get first-hand knowledge of anything that could be an animal welfare concern.

- In the United Kingdom, it is a standard protocol to have appointed animal technicians serve as full, voting members on the ethical committees—the equivalent to the IACUCs in America.

- The situation is similar in Switzerland where lab technicians, dealing with the animals on a daily basis, are full members of the IACUC.

killing animals

When you work with individual animals or with a group of animals—be it mice, cats, monkeys, or any other species—for an extended period of time, chances are that you develop personal relationships with them; that means you get attached. Once you get attached to an animal or a group of animals in the research lab setting, you may find it sad or painful when the time comes to kill them or have them killed. If this is an issue for you, how do you deal with it?

- This is an important and difficult subject. I have been present at the final moment of some dogs who, I feared, would be frightened with strange people. It was hard and there was of course some crying, but I felt relief in the fact that I could offer these animals, who were so close to me, some comfort; it was worth the tears!

- I would worry if I ever found that I wasn't disturbed by the thought of having to kill any creature, but it is much more difficult when you've become friends with an animal, and this happens to me quite often even though the animals in our lab are with us only for a short term. After 40 years in the business, I still find it difficult. Yet, I do get involved in the killing process because I strongly believe that it provides some comfort to the individual animal to have someone familiar present who maintains kind and gentle vocal contact up to the very end.

• I am currently a second year PhD student working with feed-restricted broiler breeders. I had no previous experience in this sort of setting/environment. Before that I was a vet nurse for circa eight years so I was used to assisting with and performing euthanasia.

When I had my interview with my funding committee, one of the first questions I was asked was how I feel about euthanizing my chickens at the end of the study. My reply at the time was that it was evil to kill, but a necessary evil and the lesser of two evils. At that point I had made my peace with this issue. However, it does come at some cost as I am now constantly being reminded—by myself!—that I personally am responsible for the deaths of my birds; there is no distancing myself from this fact. I often feel that there is some kind of cognitive dissonance going on in my head. Almost my whole life has been spent trying to help the individual animal and now I am sacrificing individuals for the greater good and, while I find it easy to rationalize this at a distance, it is definitely much harder when you work closely with these individuals day in and day out. Before starting, I had rationalized this at the level of the individual animal: these birds are constantly hungry so what sort of life would they have if I kept them alive? But when you then spend time with them and realize that there is so much more to these birds than simply an unrequited desire for food, it does become difficult—very difficult. Knowing an individual's personality makes

it so hard. My chickens weren't/aren't just hungry birds to me anymore—they are characters for which hunger is only a shaping force. I am not sure that I will ever get over this hurdle and, to be honest, I am not convinced that I want to. I always said that I would get out of nursing if I ever got to the point where I just didn't care anymore, and I think the same applies here. If I wouldn't feel for these birds, I would have lost all compassion.

How do I cope? Firstly, I take full responsibility for the manner in which my birds are dying. I euthanize them myself, and it is important to me that I do this. On the one occasion when I haven't done so I got greatly upset. For me, I need to know that they have died peacefully, been given the best possible death (unpalatable phrase) that I could give them. This includes them being handled by somebody they are familiar with and are comfortable being handled by. I also have created a ritual specifically for my birds. They are generally feed restricted so, on the last day, I give them a last supper in which they can eat freely; I euthanize them only once they are satisfied and stop eating. I mentally switch off and try to treat this all as any other routine event, focusing my mind on other issues. Anybody observing me would probably think that I just don't really care and that I am not emotionally affected by euthanizing my birds. To be honest, I do care but I am not affected emotionally as *there is a great big wall around me* that protects me from getting overwhelmed by what I am actually doing! It generally hits me a few days later when I feel tearful but, as my housemate would testify, I am generally grumpy and bad tempered that night and just want to be alone.

I find that spending time with my pet dogs afterwards helps; I will usually go and have a play session with them or give them a special treat or something like that. I probably compensate for feeling bad by being overly good with other animals, to remind myself that I am an animal lover.

Talking to others definitely doesn't help me; I get irritated if people come out with trite phrases that they think will help. Finally, I remind myself of why I am doing the PhD and focus on the perceived animal welfare benefits.

• When you love animals, you are bound to develop a close relationship with them; this makes it very hard to put an animal down. I was very close to all the marmosets of our colony as I trained them during many, many sessions and worked with them over a period of four years. There were several marmosets who had serious health problems; we tried very hard to turn their conditions around, in some cases for as long as six months, but it was finally decided to relieve them from their pain and suffering.

I ended up placing the femoral needle that would deliver the euthanasia solution. During the procedure I focused on proper needle placement, trying to avoid any extra stress or distress to that animal. I preferred to let the vet actually deliver the lethal dose; this is probably my coping strategy, it makes me feel a little bit better. After euthanasia of one of my animals I was always very sad for several days.

To put down an animal, for whatever reason, has always been the toughest part of my job; no question. I wish the animal rights groups would understand just how much we really care and love the animals that we all work with.

- I get terribly upset when it comes time to euthanize one of our macaques. I am the one who takes care of them day in and day out, feeds them, medicates them, grooms them if they ask for it, and euthanizes them. It is very difficult because I know the animals so well and, unavoidably, get attached to each one of them.

  I don't feel like there is anyone here to talk to about this dilemma, so I deal with it on my own. I have cats and a bunny at home; they are my therapists so to speak. I do my best to be professional at work but it does show on my face that I am very upset. Everyone is usually very good in giving me space and allowing me to deal with it in my own way.

I am lucky that not only do we not euthanize often, but some of our investigators are moving towards retirement rather that euthanasia. My dream is to open a retirement center for macaques who are no longer needed for research.

- I have almost left my job a few times in my 24-year career while working with dogs in chronic studies. It can be very hard when an animal is euthanized with whom you have worked for quite some time and for whom you have developed affection and compassion. It helps me to share my feelings with others who have similar experiences, and to know that I am not alone but that it is okay to feel very sad and frustrated. I firmly believe that the feelings and emotions we carry for these little critters help us to make their lives as good as possible while they are in our care!

- It can be tough, very tough at times to deal with the realities that animals are facing, by the millions, daily in research labs. I worked in this environment for 25 years. After a few months, I got so disillusioned that I vowed to myself never again to kill an animal for scientific reasons. I kept this vow, missed job opportunities but kept ease of mind and heart.

death and dying

Could it be that animals are aware of their mortality and afraid of dying when they face a life-threatening situation, for example, monkeys who are forcefully restrained by the human predator during a painful procedure?

- It is probably more an issue of survival instinct than fear of death.

- The idea of death and dying may not exist for animals. Unlike humans, animals do not give the impression that they identify with the body, hence there is nobody there to actually experience anxiety at the prospect of the body's decay. The survival instinct takes care of the body; it's an unconscious process. At the sight of an unexpected danger—for example a fast approaching car—the survival instinct takes over also in humans, and you do exactly what needs to be done to protect the body—no thoughts, no fear, no anxiety, just right action. Under normal circumstances, however, humans rely on the mind for taking care of the body; this consciously taking care of a vulnerable, complex organism that is constantly exposed to a rather dangerous environment leads to incessant restlessness, fear and anxiety which, I think, animals don't suffer from.

Humans tend to have a feeling of insecurity most of the time, as neither the body nor the external environment are, ultimately, under their control. Animals probably don't have this problem. This is perhaps one reason why being with animals can have such a healing effect on the human psyche.

- I think that an animal who tries to escape from a predator has some feeling of being in peril. Even though the animal has probably no abstract notion of ceasing to exist, I would call that feeling fear of death.

- It seems to me that animals have an instinct for living, and thereby preserving the species. An animal probably avoids a situation, such as being captured or receiving an injection that is remembered as threatening his or her life in the past. Even the memory of such a situation inflicts suffering if the animal is facing the same situation again.

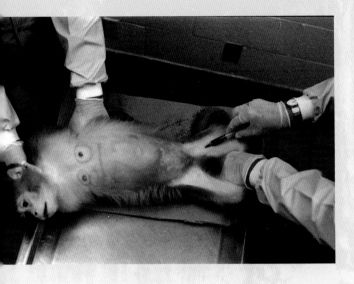

- This implies that animals in laboratories are often suffering intense fear when an investigator or technician enters the room to subject one of them to a procedure that was experienced as life-threatening in the past. Most of the common procedures are life-threatening for animals, just as they would be for humans: the subject is first captured by a predator, then immobilized by the predator and finally forced to hold still while being handled by the predator. This must be quite a terrible experience, so animals in research laboratories are, therefore, likely to live in terror much of their lives.

self-awareness

I wonder, do monkeys have a sense of self and identify with their bodies?

- When a monkey looks in a mirror, he or she probably thinks that the reflection is another monkey. This would suggest that the monkey does not have a sense of self.

- Doesn't the fact that macaques develop stable dominance-subordinance relationships imply that the individual group member must have a feeling of self, *I* versus *you*. I would even go one step further and argue that macaques—similar to humans—also have a sense of *us*. This identification with a group is the basic driving force of xenophobia in nonhuman primates, and war in human primates.

- I regularly see macaques threaten or lip smack their mirrors as if they are communicating with another monkey, but I have also made many observations of macaques using mirrors to look at and clean their own head implants. Does this not suggest that there is some recognition of self?

- Having worked with macaques for around 14 years, I strongly believe they do have a feeling of self. I have one monkey who demonstrates this quite clearly: he actually grooms his little face while looking at his reflection in the mirror. If he wouldn't identify with the image in the mirror, he would probably touch/groom the mirror but not himself; after all he cannot possibly see himself directly.

- Your observation is very similar to mine of Annie, a cynomolgus female, who looked in the mirror and examined her own teeth. She used her fingers to pull her lip down to get a better look at the teeth, with her face close to the mirror. She noticed a small piece of raisin stuck to her tooth and used the mirror to direct her fingers to remove it. Annie didn't reach to the raisin image in the mirror; she reached to the raisin piece stuck to her tooth as she looked in the mirror, and removed it. Recently we put a red dot on Annie's forehead while she was under for medical procedures, and then later took her to the mirror. She put her

face very close to the mirror and looked at the dot for some time. Then she reached up to the dot on her forehead with her fingers, as she continued looking at it in the mirror, and tried to groom it off (Schultz, 2006).

- I have also seen monks who use the mirror to groom themselves, indicating that they are aware that they are looking at themselves.

- Anyone who has worked with a large number of macaques in any close relationship can attest that some have very apparent self-awareness, while others do not. With respect to mirrors, I think young animals cannot recognize the image as self, but many adults do seem to understand the reflection.

- Formal studies using the mirror test in chimpanzees have shown that certain individuals seem to recognize themselves in the mirror and other individuals don't [Gallup, 1970; Lethmate & Dücker, 1973].

- This is one of the complications of research on animal cognition. If one animal can perform the required task, does that mean all members of that species have the same cognitive ability? Or, do several/all animals tested have to perform to criterion for statistical significance to indicate that the species has that capacity? A colleague once had some extremely interesting results on cognition in pigs rejected for publication because only one of the six pigs performed the task. What if the other five pigs were just being lazy, distracted or did not perform the task for some other reason?

- Do we know for sure that each and every psychologically healthy adult human identifies with the reflection she or he sees in the mirror? I am not quite so sure. Have you ever looked into the mirror and seriously asked yourself "Who is that?" and then pondered about an answer that makes sense?

- Even though the question of self-awareness is not really relevant on this forum, it is interesting because we humans have the tendency to try very hard to find human-specific characteristics that distinguish *us* from *them*—the animals. I remember when people had a hard time coming to grips with the fact that nonhuman primates not only fabricate and use tools, but that they can also learn a sign language and then kind of talk with you if you also know sign language.

  There is no good reason to believe that only humans have a sense of self.

humor

Do animals have a sense of humor?

- When I see how our cat enjoys it when he can make our dog run without even getting up, I have no doubt that he has a sense of humor.

- When I paired aged rhesus macaques with surplus infants from a breeding colony, I noticed several infants who got a kick out of quickly touching their *opas* or *omas* as if inviting them to play, and then jumping up on the high perch out of reach of the seniors who, with the frequent repetition of this game, got a bit annoyed; but what could they do? When enticing their partners, the kids showed the typical play face, which includes laughing, and they sure gave the impression of having fun. Jack, a 33-year-old male got a bit distressed by his little companion's constant teasing, so I finally exchanged the kid with another *oma*, who did not try to play with the old guy but groomed him at length to his great delight.

- I remember the tale told by Miriam Rothschild about her parrot who called the dog's name and whistled; the dog dutifully turned up, and then the parrot laughed. It seems to me that this parrot did have a sense of humor.

- As for parrots with a sense of humor, I would say absolutely yes! I had a greenwing macaw whom I used to bring to work with me. One of Sam's favorite things to do was walk into a dark office and make ghost sounds to anyone walking by. He would poke his head out and laugh at anyone that he was able to make scream. Of course he also loved to quasi-ask for scratches, only to bite and laugh at the person who obliged.

- We have a fairly tame garden robin at home who teases our cat by persistently sitting in the tree a few feet above the cat's head:
  Cat starts climbing the tree stalking Robin until she's a few feet away, when Robin moves up a bough;
  Cat repeats process and so does Robin. When neither of them can get any higher,
  Robin flies down to the bottom and helps himself to cat food;
  Cat ponderously works her way down the tree—she's 19 years old and should know better!
  Robin flies up into the tree;
  Cat collapses from exhaustion;
  Robin comes back down and pulls hair from Cat's coat;
  Cat has no teeth, so Robin is in no real danger.
  I should add that at no time is Robin any more than one branch ahead of Cat and that he never tries this game with any of the younger, more agile neighbor cats who pass through the garden from time to time. I suspect that I am endowing Robin with more credit than perhaps nature intended but it's fascinating to watch. I end up removing our cat to the safety of the house, as I'm worried that she'll die from frustration.

- Your observations make me recall a scene that once unfolded in our yard.
  A turtle was making her way across the lawn toward the cranberry bogs when a very young squirrel discovered what,

262

I'm sure, seemed like a moving rock. The squirrel would tap the top of the shell, causing the turtle to pull her arms and legs in. After a few minutes the turtle would slowly extend her limbs out and start walking again, whereby the little squirrel—who had patiently waited during this interim—bopped on the shell again and caused the turtle to pull herself into the shell again. This happened several times during the course of an hour, so I can only imagine that the young squirrel found this interaction very interesting and fun. The whole thing was surreal to watch; it was like a peek into a real-life Gary Larson cartoon.

• Many years ago, when I managed a pet store, I had a scarlet macaw who would always wait until I had swept the floor and then proceeded to scoop with his beak the seeds out of his bowl and fling it across the floor. When the bowl was empty, he would stick his head upside down in it and laugh as loud as he could—he liked the echo of the bowl—until I swept it all up. I would wait a while, refill his bowl and the whole scenario would start over again. That bird sure had me trained.

• I had an Amazon parrot who liked to sing *You are My Sunshine* whenever I had the vacuum cleaner on. One day, I went to answer the phone and, after a moment, heard the vacuum on and the bird singing. I first thought a coworker was cleaning, but then quickly remembered that everybody was at lunch. When I went to investigate, I found that the bird had unlocked her cage, turned on the vacuum and was sitting on top singing her little heart out. Was it an expression of humor? I don't really care to know but it was fascinating to witness this funny scene.

• My friend had a parrot named Baby who would act very sweet and try to get you to pet his head through the cage bars. When you did, he would bite you very hard and scream "bad Baby!" Obviously, this is what people had previously said whenever he had behaved in this manner. It's hard to say whether this was just a learned response, or had an element of humor or amusement in it. But he seemed to get a kick out of it!

- Even if animals—and for that matter also humans—*learn* to respond to a certain situation in order to trigger a predictable, albeit futile reaction in another partner, this does not exclude the possibility that the learned response is an expression of humor/amusement/fun. There is no convincing reason to believe that animals do not have a sense of humor and derive amusement and fun from a certain situation, just as humans do.

- I believe many animals have a sense of humor. It is my experience with pigs that they sometimes exhibit behaviors that serve no purpose other than getting people to react.

    My favorite example is from almost 17 years ago. In our lab we used to exercise the pigs in the afternoons in the dirty hallway. The pigs would run up and down the hallway and greet anyone who exited an animal room with a big slobbery tug on their clothes.

    There was an understanding that you did not bring visitors to the facility after 2 p.m. without an appointment because the pigs would be out—and therefore some feces was likely to be in the corridor; not a good image for a guest.

I got a new boss during a group shift. He was a scientist who had never supervised an animal group. I explained the need for an appointment for afternoon visits which he said he understood. About a month later at 3 p.m. one afternoon, I hear two of our pig ladies hauling down the hallway, oinking and grunting gleefully. Then I hear the commotion of several voices. I turn the corner and my new boss in his suit and several suited visitors are standing kind of stuck against the wall with two 125 lb piggies tugging on their suits leaving drool marks, brushing up against them and grunting. The pigs had very happy looks on their faces while the visitors were not amused. I refrained from laughing and called the two ladies off with a treat. The visitors in their slobbered, smelly suits walked gingerly down the hallway, I gave them the rest of the tour and they left. My boss never came down again without an appointment. I think those two pigs laughed about that for weeks! They were very amused.

• Jo, one of our breeder rhesus amuses himself by peeing on you while you are bending down under his upper-row cage to check another animal in the bottom row. I don't think it's funny but he probably does. You have to watch out for him: he will sit on his perch up front and casually put his hand in the urine stream, directing it right on you. You will feel sprinkles on your head and on your scrub pants, and when you get up and give Jo a piece of your mind, he will just look at you like an innocent baby; but I know, deep inside he laughs and already waits for the next opportunity to get you. I would call that a sense of humor.

• I had a most memorable experience a while back when I worked with young chimpanzees. One female would often take a blanket and put it over her head, like a little ghost. She would then chase the other chimps around who would run away, screaming and smiling. The little "ghost" would then suddenly pull the blanket off, and the other chimps would laugh and laugh. It looked like a human game of tag, and they definitely seemed to enjoy it. I am always thankful for the time I had with them; they were amazing.

References

Ackerley ET and Stones PB 1969 Safety procedures for handling monkeys. *Laboratory Animal Handbooks 4*: 207-211

Aidara D, Tahiri-Zagret C and Robyn C 1981 Serum prolactin concentrations in mangabey (*Cercocebus atys lunulatus*) and patas (*Erythrocebus patas*) monkeys in response to stress, ketamine, TRH, sulpiride and levodopa. *Journal of Reproduction and Fertility 62*: 165-172

Altman NH 1970 Restraint of monkeys in clinical examination and treatment. *Journal of the American Veterinary Medical Association 159*: 1222

American Psychiatric Association *1987 Diagnostic and Statistical Manual of Mental Disorders*, 3rd Edition. American Psychiatric Association: Washington, DC

Animal Welfare Act 2002 *United States Code, Title 7, Chapter 54, Sections 2131-2159*. U.S. Government Printing Office: Washington, DC
http://cofcs66.aphis.usda.gov:80/ac/awapdf.pdf

Arendash GW, Garcia MF, Costa DA, Cracchiolo JR, Wefes IM and Potter H 2004 Environmental enrichment improves cognition in aged Alzheimer's transgenic mice despite stable beta-amyloid deposition. *Neuroreport 15*: 1751-1754

Baker KC, Bloomsmith M, Neu K, Griffis C, Oettinger B, Schoof V, Clay A and Maloney M 2008 Benefits of isosexual pairing of rhesus macaques (*Macaca mulatta*) vary with sex and are limited by protected contact but not by frequent separation. *American Journal of Primatology 70*(Supplement): 44

Baker KC, Weed JL, Crockett CM and Bloomsmith MA 2007 Survey of environmental enhancement programs for laboratory primates. *American Journal of Primatology 69*: 377-394

Baldwin AL, Schwartz GE and Hopp DH 2007 Are investigators aware of environmental noise in animal facilities and that this noise may affect experimental data? *Journal of the American Association for Laboratory Animal Science 46*(1): 45-51

Barbiers RB 1985 Orangutans' color preference for food items. *Zoo Biology 4*: 287-290

Barrett AM and Stockham MA 1996 The effect of housing conditions and simple experimental procedures upon corticosterone level in the plasma of rats. *Journal of Endocrinology 26*: 97-105

Basile BM, Hampton RR, Chaudhry AM and Murray EA 2007 Presence of a privacy divider increases proximity in pair-housed rhesus monkeys. *Animal Welfare 16*: 37-39

Bayne K and McCully C 1989 The effect of cage size on the behavior of individually housed rhesus monkeys. *Lab Animal 18*(1): 25-28

Bennett EL, Rosenzweig MR and Diamond MC 1969 Rat brain: Effects of environmental enrichment on wet and dry weights. *Science 163*: 825-826

Bentson KL, Crockett CM, Montgomery HB and Ha JC 2004 Cage level has little effect on behavior of macaques (*M. fascicularis, M. nemestrina*, and *M. mulatta*). *American Journal of Primatology 62*(Supplement): 85-86

Bertrand F, Seguin Y, Chauvier F and Blanquié JP 1999 Influence of two different kinds of foraging devices on feeding behaviour of rhesus macaques (*Macaca mulatta*). *Folia Primatologica 70*: 207

Boinski S, Swing SP, Gross TS and Davis JK 1999 Environmental enrichment of brown capuchins *(Cebus apella)*: Behavioral and plasma and fecal cortisol measures of effectiveness. *American Journal of Primatology 48*: 49-68

Burgdorf J and Panksepp J 2001 Tickling induces reward in adolescent rats. *Physiology and Behavior 72*: 167-173

Burwell AK 2006 Do audible and ultrasonic sounds of intensities common in animal facilities affect the autonomic nervous system of rodents? *Journal of Applied Animal Welfare Science 9*: 179-200

Campo JL, Gil MG and Dávila SG 2005 Effects of specific noise and music stimuli on stress and fear levels of laying hens of several breeds. *Applied Animal Behaviour Science 91*: 75-84

Cancedda L, Putignano E, Sale A, Viegi A, Berardi N and Maffei L 2004 Acceleration of visual system development by environmental enrichment. *Journal of Neuroscience 24*: 4840-4848

Carter RJ, Morton J and Dunnett SB 2001 Motor coordination and balance in rodents. *Current Protocols in Neuroscience Chapter 8*: Unit 8.12.

Carughi A, Carpenter KJ and Diamond MC 1989 Effect of environmental enrichment during nutritional rehabilitation on body growth, blood parameters and cerebral cortical development of rats. *Journal of Nutrition 119*: 2005-2016

Choi GC 1993 Humans enrich the lives of lab baboons. *WARDS (Working for Animals Used in Research, Drugs and Surgery) Newsletter 4*: 3-7 & 13

Christenson GA and Mansueto CS 1999 Trichotillomania: descriptive characteristics and phenomenology. In: Stein DJ, Christenson GA and Hollander E (eds) *Trichotillomania* pp. 1-41. American Psychiatric Press: Washington, DC

Clarke AS, Czekala NM and Lindburg DG 1995 Behavioral and adrenocortical responses of male cynomolgus and lion-tailed macaques to social stimulation and group formation. *Primates 36*: 41-46

Coe CL, Franklin D, Smith ER and Levine S 1982 Hormonal responses accompanying fear and agitation in the squirrel monkey. *Physiology and Behavior 29*: 1051-1057

Council of Europe 2002 *Proposals for the revision of Appendix A of the Convention: Species-specific provisions for Non-human Primates.* Council of Europe: Strasbourg, France
http://www.eslav.org/appendixa/appendix-A.htm

Council of Europe 2006 *Appendix A of the European Convention for the Protection of Vertebrate Animals Used for Experimental and Other Scientific Purposes (ETS No. 123) enacted June 15, 2007.* Council of Europe: Strasbourg, France
http://conventions.coe.int/Treaty/EN/Treaties/PDF/123-Arev.pdf

Cooper RM and Zubek JP 1958 Effects of enriched and restricted early environments on the learning ability of bright and dull rats. *Canadian Journal of Psychology 12*: 159-164

Crockett CM, Bowers CL, Shimoji M, Leu M, Bellanca RU and Bowden DM 1993 Appetite and urinary cortisol responses to different cage sizes in female pigtailed macaques. *American Journal of Primatology 31*: 305

Crockett CM, Shimoji M and Bowden DM 2000 Behavior, appetite, and urinary cortisol responses by adult female pigtailed macaques to cage size, cage level, room change, and ketamine sedation. *American Journal of Primatology 52*: 63-80

Crockett CM, Koberstein D and Heffernan KS 2001 Compatibility of laboratory monkeys housed in grooming-contact cages varies by species and sex. *American Journal of Primatology 54*(Supplement): 51-52
http://www.asp.org/asp2001/abstractDisplay.cfm?abstractID=112&confEventID=26

Crockett CM, Lee GH and Thom JP 2006 Sex and age predictors of compatibility in grooming-contact caging vary by species of laboratory monkey. *International Journal of Primatology 27*(Supplement): 417

Cross N, Pines MK and Rogers LJ 2004 Saliva sampling to assess cortisol levels in unrestrained common marmosets and the effect of behavioral stress. *American Journal of Primatology 62*: 107-114

Cummings BJ, Engesser-Cesar C, Cadena G and Anderson AJ 2007 Adaptation of a ladder beam-walking task to assess locomotor recovery in mice following spinal cord injury. *Behavioral Brain Research 177*: 232-241

Davenport MD, Lutz CK, Tiefenbacher SNMA and Meyer JS 2008 A rhesus monkey model of self-injury: effects of relocation stress on behavior and neuroendocrine function. *Biological Psychiatry 63*: 990-996

Dellinger-Ness LA and Handler L 2006 Self-injurious behavior in human and non-human primates. *Clinical Psychology Review 26*: 503-514

Diamond MC, Krech D and Rosenzweig MR 1964 The effects of an enriched environment on the rat cerebral cortex. *Journal of Comparative Neurology 123*: 111-119

Donnelly MJ 2008 Capturing and handling marmosets. *Laboratory Primate Newletter 47*(4): 6-7
http://www.brown.edu/Research/Primate/

Doyle LA, Baker KC and Cox LD 2008 Physiological and behavioral effects of social introduction on adult male rhesus macaques. *American Journal of Primatology 70*: 542-550

Drescher B and Loeffler K 1991 Einfluß unterschiedlicher Haltungsverfahren und Bewegungsmöglichkeiten auf die Kompakta der Röhrenknochen von Versuchs- und Fleischkaninchen [German text with English abstract]. *Tierärztliche Umschau 46*: 736-741

Eaton GG, Kelley ST, Axthelm MK, Iliff-Sizemore SA and Shiigi SM 1994 Psychological well-being in paired adult female rhesus (*Macaca mulatta*). *American Journal of Primatology 33*: 89-99

Emond M, Faubert S and Perkins M 2003 Social conflict reduction program for male mice. *Contemporary Topics in Laboratory Animal Science 42*(5): 24-26

Ferchmin PE, Eterovic VA and Caputto R 1970 Studies of brain weight and RNA content after short periods of exposure to environmental complexity. *Brain Research 20*: 49-57

Fernandez-Teruel A, Gimenez-Llort L, Escorihuela RM, Aguilar R, Steimer T and Tobena A 2002 Early-life handling stimulation and environmental enrichment: are some of their effects mediated by similar neural mechanisms? *Pharmacology Biochemistry and Behavior 73*: 233-245

Festing MFW and Greenwood R 1976 Home-cage wheel activity recording in mice. *Laboratory Animals 10*: 81-85

Forkman B, Boissy A, Meunier-Salaün MC, Canali E and Jones RB 2007 A critical review of fear tests used on cattle, pigs, sheep, poultry and horses. *Physiology and Behavior 92*: 340-374

Fox C, Merali Z and Harrison C 2006 Therapeutic and protective effect of environmental enrichment against psychogenic and neurogenic stress. *Behavioral Brain Research 175*(1): 1-8

Fredericson E 1953 The wall-seeking tendency in three inbred mouse strains (*Mus musculus*). *Journal of Genetic Psychology 82*: 143-146

Galef BG and Durlach P 1993 Should large rats be housed in large cages? An empirical issue. *Canadian Psychology 34*: 203-207

Galef BG and Sorge RE 2000 Use of PVC conduits by rats of various strains and ages housed singly and in pairs. *Journal of Applied Animal Welfare Science 3*: 279-292

Gallup GG 1970 Chimpanzees: Self-recognition. *Science 167*: 86-87

Gaskill BN, Rohr SA, Pajor EA, Lucas JR and Garner JP 2009 Some like it hot: Mouse temperature preferences in laboratory housing. *Applied Animal Behaviour Science 116*: 279-285

Gauthier C 2004 Overview and analysis of animal use in North America. *ATLA* [Alternatives to Laboratory Animals] *32*(Supplement): 275-285
http://www.worldcongress.net/2002/proceedings/C1 Gauthier.pdf

Gerson P 2000 The modification of "traditional" caging for experimental laboratory rabbits and assessment by behavioural study. *Animal Technology 51*: 13-36

Gisler DB, Benson RE and Young RJ 1960 Colony husbandry of research monkeys. *Annals of the New York Academy of Sciences 85*: 758-568

Hall CS and Ballachey EL 1932 A study of the rat's behavior in a field: A contribution to method in comparative psychology. *University of California Publications in Psychology 6*: 1-12

Hartner MK, Hall J, Penderhest J and Clark LP 2001 Group-housing subadult male cynomolgus macaques in a pharmaceutical environment. *Lab Animal 30*(8): 53-57

Henrickson RV 1976 The nonhuman primate. *Lab Animal 5*(4): 60-62

Hite M, Hanson HM, Bohidar NR, Conti PA and Mattis PA 1977 Effect of cage size on patterns of activity and health of beagle dogs. *Laboratory Animal Science 27*: 60-64

Hughes HC, Campbell S and Kenney C 1989 The effects of cage size and pair housing on exercise in beagle dogs. *Laboratory Animal Science 39*: 302-305

IACUC Certification Coordinator 2008 Restraint. *IACUC Learning Module - Primates (Web site)*: Accessed 02/11/2008
http://www.iacuc.arizona.edu/training/primate/rest.html

Iglesias D and Gil-Burmann C 2002 Environmental enrichment program for squirrel monkeys (*Saimiri sciureus and Saimiri boliviensis*) in captivity. *Folia Primatologica 73*: 291-292

International Primatological Society 2007 *IPS International Guidelines for the Acquisition, Care and Breeding of Nonhuman Primates*. International Primatological Society: Bronx, NY
http://www.internationalprimatologicalsociety.org/docs/IPS_International_Guidelines_for_the_Acquisition_
Care_and_Breeding_of_Nonhuman_Primates_Second_Edition_2007.pdf

Jain M and Baldwin AL 2003 Are laboratory animals stressed by their housing environment and are investigators aware that this stress can affect physiological data? *Medical Hypotheses 60*: 284-289

Johns Hopkins University and Health System 2001 Restraint techniques for animals—Nonhuman primates. *Animal Care and Use Training (Web site)*: Accessed 02/11/2008
http://www.jhu.edu/animalcare/training_procedures_restraint.html

Kallai J, Makany T, Csatho A, Karadi K, Horvath D, Kovacs-Labadi B, Jarai R, Nadel L and Jacobs JW 2007 Cognitive and affective aspects of thigmotaxis strategy in humans. *Behavioral Neuroscience 21*: 21-30

Kavanau JL and Rischer CE 1968 Program clocks in small mammals. *Science 161*: 1256-1259

Kelley ST and Hall AS 1995 Housing. In: Bennett BT, Abee CR and Henrickson R (eds) *Nonhuman Primates in Biomedical Research* pp. 193-209. Academic Press: New York, NY

Kelly J 2008 Implementation of permanent group housing for cynomolgus macaques on a large scale for regulatory toxicological studies. *AATEX* [Alternatives to Animal Testing and Experimentation] *14*(Special Issue): 107-110
http://altweb.jhsph.edu/wc6/

Knezevich M and Fairbanks L 2004 Tooth blunting as a wound reduction strategy in group living vervet monkeys (*Chlorocebus aethiops*). *American Journal of Primatology 62*(Supplement): 45
http://www.asp.org/asp2004/abstractDisplay.cfm?abstractID=744&confEventID=722

Lamprea MR, Cardenas FP, Setem J and Morato S 2008 Thigmotactic responses in an open-field. *Brazilian Journal of Medical and Biological Research 41*: 135-140

Landi S, Cenni MC, Maffei L and Berardi N 2007 Environmental enrichment effects on development of retinal ganglion cell dendritic stratification require retinal BDNF. *PLoS One 2*(4): e346

Lethmate J and Dücker G 1973 Studies on self-recognition in a mirror in orang-utans, chimpanzees, gibbons and various other monkey species. *Zeitschrift für Tierpsychologie 33*: 248-269

Line SW, Morgan KN, Markowitz H and Strong S 1989 Influence of cage size on heart rate and behavior in rhesus monkeys. *American Journal of Veterinary Research 40*: 1523-1526

Line SW, Morgan KN, Markowitz H and Strong S 1990a Increased cage size does not alter heart rate or behavior in female rhesus monkeys. *American Journal of Primatology 20*: 107-113

Line SW, Morgan KN, Markowitz H, Roberts J and Riddell M 1990b Behavioral responses of female long-tailed macaques (*Macaca fascicularis*) to pair formation. *Laboratory Primate Newsletter 29*(4): 1-5
http://www.brown.edu/Research/Primate/lpn29-4.html#line

Line SW, Markowitz H, Morgan KN and Strong S 1991 Effect of cage size and environmental enrichment on behavioral and physiological responses of rhesus macaques to the stress of daily events. In: Novak MA and Petto AJ (eds) *Through the Looking Glass. Issues of Psychological Well-being in Captive Nonhuman Primates* pp. 160-179. American Psychological Association: Washington, DC

Lukas KE, Hamor G, Bloomsmith MA, Horton CL and Maple TL 1999 Removing milk from captive gorilla diets: The impact on regurgitation and reingestion (R/R) and other behaviors. *Zoo Biology 18*: 515-528

Lutz CK, Davis EJ, Suomi SJ and Novak MA 2007 The expression of self-injurious behavior in *Macaca mulatta*: prevalence, risk factors, and context. *American Journal of Primatology 69*(Supplement): 38

Major CA, Kelly BJ, Novak MA, Davenport MD, Stonemetz KM and Meyer JS 2009 Self-directed biting in male rhesus monkeys (*Macaca mulatta*) with self-injurious behavior (SIB) increases following acute treatment with the anxiogenic drug FG7142. *American Journal of Primatology 71*(Supplement): 89

Matsuda Y and Kurosawa TM 2002 Transition of animal numbers used for experiments and recent trends in Japan. *Proceedings of the World Congress on Alternatives and Animal Use in the Life Sciences*: 127 http://www.worldcongress.net/2002/abstract-book/contents.htm

McDermott J and Hauser MD 2007 Nonhuman primates prefer slow tempos but dislike music overall. *Cognition 104*: 654-668

McDonald KM and Ratajeski MA 2005 Pair-housing of monkeys on behavioral studies. *American Association for Laboratory Animal Science* [AALAS] *Meeting Official Program*: 133

McGlone JJ, Anderson DL and Norman RL 2001 Floor space needs for laboratory mice: BALB/cJ males or females in solid-bottom cages with bedding. *Contemporary Topics in Laboratory Animal Science 40*(3): 21-25

McKinley J, Buchanan-Smith HM, Bassett L and Morris K 2003 Training common marmosets (*Callithrix jacchus*) to cooperate during routine laboratory procedures: Ease of training and time investment. *Journal of Applied Animal Welfare Science 6*: 209-220

Mori Y, Franklin PH, Petersen B, Enderle N, Congdon WC, Baker B and Meyer S. 2006 Effect of ketamine on cardiovascular parameters and body temperature in cynomolgus monkeys. *American Association for Laboratory Animal Science* [AALAS] *Meeting Official Program*: 178

Murchison MA 1995 Forage feeder box for single animal cages. *Laboratory Primate Newsletter 34*(1): 1-2 http://www.brown.edu/Research/Primate/lpn34-1.html#forage

Naff KA, Riva CM, Craig SL and Gray KN 2007 Noise produced by vacuuming exceeds the hearing thresholds of C57Bl/6 and CD1 mice. *Journal of the American Association for Laboratory Animal Science 46*(1): 52-57

National Research Council 1996 *Guide for the Care and Use of Laboratory Animals, 7th Edition*. National Academy Press: Washington, DC http://www.nap.edu/readingroom/books/labrats/

Neugebauer NM, Cunningham ST, Zhu J, Bryant RI, Middleton LS and Dwoskin LP 2004 Effects of environmental enrichment on behavior and dopamine transporter function in medial prefrontal cortex in adult rats prenatally treated with cocaine. *Brain research 153*: 213-223

Novak MA, Davenport MD and Meyer JS 2008 Biobehavioral factors in the development and maintenance of self injurious behaviour in rhesus monkeys (*Macaca mulatta*). *Primate Eye 96*: 465

O'Connor E and Reinhardt V 1994 Caged stumptailed macaques voluntarily work for ordinary food. *In Touch 1*(1): 10-11 http://labanimals.awionline.org/Lab_animals/biblio/tou-food.htm

Ogura T and Tanaka M 2008 Preferred contents of movies as an enrichment method for Japanese macaques. *Primate Eye 96*: 99

Ormandy EH, Schuppli CA and Weary DM 2009 Worldwide trends in the use of animals in research: The contribution of genetically-modified animal models. *ATLA* [Alternatives to Laboratory Animals] *37*(1): 63-68

Panksepp J 2007 Neuroevolutionary sources of laughter and social joy: modeling primal human laughter in laboratory rats. *Behavioural Brain Research 182*: 231-244

Panneton M, Alleyn S and Kelly N 2001 Chair restraint for squirrel monkeys. *American Association for Laboratory Animal Science* [AALAS] *Meeting Official Program*: 92

Phoenix CH and Chambers KC 1984 Sexual behavior and serum hormone levels in aging rhesus males: Effects of environmental change. *Hormones and Behavior 18*: 206-215

Pines MK, Kaplan G and Rogers LJ 2004 Stressors of common marmosets (*Callithrix jacchus*) in the captive environment: Effects on behaviour and cortisol levels. *Folia Primatologica 75*(Supplement): 317-318

Poffe A, Melotto S and Gerrard PA 1995 Comparison of four environmental enrichment strategies in captive common marmosets (*Callithrix jacchus*). *Primate Report 42*: 24-25

Prusky GT, Harker KT, Douglas RM and Whishaw IQ 2002 Variation in visual acuity within pigmented, and between pigmented and albino rat strains. *Behavioral Brain Research 136*: 339-348

Public Health Service (PHS) 1996 U.S. Government Principles for the Utilization and Care of Vertebrate Animals Used in Testing, Research, and Training. In: National Research Council *Guide for the Care and Use of Laboratory Animals, 7th Edition* pp. 117-118. National Academy Press: Washington, DC

Quinn LP, Perren MJ, Brackenborough KT, Woodhams PL, Vidgeon-Hart M, Chapman H, Pangalos MN, Upton N and Virley DJ 2007 A beam-walking apparatus to assess behavioural impairments in MPTP-treated mice: pharmacological validation. *Journal of Neuroscience Methods 164*: 34-39

Rasmussen S, Glickman GNR, Quimby FW and Tolwani RJ 2009 Construction noise decreases reproductive efficiency in mice. *Journal of the American Association for Laboratory Animal Science 48*(4): 363-370

Reasinger DJ and Rogers JR 2001 Ideas of improving living conditions of non-human primates by improving cage design. *Contemporary Topics in Laboratory Animal Science 40*(4): 89

Reinhardt V 1989 Behavioral responses of unrelated adult male rhesus monkeys familiarized and paired for the purpose of environmental enrichment. *American Journal of Primatology 17*: 243-248
http://www.brown.edu/Research/Primate/lpn27-4.html#vik

Reinhardt V 1990 Social enrichment for laboratory primates: A critical review. *Laboratory Primate Newsletter 29*(3): 7-11
http://www.brown.edu/Research/Primate/lpn29-3.html#rev

Reinhardt V 1991a Social enrichment for aged rhesus monkeys who have lived singly for many years. *Animal Technology 43*: 173-177
http://labanimals.awionline.org/Lab_animals/biblio/at173.htm

Reinhardt V 1991b Uncommon tool usage by captive primates. *International Zoo News 38*(5): 13-14

Reinhardt V 1991c Training adult male rhesus monkeys to actively cooperate during in-homecage venipuncture. *Animal Technology 42*: 11-17

http://labanimals.awionline.org/Lab_animals/biblio/at11.htm

Reinhardt V 1992 Are rhesus macaques really so aggressive? *International Zoo News 39*(1): 14-19

http://labanimals.awionline.org/Lab_animals/biblio/izn.htm

Reinhardt V 1993a Using the mesh ceiling as a food puzzle to encourage foraging behaviour in caged rhesus macaques (*Macaca mulatta*). *Animal Welfare 2*: 165-172

http://labanimals.awionline.org/Lab_animals/biblio/aw3mesh.htm

Reinhardt V 1993b Enticing nonhuman primates to forage for their standard biscuit ration. *Zoo Biology 12*: 307-312

http://labanimals.awionline.org/Lab_animals/biblio/zb12-30.htm

Reinhardt V 1993c Promoting increased foraging behaviour in caged stumptailed macaques. *Folia Primatologica 61*: 47-51

Reinhardt V 1994a Pair-housing rather than single-housing for laboratory rhesus macaques. *Journal of Medical Primatology 23*: 426-431

http://labanimals.awionline.org/Lab_animals/biblio/jmp23.htm

Reinhardt V 1994b Caged rhesus macaques voluntarily work for ordinary food. *Primates 35*: 95-98

http://labanimals.awionline.org/Lab_animals/biblio/primat~1.htm

Reinhardt V 1999 Pair-housing overcomes self-biting behavior in macaques. *Laboratory Primate Newsletter 38*(1): 4

http://www.brown.edu/Research/Primate/lpn38-1.html#pair

Reinhardt V 2005 Hair pulling: a review. *Laboratory Animals 39*: 361-369

Reinhardt V, Reinhardt A, Eisele S, Houser WD and Wolf J 1987 Control of excessive aggressive disturbance in a heterogeneous troop of rhesus monkeys. *Applied Animal Behaviour Science 18*: 371-377

Reinhardt V, Cowley D, Eisele S and Scheffler J 1991 Avoiding undue cortisol responses to venipuncture in adult male rhesus macaques. *Animal Technology 42*: 83-86

http://labanimals.awionline.org/Lab_animals/biblio/at83.htm

Reinhardt V and Reinhardt A 1999 The monkey cave: The dark lower-row cage. *Laboratory Primate Newsletter 38*(3): 8-9

http://www.brown.edu/Research/Primate/lpn38-3.html#cave

Reinhardt V and Garza-Schmidt M 2000 Daily feeding enrichment for laboratory macaques: Inexpensive options. *Laboratory Primate Newsletter 39*(2): 8-10

http://www.brown.edu/Research/Primate/lpn39-2.html#vik

Reinhardt V and Reinhardt A 2008 *Environmental Enrichment and Refinement for Nonhuman Primates Kept in Research Laboratories - A Photographic Documentation and Literature Review (Third Edition)*. Animal Welfare Institute: Washington, DC
http://www.awionline.org/ht/a/GetDocumentAction/i/4569

Richards MPM 1966 Activity measured by running wheels and observation during the oestrus cycle, pregnancy and pseudopregnancy in the Golden hamster. *Animal Behaviour 14*: 450-458

Richmond J 2002 Animal use in the United Kingdom. *Proceedings of the World Congress on Alternatives and Animal Use in the Life Sciences*: 126
http://www.worldcongress.net/2002/abstract-book/contents.htm

Richter CP 1927 Animal behavior and internal drives. *Comparative Psychology Monographs 1*: 1-55

Roper TJ 1976 Sex differences in circadian wheel running rhythms in the Mongolian gerbil. *Physiology and Behavior 17*: 549-551

Rothfritz P, Loeffler K and Drescher B 1992 Einfluß unterschiedlicher Haltungsverfahren und Bewegungsmöglichkeiten auf die Spongiosastruktur der Rippen sowie Brust- und Lendenwirbel von Versuchs- und Fleischkaninchen [German text with English abstract]. *Tierärztliche Umschau 47*: 758-768

Sarna JR, Dyck RH and Whishaw IQ 2000 The Dalila effect: C57BL6 mice barber whiskers by plucking. *Behavioural Brain Research 108*: 39-45

Savane S 2008 Use of flashlights in Old World nonhuman primate health monitoring. *American Association for Laboratory Animal Science [AALAS] Meeting Official Program*: 103

Schapiro SJ and Bushong D 1994 Effects of enrichment on veterinary treatment of laboratory rhesus macaques (*Macaca mulatta*). *Animal Welfare 3*: 25-36
http://labanimals.awionline.org/Lab_animals/biblio/aw3-25.htm

Schapiro SJ, Nehete PN, Perlman JE and Sastry KJ 1997 A change in housing condition leads to relatively long-term changes in cell-mediated immune responses in adult rhesus macaques. *American Journal of Primatology 42*: 146

Schapiro SJ, Nehete PN, Perlman JE and Sastry KJ 2000 A comparison of cell-mediated immune responses in rhesus macaques housed singly, in pairs, or in groups. *Applied Animal Behaviour Science 68*: 67-84

Schultz P 2006 I see myself. *AWI [Animal Welfare Institute] Quarterly 55*(3): 6
http://www.awionline.org/ht/display/ContentDetails/i/1970/pid/2500

Sharp J, Azar T and Lawson D 2005 Effects of a cage enrichment program on heart rate, blood pressure, and activity of male Sprague-Dawley and spontaneously hypertensive rats monitored by radiotelemetry. *Contemporary Topics in Laboratory Animal Science 44*(2): 32-40

Sodaro C and Mellen J 1997 Behavioral biology. In: Sodaro C. (ed) *Orangutan Species Survival Plan Husbandry Manual* pp. 17-25. Atlanta Orangutan SSP: Atlanta, GA

Steinbacher EA, Setser JJ, Morris TD and Gumpf D 2006 Development and implementation of a program for the social housing of nonhuman primates on toxicology studies. *American Association for Laboratory Animal Science* [AALAS] *Meeting Official Program*: 157

Taylor K, Gordon N, Langley G and Higgins W 2008 Estimates for worldwide laboratory animal use in 2005. *ATLA* [Alternatives to Laboratory Animals] *36*: 327-342

Turner JG, Bauer CA and Rybak LP 2007 Noise in animal facilities: why it matters. *Journal of the American Association for Laboratory Animal Science 46*(1): 10-13

United States Department of Agriculture 1989 Animal Welfare; Final Rules; 9 CFR Parts 1 and 2. *Federal Register 54*(168): 36112-36163
http://www.nal.usda.gov/awic/legislat/awafin.htm

United States Department of Agriculture 1995 *Regulations under the Animal Welfare Act as Amended - 7 USC, 2131-2156) - 9 CFR Ch. 1 (1-1-95 Edition)*. U.S. Government Printing Office: Washington, DC
http://www.access.gpo.gov/nara/cfr/waisidx_00/9cfr2_00.html

United States Department of Agriculture 2002 *Animal Welfare Regulations Revised as of January 1, 2002 - Code of Federal Regulations, Title 9, Chapter 1, Parts 1-4*. U.S. Government Printing Office: Washington, DC
http://www.access.gpo.gov/nara/cfr/waisidx_02/9cfrv1_02.html

United States Department of Agriculture 2007 *Animal Care Annual Report of Activities - FY 2007*. United States Department of Agriculture: Riverdale, MD
http://www.aphis.usda.gov/publications/animal_welfare/content/printable_version/2007_AC_Report.pdf

Valerio, DA, Miller, RL, Innes, JRM, Courntey, KD, Pallotta, AJ and Guttmacher, RM 1969 *Macaca mulatta: Management of a Laboratory Breeding Colony*. Academic Press: New York, NY

Van de Weerd HA, van Loo PLP, van Zutphen LFM, Koolhaas JM and Baumans V 1997 Nesting material as environmental enrichment has no adverse effects on behavior and physiology of laboratory mice. *Physiology and Behavior 62*: 1019-1028
http://www.library.uu.nl/digiarchief/dip/diss/01801846/c6.pdf

Van de Weerd HA, Van Loo PL and Baumans. V. 2004 Environmental enrichment: room for reduction? *ATLA* [Alternatives to Laboratory Animals] *32*(Supplement): 69-71

Van Loo PLP, Kruitwagen CLJJ and Van Zutphen LFM 2000 Modulation of aggression in male mice: Influence of cage cleaning regime and scent marks. *Animal Welfare 9*: 281-295

Van Loo PLP, Mol JA, Koolhaas JM, Van Zutphen LFM and Baumans V 2001 Modulation of aggression in male mice - Influence of group size and cage size. *Physiology and Behavior 72*: 675-683

Van Loo PLP, Van Zutphen LFM and Baumans V 2003 Male management: coping with aggression problems in male laboratory mice. *Laboratory Animals 37*: 300-313

Weed JL, Wagner PO, Byrum R, Parrish S, Knezevich M and Powell DA 2003 Treatment of persistent self-injurious behavior in rhesus monkeys through socialization: A preliminary report. *Contemporary Topics in Laboratory Animal Science 42*(5): 21-23

Wells DL, Graham L and Hepper PG 2002 The influence of auditory stimulation on the behaviour of dogs housed in a rescue shelter. *Animal Welfare 11*: 385-393

White WJ, Balk MW and Lang CM 1989 Use of cage space by guinea pigs. *Laboratory Animals 23*: 208-214

Wickings EJ and Nieschlag E 1980 Pituitary response to LRH and TRH stimulation and peripheral steroid hormones in conscious and anaesthetized adult male rhesus monkeys *(Macaca mulatta)*. *Acta Endocrinologica 93*: 287-293

Wolfensohn, SE and Lloyd, M 1994 *Handbook of Laboratory Animal Management and Welfare*. Oxford University Press: New York, NY

Photo Credits

page 17: Sarah Sosiak | www.flickr.com/photos/secret_canadian/

page 19: **left:** Viktor Reinhardt
right: Scott | www.flickr.com/photos/25993745@N05/

page 21: Compassion in World Farming | www.flickr.com/photos/ciwf/

page 22: Bob Dodsworth

page 23: Allen Lee | www.flickr.com/photos/23054626@N02/

page 24: **top:** Tom Sparks | www.flickr.com/photos/choirmaster/
bottom: Beverly | www.flickr.com/photos/walkadog/3353936487/sizes/o/

page 25: **top:** Scott Wyngarden | www.flickr.com/photos/antidale/
bottom: Jon Hurd | www.flickr.com/photos/jonhurd/

page 29: Antonio Viva | www.flickr.com/photos/antonioviva/

page 33: Tatiana Bulyonkova | www.flickr.com/photos/ressaure/

page 34: **left top:** Marko Savic | www.flickr.com/photos/marsavic/page4/
left bottom: Lindsay | www.flickr.com/photos/30097147@N04/2820747143/sizes/o/
right top: Ashley | www.flickr.com/photos/sweetassugar/3560094065/
right bottom: Micah Sittig | www.flickr.com/photos/msittig/

page 35: **left:** Ryan Owens | www.flickr.com/photos/10257524@N08/
right: Dennis S. Hurd | www.flickr.com/photos/dennissylvesterhurd/

page 36: Audra | www.flickr.com/photos/braindamaged217/

page 37: **left:** Lucy | www.flickr.com/photos/lucy_baxter/sets/72157617263040845/
right top: Peter Kemmer | www.flickr.com/photos/pkmousie/
right bottom: Splodgy Pig | www.flickr.com/photos/splodgypig/

page 38: Lindsay | www.flickr.com/photos/30097147@N04/2821584866/sizes/o/

page 39: T.P. Rooymans (Utrecht University)

page 40: **left:** Jessica Smith | www.flickr.com/photos/silverpasta/3923204588/
right: Toby Sanderson | www.flickr.com/photos/minimilkus/

page 41: **left:** Richard Masoner | www.flickr.com/photos/bike/
right: Deborah Silverbees | www.flickr.com/photos/silverbees/

page 42: Rattyroo | www.flickr.com/photos/rattyroo/260533855/sizes/o/

page 43: Lindsay | www.flickr.com/photos/30097147@N04/2820745829/sizes/o/

page 45: **left top:** Kai Schreiber | www.flickr.com/photos/genista/
left bottom: Lindsay | www.flickr.com/photos/30097147@N04/2820747053/sizes/o/
right: Jim Kenefick | www.flickr.com/photos/stark23x/

page 46: Kai Schreiber | www.flickr.com/photos/genista/

page 47: Audra | www.flickr.com/photos/braindamaged217/252465967/sizes/o/

page 48: **left:** Hjem | www.flickr.com/photos/hjem/
right: Michael Fivis | www.flickr.com/photos/dehgenog/

page 49: Doug Beckers | www.flickr.com/photos/dougbeckers/

page 51: **top:** Kailash Gyawali | www.flickr.com/photos/klash/
bottom: Jakub Hlavaty | www.flickr.com/photos/jakub_hlavaty/

page 52: Reg Mckenna | www.flickr.com/photos/whiskymac/

page 53: Lydia Troc | LAREF

page 54: Pehpsii Altemark | www.flickr.com/photos/pepsii/

page 57: **top:** Sassy Frassy Lassie | www.flickr.com/photos/dystopian/
bottom: Nigel Jones | www.flickr.com/photos/insectman/

page 58: **top:** Joy | www.flickr.com/photos/joysaphine/3170780030/
bottom: T.P. Rooymans (Utrecht University)

page 60: **left:** Scorpions and Centaurs | www.flickr.com/photos/sshb/
right: Pehpsii Altemark | www.flickr.com/photos/pepsii/

page 61: Grégory Millasseau | www.flickr.com/photos/gregseth/

page 70: Grégory Millasseau | www.flickr.com/photos/gregseth/

page 71: **left:** Penny | www.flickr.com/photos/pengrin/2499700830/
right: Chuck Seggelin | www.flickr.com/photos/plastereddragon/2286268244/

page 75: **top:** Anita Martinz | www.flickr.com/photos/annia316/
bottom: Lucy | www.flickr.com/photos/lucy_baxter/sets/72157617263040845/

page 76: Kyle Kesselring | www.flickr.com/photos/12249926@N06/

page 77: **top:** Claudio | www.flickr.com/photos/monky/533890540/
bottom: Pietro Izzo | www.flickr.com/photos/pietroizzo/

page 78: Andy the Loser | www.flickr.com/photos/lsthree/

page 79: Patrick Ellis | www.flickr.com/photos/pellis/

page 80: Photon | www.flickr.com/photos/photon_de/3050370414/

page 81: **top:** Mad_m4tty | www.flickr.com/people/mad_m4tty/
bottom: Motodraconis | www.flickr.com/photos/motodraconis/

page 82: **left:** Kawisign | iStockphoto
right: Lee Turner | www.flickr.com/photos/leeturner/

page 83: **top:** Cláudio Dias Timm | www.flickr.com/photos/cdtimm/
bottom: Vovchychko | www.flickr.com/photos/schneelocke/460302664/

page 84: **left:** Keithius | www.flickr.com/people/keithius/
right: The Sharpteam | www.flickr.com/photos/sharpteam/

page 85: Silke | www.flickr.com/photos/8930168@N06/sets/72157601696770722/

page 87: **top:** Joe Carroll | www.flickr.com/photos/joecarroll/
bottom: Maggie Champaigne | Flickr

page 88: **left:** Pehpsii Altemark | www.flickr.com/photos/pepsii/
right: Shawn Thorpe | www.flickr.com/photos/shawno/

page 89: **top:** Gary Van Fleet | www.flickr.com/photos/32466858@N06/3140254848/
bottom: Max Maass | www.flickr.com/photos/malexmave/

page 91: **left:** Craig Elliott | www.flickr.com/photos/tjflex/
right: Pehpsii Altemark | www.flickr.com/photos/pepsii/

page 92: **left:** Doron Tilleman | www.flickr.com/photos/21463982@N00/
right: Craig Elliott | www.flickr.com/photos/tjflex/

page 95: Boers K.

page 96: Silke | www.flickr.com/photos/8930168@N06/sets/72157601696770722/

page 98: **left:** Maria Pratt

right: Joe Carroll | www.flickr.com/photos/joecarroll/

page 99: Silke | www.flickr.com/photos/8930168@N06/sets/72157601696770722/

page 101: Bob Dodsworth

page 102: Viktor Reinhardt

page 105: Viktor Reinhardt

page 107: **top:** Viktor Reinhardt

bottom: Volker Otten | Getty Images

page 111: Basile Ben

page 112: Viktor Reinhardt

page 114: Viktor Reinhardt

page 116: Martin Ng | www.flickr.com/photos/minghong/

page 117: Peter Rinblad | www.flickr.com/photos/rinblad/

page 118: Viktor Reinhardt

page 119: **top:** Jeff Utecht | www.flickr.com/photos/jutecht/

bottom: Viktor Reinhardt

page 120: Valerie Schoof

page 121: Viktor Reinhardt

page 123: Moshe Bushmitz

page 125: Ivan Lanin | www.flickr.com/photos/ivanlanin/

page 126: Mark Abel | www.flickr.com/photos/markabel/4051071648/

page 127: Richard Lynch

page 128: Viktor Reinhardt

page 129: Viktor Reinhardt

page 130: Viktor Reinhardt

page 131: **left:** Amber MacPherson | www.flickr.com/photos/ambergris/
right: Eric Kilby | www.flickr.com/photos/ekilby/

page 132: Viktor Reinhardt

page 133: Viktor Reinhardt

page 134: Viktor Reinhardt

page 135: Viktor Reinhardt

page 136: Pirate Lemur | www.flickr.com/photos/piratelemur/

page 137: Sudar Muthu | www.flickr.com/photos/sudarmuthu/

page 138: **top:** Brandi | www.flickr.com/people/70109157@N00/
bottom: Tracy and Maneesha | www.flickr.com/photos/tracyandmaneesha/

page 139: Viktor Reinhardt

page 141: **top:** Lisa Knowles
bottom: Shira Golding | www.flickr.com/photos/boojee/

page 142: **top:** Andrea Aplasca | www.flickr.com/photos/13695597@N06/
bottom: Arnold Chamove

page 143: Joachim S. Müller | www.flickr.com/photos/joachim_s_mueller/

page 144: Philipp Roth | www.flickr.comphotosfipsy

page 145: **top:** Philipp Roth | www.flickr.comphotosfipsy
bottom: Viktor Reinhardt

page 146: Jörg Spiegel | www.flickr.com/photos/jotespe/2501612651/

page 147: **left:** Viktor Reinhardt
right: Christopher Chan | www.flickr.com/photos/chanc/

page 148: **left:** Joachim S. Müller | www.flickr.com/photos/joachim_s_mueller/
right: Michael Keen | www.flickr.com/photos/michaelkeen/

page 149: Arno Meintjes | www.flickr.com/photos/arnolouise/

page 150: **top:** Magnus Franklin | www.flickr.com/photos/adjourned/
bottom: Jörg Woltemade | www.flickr.com/photos/woltemade/

page 151: Scorpions and Centaurs | www.flickr.com/photos/sshb/

page 152: piX dust | www.flickr.com/photos/21173961@N07/2835940481/

page 153: Brian Wilson | www.flickr.com/photos/bgwilson89/2877294720/

page 154: Jennifer Powers | www.flickr.com/photos/justpowers/2202451988/

page 155: Paula Goodale | www.flickr.com/photos/riotcitygirl/

page 156: Sherman Wang | www.flickr.com/photos/oopsilon/

page 157: Sscchhaaeeff | www.flickr.com/photos/14441993@N06/4148115765/

page 158: **top:** Marie-Claude Labbé | LAREF
middle: Jennifer Green | LAREF
bottom: Joey A. Rodriguez | www.flickr.com/photos/huedge28/3029388398/

page 160: Christopher Cummings | www.flickr.com/photos/poxod/2942684170/

page 161: Christopher Cummings | www.flickr.com/photos/poxod/2942684170/

page 162: Peggy O'Neill-Wagner

page 163: Tadatoshi Ogura | LAREF

page 165: Viktor Reinhardt

page 169: Viktor Reinhardt

page 173: Evan MacLean

page 176: Viktor Reinhardt

page 178: Viktor Reinhardt

page 181: Viktor Reinhardt

page 184: Viktor Reinhardt

page 185: Bob Dodsworth

page 190: Tracy | www.flickr.com/photos/plasticbat/2691542507/

page 218: Aziz Cetinsu

page 219: **top:** Anssi Koskinen | www.flickr.com/photos/ansik/
bottom: Jennifer Lamb | www.flickr.com/photos/lambj/

page 220: Viktor Reinhardt

page 221: **left top:** Giane Portal | www.flickr.com/photos/fofurasfelinas/
left bottom: Stas Kulesh | www.flickr.com/photos/piterpan/
right top: Jerry | www.flickr.com/photos/jerry7171/388369145/
right bottom: Leeighla | www.flickr.com/photos/lmlipscomb/

page 222: **left:** Bill Liao | www.flickr.com/photos/liao/
right: Seven Morris | www.flickr.com/photos/sevenmorris/3273893126/

page 223: Melvin Schlubman | www.flickr.com/photos/pauldineen/4015710342/

page 224: Mark Thaden | www.flickr.com/photos/28158018@N08/2901231777/

page 225: **top:** Angeline Evans | www.flickr.com/photos/cattoo/
middle: Dave | www.flickr.com/photos/19673572@N00/
bottom: Jeffrey Beall | www.flickr.com/photos/denverjeffrey/460563216/

page 226: **left:** Rachel Wente-Chane | www.flickr.com/photos/rwentechaney/
right: Mattkiazyk | www.flickr.com/photos/mattkiazyk/
bottom: Dave | www.flickr.com/photos/19673572@N00/

page 227: Emma.maria | www.flickr.com/photos/emma_maria/

page 230: Liddy Roberts | www.flickr.com/photos/duchessoftea/

page 231: Whitelines | www.flickr.com/photos/keith_clubb/

page 232: Nicole Laukhart | www.flickr.com/photos/nicolelaukhart/

page 233: **left middle:** Jim Champion | www.flickr.com/photos/treehouse1977/
left bottom: Jon Glittenberg | www.flickr.com/photos/jglitten/3611823859/
right: Canolais | www.flickr.com/photos/canolais/

page 234: **left:** Roger Moffatt | www.flickr.com/photos/rogermoffatt/
right: Walter Jeffries | www.flickr.com/photos/sugarmtnfarm/

page 235: **left:** Jim Reynolds | www.flickr.com/photos/revjim5000/

right: Lisa Rasmussen | www.flickr.com/photos/41879561@N02/

page 236: Romorga | www.flickr.com/photos/romorgan/

page 237: **left:** Thomas Mues | www.flickr.com/photos/garibaldi/

right: Francisco Martins | www.flickr.com/photos/betta_design/

page 238: Lynne | www.flickr.com/photos/your_teacher/3231591866/

page 239: **left:** Nancy | www.flickr.com/photos/turtlemom_nancy/3820868968/

right top: Robbie | www.flickr.com/photos/photo_art/334553541/

right middle: Peter | www.flickr.com/photos/peterallen/

right bottom: Michael Smith | www.flickr.com/photos/michaeledwardsmith/

page 240: Ecoagriculture Partners | www.flickr.com/photos/ecoagriculture/2604488659/

page 241: Annie Reinhardt

page 243: Genaro Orengo | www.flickr.com/photos/orengophotography/3326735359/

page 244: Dead Roxy | www.flickr.com/photos/deadroxy/

page 246: Viktor Reinhardt

page 249: Viktor Reinhardt

page 253: Bullcitydogs | www.flickr.com/photos/bullcitydogs/

page 254: Nicola Gothard | LAREF

page 255: Kit Logan | www.flickr.com/photos/kitlogan/sets/

page 258: Viktor Reinhardt

page 259: **top:** Flickmor | www.flickr.com/photos/mmoorr/1921632741/

bottom: Camilla Solum | www.flickr.com/photos/26023607@N00/1305755221/

page 260: Matt Kemberling | www.flickr.com/photos/mek22/

page 261: **left:** Jeff McCann | www.flickr.com/photos/45519093@N00/4735707091/

right top: viajar24h | www.flickr.com/photos/soschilds/

right bottom: Wanja Krah | www.flickr.com/photos/wanjakrah/

page 262: Snuzzy | www.flickr.com/photos/snuzzy/2564114582/

page 265: Tambako | www.flickr.com/photos/tambako/3997857214/#

Index

How Can You Join the Laboratory Animal Refinement & Enrichment Forum?

The purpose of this electronic discussion forum is the factual exchange of experiences about ways to refine the conditions under which animals are housed and handled in research institutions. The group is intended to serve the international animal care community in its attempt to promote animal welfare and improve scientific methodology by avoiding or eliminating husbandry-related stress situations. The forum is open to animal care personnel, animal technicians, students, attending veterinarians and researchers who have or had first-hand experience in the care of animals kept in research and education facilities.

LAREF is managed and moderated by Viktor Reinhardt, who reserves the right to accept or reject subscribers. If you want to join LAREF, please send a message to viktorawi@yahoo.com indicating briefly your practical experience with animals kept in research laboratories, your current professional affiliation, and your interests as they pertain to the discussion group.